Praise for *Madonna & Me*

"For someone who has spent the past ⋯
to whoever would listen, Madonna ⋯
Reading these smart, funny, and mo⋯
influenced by the material girl brought me right back to my school
years, when I was touched by Madonna for the very first time."

—DEBBIE STOLLER, co-founder and editor-in-chief
of *BUST* magazine

"Sure, one Madonna gave birth to Jesus—but our Madonna gave
birth to femme-inism. If you've forgotten why you should worship
Madge, this hilarious, provocative collection is like a prayer to the
patron saint of girl power."

—JENNIFER BAUMGARDNER, author of *Manifesta: Young
Women, Feminism and the Future, Look Both Ways: Bisexual Politics*, and
F' em!: Goo Goo, Gaga, and Some Thoughts on Balls

"When I first heard the song 'Everybody' in 1982, I ran right out and
bought the 'cas-single.' Now, thirty years later, I greedily read everything about Madonna I can get my hands on. Madonna is one of
those rare public figures who elicit a lifelong, intensely personal
fixation, making this collection of essays a giddy pleasure. By turns
hilarious, thought-provoking, and touching, *Madonna & Me* is a fitting salute to the smart, brash, occasionally infuriating provocateur, who is always offering us something new."

—JANCEE DUNN, music journalist for *Rolling Stone*,
Vogue, and *The New York Times*, and author of *Why Is My Mother
Getting a Tattoo? And Other Questions I Wish I Never Had to Ask*

"Finally, an anthology that speaks to the blisteringly potent influence
Madonna has had on women of our generation."

—JULIE KLAUSNER,
author of *I Don't Care About Your Band*

"Madonna & Me is a collection as saucy and savvy as Madonna herself. In heartfelt and incisive ways, the contributors engage with an icon who deeply impacted the identities, sexual and otherwise, of an entire generation of girls."

—JILLIAN LAUREN,
New York Times-bestselling author of
Some Girls: My Life in a Harem

"Though it was written entirely by women, *Madonna & Me* can easily hold the interest of non-Madonna fans and even male readers, which is (sadly) no small feat. Highly recommended for anyone interested in music, pop culture, women's lives, and smart personal essays with heart."

—SCOTT LAPATINE, founder and editor-in-chief of Stereogum,
named one of *Entertainment Weekly's* Best Music Websites

"The writers in *Madonna & Me* explore all that Madonna has meant to more than one generation of feisty, feminist, powerful women. They dive into her music, persona, and legacy, expressing themselves in ways that would surely give even Her Madgesty food for thought."

—RACHEL KRAMER BUSSEL,
editor of *Women in Lust and Best Sex Writing 2012*

"In *Madonna & Me*, editor Laura Barcella shows how Madonna has become a cultural benchmark for women of varying backgrounds. Reaching far beyond pop-culture critique, the essays in this book examine Madonna—both the woman and the legend—as an allegory of the modern female experience."

—STEVE LOWENTHAL,
music writer for *SPIN and the Village Voice*, and
founder of *Swingset* magazine

MADONNA & ME

Women Writers on the
QUEEN OF POP

Edited by LAURA BARCELLA • Foreword by JESSICA VALENTI

SOFT SKULL PRESS | BERKELEY
AN IMPRINT OF COUNTERPOINT

Madonna and Me © Laura Barcella 2012
Foreword © Jessica Valenti 2012

"Justify My Love" by Emily Nussbaum was reprinted with permission from New York magazine.
"Touched for the Very First Time" by Rebecca Traister was reprinted with permission from Salon.com.
A version of "Madonna and Me" by Susan Shapiro was originally published in The Jewish Forward.

Library of Congress Cataloging-in-Publication Data is available.

ISBN: 978-1-59376-429-6

Printed in the United States of America

SOFT SKULL PRESS
An Imprint of COUNTERPOINT
1919 Fifth Street
Berkeley, CA 94710
www.softskull.com

Distributed by Publishers Group West

10 9 8 7 6 5 4 3 2 1

Contents

Track 3: BURNING UP

Track 4: KEEP IT TOGETHER

Track 5: LUCKY STAR

Track 6: FIGHTING SPIRIT

Bonus Track: NOW I'M FOLLOWING YOU

Foreword

Jessica Valenti

THERE'S SOMETHING ABOUT Madonna.

For nearly thirty years Madonna has fascinated people on a global scale—especially drawing the attention (and sometimes ire) of women, who seem to love and hate her in equal amounts. Me, I'm not so sure.

My first glimpse of the pop icon came in the form of her "Papa Don't Preach" music video in 1986. I was eight years old, too young to fully grasp the meaning behind the song—and the fabulous "Italians Do It Better" T-shirt—but even then I could glean that she was singing about rebellion in the face of paternalism. (Though naturally it would take more than a decade and a few women's studies classes before I used that word to describe it!) It was a seductive message, one that resonated with a burgeoning feminist—oh yeah, and millions of other girls and women.

In the years that followed, even though my musical tastes were more hip-hop than pop, I kept coming back to Madonna. I bought her records and sometimes emulated her style. The funny thing was, save for a few songs, I wasn't really all that crazy about her music. It was her—her persona, more accurately—that drew me in. I wasn't necessarily rocking out to her, but I was watching.

I think what made Madonna endlessly fascinating to me—and still does—is her ability to be a pop-culture chameleon. And unlike current celebrity reinventions, it never seems to matter if Madonna is sporting lace gloves, a spiked bra, a cowboy hat, or a dominatrix whip—all of her selves appear authentic. (All right, maybe not that faux-European accent she had going for a while—but hey, give a girl a break.) Or perhaps it wasn't that these identities were authentic, but that they were so obviously created and carefully formed that the ease with which she slid into each incarnation of herself was amazing in and of itself.

It's also hard not to love the way Madonna confounds expectations: She's survived and thrived in an industry that reviles both female aging and sexuality that isn't male-controlled. There's something appealing and awe-inspiring about the way Madonna simultaneously titillates and terrorizes the public—after all, there's little that American men fear more than a sexually powerful woman. Even when it's playful, or a performance! (See Emily Nussbaum's essay "Justify My Love," page 268, and Laura Barcella's "My Pocket Madonna," page 86, for more discussion about male Madonna-fear).

That's why it's no surprise that, as this anthology indicates, there's such a wide range of women's thought around Madonna. Madge—arguably the most well-known female musician in the world—embodies feminist issues from performativity and sexuality to celebrity and power.

Take the 1990 *New York Times* op-ed, where firebrand Camille Paglia called Madonna "the true feminist":

"Madonna has taught young women to be fully female and sexual while still exercising total control over their lives. She shows girls how to be attractive, sensual, energetic, ambitious, aggressive, and funny—all at the same time."

Of course, instead of Paglia seeing this as in line with feminist thought, she saw Madonna as the antidote to American feminist whininess. She argued that feminism had a "man problem," and that unlike Madonna—who let men be masculine—feminists "fear and despise" the masculine. "The academic feminists think their nerdy bookworm husbands are the ideal model of human manhood," she wrote. (An odd stance when one considers the gender–bending and androgyny Madonna so often embraced, but that's a discussion for another essay!)

Bell hooks sees Madonna as someone whose performance of sexuality means little to women of color. In her essay "Madonna: Plantation Mistress or Soul Sister?" hooks wrote that though she sometimes admires Madonna for creating "a culture space where she can invent and reinvent herself," the singer co-opts black culture and engages in a public sexuality that's mired in white privilege. (More than one writer in these pages also explores these themes—see J. Victoria Sanders' essay "The Black Madonna," page 55, Jamia Wilson's "Are You There God? It's Me, Madonna," page 43, and Maria Raha's "Borderline," page 216)

Hooks writes, "In part, many black women who are disgusted by Madonna's flaunting of sexual experience are enraged because the very image of sexual agency that she is able to project and affirm with material gain has been the stick this society has used to justify its continued beating and assault on the black female body. The vast majority of black women in the United States, more concerned with projecting images of respectability than with the idea of female sexual agency and transgression, do not often feel we have the 'freedom' to act in rebellious ways in regards to sexuality without being punished."

When it comes to Madonna, there's nary a woman who lacks for an opinion. For me, though, I think something different every time I read something new about her, any time I hear a new album or see a new video. I love that while other pop culture divas have honed their performances and public identities to the whims of the time, Madonna has created her own narratives and set the pop culture agenda. I hate that without her performance of sexuality (be it consumer-driven or self-created) we wouldn't be so entranced with her.

But maybe my ever-changing mind on Madonna and what she means for women and feminism is part of the point. She's not stagnant, so why should any of our thoughts about her be? Whether you think Madonna is an appropriator or an inspiration, perhaps what makes her so outstanding is that one person can mean something so different to so many people.

That she doesn't just make us dance and sing around with a hairbrush (guilty as charged) but that she makes us angry, that she makes us horny, that she makes us think.

Introduction

Who's That Girl?

Laura Barcella

> *I'd love to be a memorable figure in the history of entertainment in some sexual, comic, tragic way. I'd like to leave the impression that Marilyn Monroe did, to be able to arouse so many different feelings in people.*
>
> —MADONNA

I'D LIKE TO think I knew exactly where I was the first time I heard her. It was 1984, so I must have been around six. I was in the backseat of my grandmother's clangy old navy-blue Cutlass, driving through Rock Creek Park in my hometown of Washington, D.C. It was hot outside, and the backs of my sweaty knees stuck to the faux-leather seat.

Because I was a budding pop-music aficionado, my parents let me listen to D.C.'s trendy pop radio station, Q107, whenever we were in the car. I knew nearly every word of nearly every song played that year, and as I listened to the lyrics from the back seat, I would stare out the window, daydreaming. I loved almost all of it—even the questionable stuff, like Sheila E., Scandal, and Corey Hart.

And then it happened. A new song appeared between the usual suspects, one that struck me with its sweet, plaintive, but optimistic opening keyboard notes. These were followed by a voice I'd never heard before—thin but throaty, with just a hint of darkness seeping through. I broke out in chills: I felt magnetically drawn to the song with laser-like focus. "That was Madonna, with her new top-ten hit, 'Borderline,'" rasped the announcer after the song ended.

I was hooked. "Borderline" stuck with me for days. I immediately memorized all the words, singing along joyfully in my head (I was too shy to croon aloud, at least when other people were around) whenever it played on the radio, which was often. I imagined the frustrating off-and-on relationship Madonna was singing about; I conjured up an image of the bad-boy heartbreaker she was singing to. In my daydream, she looked like a cute, spritely teenager. (Oh, how I longed to become a teenager! The freedom, the independence, the romance, the danger . . . Sigh.)

My fixation only grew when I finally put a face to that gravelly voice via Madonna's "Lucky Star" video on MTV—the messy hair, the mesh tank top, the jelly bracelets, the crucifixes. Whoa. My world was rocked. She was, by far, the coolest woman I'd ever seen. (Admittedly, I hadn't seen many. I was six, and my world was pretty tiny then.)

I was the only child of busy but accommodating, well-to-do parents, and I had a small circle of close-knit friends from the private school I attended in D.C. The girls in my class (all ten or fifteen of them) were smart, small, sheltered creatures. We were sometimes shy, sometimes bratty and brash, and all well loved. But as kids tend to be, we were powerless—especially as girl children. We lived firmly under our parents' thumbs. Adult women—like my mom, and the moms of my friends Lisbeth and Nelly—were gainfully employed at respectable office jobs. They had short, sensible haircuts in warm neutral tones (and if they dyed or "frosted" their hair, they took great pains to avoid anyone knowing it—it was *never* bleached or showed dark roots). They wore slacks, not jeans. They came home at night, cooked dinner for their families, and were in bed by 10:00 PM. They didn't wear black—and certainly never black lace.

★

Madonna's glittery ascent to stardom hit me hard. In a good way. She was so powerfully different from everything I'd seen, heard, or observed about womanhood. And to the six-year-old me, she was a fascinating hybrid of a twenty-six-year-old grown-up and a rebellious teenager. She was adorable but raw. She was a challenge; she always seemed to say, even without words, "I dare you to dare me." Even in her overtly sexual songs ("Like a Virgin," "Burning Up," "Physical Attraction") her eyes bore the tiniest glint of coy naïveté—was that real or was it faked? Was she just playing us, toying with us, trying to make us want her more?

"The Girlie Show," indeed—she reveled in her femaleness, rolled around in it, slathered every inch of herself in its essence. She made no apologies for what she wanted ("to rule the world," as she explained to Dick Clark on *American Bandstand*) or how far she would go to get it. And she wouldn't be caught dead in slacks.

Totally infatuated, I not only begged my parents to buy me her album, I convinced them to buy me mesh tops, neon socks, and crucifix necklaces. I wore a lace rag in my hair, lace gloves on my hands, and stacked black jelly bracelets up my arms. My friends and I made puffy-paint T-shirts proclaiming our devotion, and then posed in ridiculous homemade photo shoots, sprawled across my bedroom rug like clueless little Lolitas. I even went to school dressed like her.

Since that fateful day when I first found her on the radio, it's been "Madonna and me." Sure, it's about admiration—I loved how she danced, sang, and gyrated her little diva-punk-princess heart out. But it wasn't just a pop-star crush or a fascination with her incredible fashion sense; it was deeper ("and deeper and deeper and deeper") than that.

Really, Madonna changed everything—the musical landscape, the '80s look du jour, and most significantly, what a mainstream female pop star could (and couldn't) say, do, or accomplish in the public eye.

A shiny new world unfolded before me, and suddenly my expectations about girls and women—what we were supposed to be—were shattered. Suddenly, sex was on the table. And money. And power. And artifice. And teen pregnancy. And "boy toys." And—*gasp!*—masturbation.

As many of the writers in this book describe in their essays, Madonna's been dramatically different people throughout different stages of her life. Who could forget the spoiled superficial material girl, the kooky Kabbalist, Dita the sexual deviant, the married Primrose Hill matriarch, the "ohm Shanti" desert guru? So many Madonnas! But like most women, including me, this is why we relate to her: she's a walking knot of contradictions. When I've needed answers in life, I've turned to my image of her, like an invisible little angel on my shoulder. *What would Madonna do?* I'd ask myself in all earnestness, when faced with tough decisions throughout my teens and twenties. (In her piece on page 14, writer Shawna Kenney recalls asking herself that same question.)

Watching her career evolve has been like watching a parallel version of me do the things I've only dared to dream about. We've grown up together. As I write this I'm thirty-four. At fifty-two, of course, she's a whole new version of herself—necessarily much more grown up than the ragamuffin twenty-six-year-old lucky star we met in 1984. She's gotten married, had babies, adopted babies, gotten divorced. Her sexuality has become a bit quieter, more refined.

It's hard to explain all the ways she's impacted me. *Madonna and Me* is homage to that impact. Her influence is just so *big*—*she's* so big. (Not physically, duh—we all know she's made of steel, or "gristle," if you ask Guy Ritchie). In a way, it feels like she belongs to me—and to you, and to all of us women. She's like a celebrity version of the proverbial Bohemian aunt who lives across the country (or across the pond). She's unconventional, unpredictable, sometimes even infuriating; sometimes we want to disown her. But we've also enviously tracked her every move, waiting for updates on her next outlandish antic, jealous but proud that we know some woman, somewhere, who has the gall to do exactly as she damn well pleases. Her freedom is our freedom.

In these pages, thirty-nine talented writers explore how Madge has changed their lives, both for good and for bad. They describe her influence on their notions of family, youth, celebrity, self-love. It's all here. Enjoy it.

This Used To Be My Playground

"Kids were quite mean if you were different. I was one of those people that people were mean to. When that happened, instead of being a doormat, I decided to emphasize my differences. I didn't shave my legs. I had hair growing under my arms. I refused to wear makeup, or fit the ideal of what a conventionally pretty girl would look like. So of course I was tortured even more, and that further validated my superiority, and helped me to survive."

—MADONNA

"Children always understand. They have open minds. They have built-in shit detectors."

—MADONNA

Before Beyoncé, Tween Thongs, and Baby Tiaras

Courtney E. Martin

MY MOM HAS an endearing habit of saving "television programs," as she calls them, on her DVR for me to watch when I come home for holidays. Sometimes it's a Tom Brokaw special or a segment from CBS *Sunday Morning*. Usually it's a particularly touching moment on *Oprah*—a family reunited, John Travolta crying, free refrigerators for everyone. My mom, weathered by my impatience, very conscientiously cues the program to just the moment that she's decided I'll be interested in.

Last Christmas, I sat down on the leather couch with a glass of Trader Joe's Two-Buck Chuck to await my mom's customized montage. She was armed with her remote (the only piece of technology she seems truly comfortable with these days) and a mischievous smile. When she hit "play," it wasn't Oprah's mantras or Charles Osgood's stately voice that greeted me, but a grainy image of my eight-year-old self standing remarkably still while the unmistakable lead-in to Madonna's "Vogue" began to play. My late-'80s habit of choreographing underwhelming dances to Madonna songs had come back to haunt me.

Oh, the jazz squares! Oh, the midriffs! Oh, the bossiness! I had clearly strong-armed my less assertive friends, Emily and Katie, into being my backup dancers. As they hopped backward, I strode forth, dressed in a sports bra and puffy mini-skirt, mouthing the words with sassy aplomb. Sometimes, and I am embarrassed to admit this, I scolded them when they missed their cues.

Poor, gangly Emily, who'd come from a strange faraway land called New Jersey and whose parents were very Christian and probably didn't allow Madonna songs to be played in their home—so pure it had wall-to-wall white carpeting. Poor Katie, whose mother had thought it a good idea to cut Katie's hair very short and then perm it until she resembled a mousy brown Orphan Annie without the endearing freckles. They each had enough to deal with. They didn't deserve me. More specifically, they didn't deserve Madonna and me.

What was it with Madonna and me? I wonder this as I watch the damning footage of my own personal homage to her. What sort of appeal did the Material Girl have for a second-grader growing up in Colorado Springs, Colorado—the motherland of the Evangelical Christian movement, home of the Air Force Academy, test city for *Fast Food Nation?*

The too-easy answer is, well, sex. Even at that young age, a neighbor boy and I had discovered my dad's stack of *Playboy* magazines in the attic. On Barbie breaks, we'd flip through them, marveling at the bushy vaginas and big breasts in soft focus. I wasn't turned on by them so much as curious about their power. They were hidden, after all. My parents—old hippies—were the kind of people that considered very few things off limits.

Madonna *was* undeniably sexy. She had that flirtatious beauty mark, that two-toned hair, that lacy glove. She let men hold her up and carry her around. She wore bras as outerwear. But as I watch myself—scantily clad and comically skinny, prancing around and striking poses—I don't remember Madonna's sexiness being what inspired my performance.

I was undeniably a child trying on a sort of adult persona, but it wasn't the sexuality that I was compelled by. In the same way that I sometimes tried on ambition as a pretend "career woman"—purse thrown over my shoulder, always in a rush, heading to very important meetings with very important people—I sometimes tried on confidence, as Madonna. Ambition, as I'd come to understand as an adult who paid rent and pitched stories, is much more complex than the purse and the rushing, just as confidence is much more layered than a midriff and bold lyrics. But at the time, it was all just one big game of pretend.

Since then, lamenting the era of "too sexy, too soon" has become a big business. My sports-bra-wearing and hip-shaking (sans actual hips) of yesteryear actually has a name these days: early sexualization. Miley Cyrus—that sweet country daughter—posed seductively in *Vanity Fair* and suddenly radical feminists and Evangelical preachers stood on common ground, both lamenting the end of young girls' innocence. Viral videos of little divas, dressed to the nines, rocking out to Beyoncé's hit "Single Ladies" caused furious typing from both the nation's progressive "mommy bloggers" as well as from church deacons. Suddenly little Lolitas were turning up everywhere—exploited, objectified, and eliciting the fury of the strangest bedfellows.

And even though Madonna, unlike Miley, was well into her twenties by the time she inspired little girls like me to vamp in their living rooms, perhaps she can be marked as the first pop figure to usher in an era of early sexualization.

I can't help but wonder—would I be seen as another tragic casualty of our highly sexualized culture were my little video to go viral today? I think there's a good possibility that I would be pitied and protected, that my gyrations might be interpreted as evidence of inappropriately early maturation. Though I might wonder why the hell my mom let me wear that sports bra, I can't help but think the embarrassing scene would be wildly misunderstood if it were characterized as something salacious.

No matter what was in that video, at school on Monday I would mostly be known as the teacher's pet—attentive, obedient, and smart. Ms. Johnson loved me, even when she sent me to the principal's office for stomping to my cubbyhole that once. I literally wrote love letters to Ms. Mulholland, the teacher's aide. She had the most beautiful smile and pretty pink sweaters. I adored these women. I wanted to emulate them, too. In addition to choreographing ridiculous dances to Madonna songs, I spent countless hours reading to a mangy pile of stuffed animals. I held the book out, just like Ms. Johnson did, so they could all see the pictures after I finished reading each page.

My models of womanhood were multitudinous. Madonna signaled brazen creativity, a flexible kind of beauty; and Ms. Johnson and Ms. Mulholland signaled intellect and kindness. She was untamable; they were fair. She was talented; they were sweet. I wanted it all, even at eight years old.

Despite my bossiness when it came to creating dance routines, as a child I was preternaturally meek, known for clinging to my mom's side at backyard parties and whispering to my brother on the playground. But these women all represented different versions of a confident femininity. I had a hunch that one day I'd be able to own this kind of confidence myself, but at first, I just needed to dress up in it and dance around a little.

In high school, I felt like my sexuality was a ticking time bomb. This was in no small part because I was surrounded by Christian leaders who preached that young women's desires were dangerous and must be tamped down, just as young men must learn to control their inevitably animalistic urges. None of us were really represented in that righteous picture of adolescent sexuality. My sweet boyfriends weren't untamable hulks, just as I wasn't a virgin or vixen. We were all just kids trying to feel good—guys and girls exploring sex and power with the brave aid of Captain Morgan rum poured in 7-Eleven Coca-Cola Slurpees.

At thirty-one, I still want it all, even as I've grown more sober about how difficult it is to contain all these parts of myself in one little life. I spend all day staring at a screen, trying to write a convincing op-ed, and then hit the bar, hoping for a really good set by a DJ who appreciates everything from '90s hip-hop to Annie Lennox to, of course, Madonna. I pay my mortgage on time and in full, but I haven't lost the taste for reckless euphoria now and again—the 4:00 AM taxi ride home, leaning on the window as I coast over the Manhattan Bridge and stare at the twinkling lights of the most mad and beautiful city on Earth. I think about having children of my own, as I also realize that I finally own my unique sexuality. I know my body. I know what I like. I understand the complexity of Madonna's plea to "Express Yourself" as only a grown woman could.

I'm not claiming that girls today aren't damaged by some of the cartoonish images of sexuality they see around them. Surely it's not good for young women to view their sexuality as defined by others' probing eyes rather than by their own instincts and senses. And of course, a culture that objectifies women at younger and younger ages is also one that trains men to objectify women at younger and younger ages.

But Madonna didn't teach me to be a heathen or a bitch or a slut, as some fear-mongers would claim. She taught me to be brazen, unapologetic, and multidimensional. She taught me to be the star of my own fantasy, not to acquiesce to others' ideas of what was appropriate or beautiful. She gave me the confidence to request that my dad get his mammoth video camera out and tape the dance moves I'd painstakingly choreographed to go with each line and beat of Madonna's best anthem of all, "Vogue." It wasn't about the miniskirt; it was about the imagination. Madonna taught me that there's nothing wrong with confusing people—to drape one's self in pearls one day and rosaries the next, clad in a pink evening gown with a leather coat, a little sweet and a little dangerous.

Articles of Faith

Shawna Kenney

AS A PUNK-ROCK girl growing up in Podunk, Maryland, Madonna was my dirty little secret. The few girlfriends I had in high school did not share my interests in slam-dancing and skateboarding, so more often than not, I found myself at shows with a steady group of guy friends. For all of our proclaimed rebelliousness, we dressed pretty much the same: baggy shorts, slip-on Vans, big T-shirts worn thin and stretched out from skating. We shaved, cut, and bleached our hair as much as our parents would allow. Old photos reveal my hairstyle as a hybrid of Tony Hawk's '80s-era signature bangs-in-the-face and the short new-wave look of the Go-Go's. I wore earrings and a bra but was otherwise as androgynous as Boy George.

Maximum RocknRoll was my bible, and I didn't kiss a boy until after graduation; if any of my peers were attracted to me, I was clueless about it. It's not that I hated my body—I just never thought about it much. Part of punk's ethos was to question authority and reject mainstream models, and in my mind, this automatically extended to what I'd seen of femininity. There were very few women in the punk scene of the '80s, and definitely none in my town. This was pre-Internet and pre–mall-punk stores—a time before bands made fitted tees or sexy tanks for girls, and a time when new wave, pop, and punk never mixed. Shirts I bought at hardcore shows came in no smaller size than a men's large, which, on my five-foot-two-inch frame, hung unflatteringly down to my knees.

Witnessing Madonna's "Holiday" video on MTV at age sixteen was a confusing revelation to me. Here was a woman strutting around confidently in a mesh half-shirt, black bra showing through, with big bleachy hair, lots of jewelry, sultry eye makeup, and a graffitied jean jacket! She *looked* kind of punk. She *acted* kind of punk, giving that cheesy photographer the brush-off and going back to her "street friends" by the end of the video. But she sounded like Minnie Mouse—so I kept my fascination with the pop sensation buried beneath the Dead Kennedys and Minor Threat throughout most of high school. Still, when a friend's five-year-old sister later pointed to the picture on the cover of Madonna's "True Blue" album and said "Shawna," I couldn't have been more (secretly) flattered.

Suddenly, I became aware of my female body, and in Madonna saw something familiar and accessible. I, too, grew up in a working-class home. I was short and muscular, shaped more like her and Paula Abdul than Whitney Houston. Like me, Madonna was also raised Catholic. Punk rock had become my church and I knew at a young age that I wanted no part of organized religion, but this was not an option in my strict Catholic home. My sister and I begrudgingly participated in church activities until we were old enough to leave home.

Our church youth group hosted a Halloween party while I was in high school and I finally decided to publicly display my adoration of Madonna. I painstakingly put together a Material Girl costume. My dad had always said her black bracelets looked like "vacuum cleaner O-rings," so I knew where to get those. I wore cropped white painter's pants splattered in pastel pink paint, which I topped with a white, navel-grazing mesh shirt over a black sports bra (the closest thing I could get to her sexy lace one). I tied a black stocking around my head as a headband, teased my blonde skater-bangs up into a bunch with my sister's Aqua Net, and threw on three sets of rosary beads as necklaces. My black-and-white checkered slip-on Vans worked well, though they weren't quite the black boots she wore in the video. The fake mole I drew above my upper lip completed my look—the cherry on an ice cream sundae.

The Halloween party was packed by the time I arrived. Loverboy blasted as I entered the little wooden community center and searched for my friends. "Nice outfit," said one girl in passing. "Sexy!" noted one of the guys. Things were looking better by the minute. I found my friends; we grabbed cups of Coke to chug while watching other people do their awful '80s dances dressed as bloody monsters, black cats, Martians, robots, and superheroes. Halfway through a fistful of chips, our youth group leader pulled me aside, saying she had to speak with me in private.

"Your belly button is showing," she whispered.

"Yeah?" I said.

"It's bothering some people. Father Duncan, in particular."

"Wh-wh . . . he doesn't like my costume?"

"I'm sorry," she sighed. "I think you look adorable, but he's asked me to ask you to go home and change, or put on a coat."

I was shocked. All night I'd felt so pretty, glammed-up in a way I'd never been before—not wearing the army shorts my mom hated so much, not wearing a shirt three sizes too big. My belly button was just too powerful, apparently, and even my rosaries couldn't save me. I drove myself home, confused and ashamed. Was I really dressed inappropriately? Would I be labeled a slut? Did God care about what I looked like? Was "sexy" never to be a word in my vocabulary? I asked myself: *What would Madonna do?* I did not have the words or guts to stand up for myself yet. I went home and changed into an oversized sweatshirt.

For a long time after the party, I just sulked. Eventually, I started mixing baggy with fitted, playing with clothing until I found my own style. I've learned that I don't need to (or want to) look like a boy to fit in. Punk wasn't just a style of music or fashion for me, but a philosophy of questioning authority and doing things as an individual. I might not rock the heavily hair-sprayed bleached hair or ride a skateboard anymore, but I still carry these beliefs with me. I've also learned that one of the most revolutionary things a woman can do is to be confident with her body. Women who are physically unabashed, especially those with body types outside of what's celebrated in the media, always get backlash. But fuck the status quo: We can make our own rules. Madonna helped me to see this as much as punk rock did.

A few years after my teenage youth-dance debacle, Madonna's "Like a Prayer" video aired to much controversy. I had grown my hair long and allowed my natural dark curls to take over. I wore a black slip-dress out to a club one night, and someone said to me, "You look like Madonna in that new video." I smiled sweetly and just said thank you.

Strike a Pose

Kim Windyka

WHEN THE 1990 music video for "Vogue" came out, I was fresh out of preschool. As a big, bad almost-kindergartener, it appealed strongly to my more mature sensibilities. From the retro black-and-white shots to the sharp dance steps, it took all the self-control I could muster not to jump through the screen every time it appeared on my living room television. I just couldn't wait until I was old enough to strike a pose and rap about Ginger Rogers—though I hadn't the faintest idea who she was, I did know that she could "dance on air."

But what really captured my attention and curiosity was the Material Girl's wacky, pointy-coned bra. I clearly had a long way to go until I developed anything close to resembling breasts, but I had a sneaking suspicion that even the majestic Madonna herself couldn't naturally possess such alert ta-tas. Was it MTV magic, or did these amazing boob-enhancers exist in real life? I wasn't content to sit idly by and ponder such important grown-up mysteries; I needed to find out for myself. Fortunately, it just so happened that Mom had to run some errands at the mall the following week. This was my big chance, and I was not going to mess it up.

Even though I was less than five years old, I did have some sense of how absurd it was to hunt for the elusive cone bra. Still, when you're that young, you don't really question your obsessions much. You are simply driven. I hadn't even thought about what I'd do if I *did* locate one; my Madonna fervor was so intense that I couldn't see past the pure, gleeful satisfaction of coming face-to-face with this fashion revelation. I'd worry about logistics later.

As we strolled through Sears, past the matronly pajama sets and slippers, I could see the promised land of lace and underwire beckoning in the distance. Acting as casually as any child on a mission might, I made a beeline for the bras and haphazardly grabbed the first black one I saw. It was massive. Upon further inspection, I also discovered that it looked nothing like Madge's avant-garde underwear. Not even a little bit. There were no real "cones" to be found, just two very big, very round cups. Yet time was certainly of the essence, and I could work with this!

Skipping past the charm and jumping right to desperate pleading, I did my best puppy-dog eyes and hugged the bra to my nearly concave chest. "Mommy, can I pleeeeeease try this on? Madonna wears this. In the 'Vogue' video. Pleeease?!" At this point in my life, my mother was both acutely aware of my Madonna obsession as well as experienced in dealing with my frequent flights of fancy. She barely batted an eyelash at my request; she knew instinctively that this was not a battle worth fighting. Calmly, with purpose, my mother strode over to the middle-aged saleswoman, and as cool and collected as could be, she asked the woman a question that I'm sure she'd never heard before—in reference to a double-D bra: "Excuse me, may my daughter try this on?" The woman glanced quizzically at her, then at me . . . then back at her again. My mom acted quickly, taking it as a yes. "Thank you so much," my mom emphasized, smiling through gritted teeth at the clearly confused woman. Bouncing with barely contained glee, I followed the two into the fitting room, preparing myself for the truly magical transformation that was about to occur. Once I removed this juvenile, constricting sweater and tried on the sultry, sexy underwear, I'd be well on my way to becoming my childhood idol. Right?

My mom held the gigantic bra in front of me, and I slipped my tiny, pasty arms through the straps. "Don't just stand there, let's get to it," I quietly sang to myself in eager impatience. I purposefully had my back to the mirror, wanting to milk the moment, yet as my mom hooked the back and then tried unsuccessfully to shorten the straps, I knew it was all wrong.

I turned toward the mirror and cocked my head. I felt as crestfallen as the double-D bra that hung from my little-girl frame.

"It doesn't fit!" I whined, scowling at my reflection. I cast a pouty glance through the mirror at my mother, who was standing behind me, struggling to remain straight-faced as she took in her four-year-old drowning in a Carol Doda bra. I doubted Madonna could even fill it out.

Of course, I looked nothing like her. As much as I wanted to see a slightly younger version of the MTV queen staring back at me, I only saw a precocious girl wearing some very odd-looking undies. After pausing for a moment to decide whether I was too proud to acknowledge such an obvious mismatch, I realized that Mom would still love and support me regardless of how fashionable I was. I also realized that I had absolutely no idea how to get this thing off.

"I'm sorry, honey. Maybe it will fit when you're older." She patted my back and held out my bubblegum-pink sweater. I reluctantly wiggled out of the lacy, va-va-voom black lingerie and sighed. "But I wanna be like Madonna!"

Leaving the store, my mind was already racing as it dreamed up ideas for my next inspired style statement (fishnet tights were vetoed, but that didn't stop me from asking for them every day for the next month). Not all of my attempts to emulate Madonna fell flat, though:

inspired by the dancing in the "Vogue" video, I took my first ballet, tap, and jazz classes the following fall and continued dancing for fourteen more years.

In retrospect, I'm still not convinced that my little cone bra phase was necessarily spurred by my desire to look and act more adult. Rather, it was Madonna's fresh, edgy style and complete confidence in executing it that drew me to her. And as I grew up and bore witness to each new iteration of the Divine Miss M—from leather-clad dominatrix and mysterious Kabbalah goddess to electro-dance queen and everything in between—I too was reinventing my identity, becoming a strong, ambitious woman, with Madonna's unwavering empowerment to guide me along the way. Though I may still lack the incredible measurements to fill out that cone bra, I'm proud to say that Madonna has enhanced my life in far more ways than any sexy lingerie could.

B-Sides

Lesley Arfin

I WAS A bossy kid. There were bossier, older kids who came before me, and when they graduated to the maturity that came with being a sixth-grader, I took the reins. I was happy to. Why not? No one else had the balls to make a decision. Would we play freeze tag or red rover? Would we go to the pool or eat ice cream on the stoop? Some days it was all of the above and some days it was none of those things.

During my tenure as Queen of the Neighborhood, I made sure there was always one particular activity on the table: dance routines. I had the pink cassette player, and I had the cassettes. Jamie Middleton's dad had a camcorder. Jen Pike took dance lessons at Jan Martin's School of Dance, so she had the moves. Her younger twin brothers came in handy as audience members, or when we wanted to include a boy in the routine. Sure, we had Debbie Gibson and Tiffany phases (and one embarrassing "Jonny B. Good" incident after seeing *Back to the Future*), but there was one album that changed all the rules.

The year was 1986. The album was Madonna's *True Blue*. After this album came out, there was simply no substitute. When we got sick of listening to it, when every song had an accompanying dance routine to go along with it, when our lips were maxed out from all the syncing, that's when I handed over my crown and retreated indoors. It was summer in my heart and summer in my eardrums.

★

The album's title track, "True Blue," was an easy routine—too easy. We had all seen the video. Put on a blue outfit and whisper fake secrets in my ear while I lip-sync, *duh*.

Next!

"White Heat" was the obvious choice. And though Jamie and Jen didn't know this song as well (I was a big fan of the lesser-known songs, or B-sides, on her albums), they soon would. Instead of blue we wore all-white. "Get up/stand tall/put your back up against the wall/my love is dangerous/this is a bust." I don't think I need to spell out the dance routine; it's all in the lyrics, as literal as they come. Still, I made them practice until we had it perfect. When we were ready to showcase our moves, we'd put lawn chairs on the grass for our mothers to sit in and watch us. They would arrive slowly, in groups of two or three, sauntering into my backyard casually, as if they were just shopping for tennis skirts. They'd pretend to notice our moves, but really they would just stand around and gossip over cups of coffee or tea. In between songs I'd yell "Mom! You're not watching!" And she'd say "I'm sorry, I'm sorry," but she still wouldn't look, she'd just keep talking to Linda Lowell, the arty suburban mom who wore black ballet flats and black leggings. After the "Papa Don't Preach" video came out, I noticed she shifted to a black-and-white striped shirt tucked into Levis with a big black belt.

One of my favorite routines was to "Open Your Heart," if for nothing else than the perfect staging. My backyard patio had a big air conditioner that was built underneath a wooden platform. It was bi-level, so two girls fit perfectly on either side of the lowest platform, and one girl fit perfectly on top, like a single candle on top of a birthday cake. That girl was usually me, unless I was feeling diplomatic.

When *Like a Prayer* came out, I got a bit more selfish. Rather than waste my time teaching endless dance routines to girls who could never quite seem to remember the lyrics anyway, I took to my bedroom and listened to *Like a Prayer* on my own. It was a darker album for darker times. I knew the burning cross in the video represented something awful because my dad complained about it and dismissed it as garbage. I thought he'd misunderstood the video entirely. I assumed Madonna wanted to burn the cross so it would stand out in the video as a cool decoration, something jazzier than your typical light bulb. Something to catch your eye. I remember thinking how sad it was that my arrogant father was wrong. It was art, dad! *Hello?*

"Spanish Eyes" was the song where I finally found my voice. The days of lip-syncing were over. I was ready to sing, and sing I did. I belted the shit out of that song. "*And if I find nothing left to show/but tears on my pillow . . .*" Those lyrics resonated with me. I was old enough to know she wasn't literally singing to me, but young enough to pretend that she kind of was. It was a gift from her that I would reopen every single night after dinner. Or after school. Or on a Sunday when there was nothing to do. It was too cold to play outside and too boring to hang out with my old neighborhood minions who, let's face it, just didn't "get it." And frankly, I didn't want them to. When I lay on my back, sinking into my soft bedroom carpet listening to "Dear Jessie," I saw those pink elephants! I saw the lemonade, candy kisses, and sunny days. I often wondered who "Jessie" was. Was she a girl Madonna babysat for? Probably. How badly did I wish that girl could be me?

All the women in my family loved Madonna. My sister was into the *Vogue/Bedtime Stories/Erotica* Madonna, while my mom still claims that her favorite movie, to this day, is *Desperately Seeking Susan.* But my Madonna will always be the B-side Madonna, the lesser-known-hits Madonna, so that when people boast of their undying love for her, we're clearly not talking about the same woman.

When I told people I was writing an essay about Madonna, everyone had something to say. I heard a lot of "Oh my God, *I* should be writing that!" and "Didn't you know? I'm *obsessed* with Madonna." Yes, yes, I thought, of course you are. Everyone loves the Material Girl. Everyone thinks her Gaultier cone bras were "sick," and everyone's favorite movie is *Truth or Dare*. I get it. You love her. But one thing I want to make clear is that *my* Madonna is different from yours. No one knows my Madonna. I might not be her biggest fan, but I'm definitely her most special because I appreciate all the songs you people gloss over. Ha! If she knew me, she'd definitely like me for that reason. She'd wink and kiss me on the cheek with her fire-engine-red lips and then we'd go shopping for polka-dot crinolines together (did I mention that my Madonna only exists in the movie *Who's That Girl?*).

I'll still make up dance routines to Madonna songs, but only if I get to choose them. And everyone has to draw a mole above their lips and wear black-lace gloves. I know that the Madonna of my Halloween-costume dreams has been gone for many years, but that's the only kind of Madonna I'm interested in talking about. The grown-up Madonna, she's for grown-ups. We can talk about *that* Madonna when I get there.

Bad Girls from Bay City

Erin Trahan

BALTIMORE HAS JOHN Waters. New Haven has George W. Bush. And Bay City, Michigan, has Madonna. And me. I'm easy to trace back to that crook of the mitten, where the thumb meets the palm, because the Trahans are known for running a funeral home there since 1934. But don't try to fact-check Madonna's roots with her people—she'll probably deny them altogether. She doesn't seem too keen to claim a connection to her home state.

That we were both born in Bay City—in the same hospital, no less—was enough for me to form a Madonna liberation mythology; something to cinch around my waist like a spelunker would use a rope to tug when she wanted out of the cavernous darkness. Not that Bay City was so bad, though Madonna calling it a "stinky little town" in 1987 is now part of its Wiki-lore. Granted, it did occasionally reek of sugar beets, but like many Midwestern municipalities it had a heyday: One could buy diamonds and fine leather gloves downtown, eat lunch with the Rotarians on Tuesdays, borrow books from a Carnegie library, and aspire to be the St. Patrick's Day Queen.

It's where my father and his father were born, where together they ran a pharmacy, and where my mother thinks the best tomatoes grow. A safe place with earnest neighbors. But before Madonna, it had no claim to fame to satiate the would-be dreams of a precocious kid like me. The Bay City Rollers had supposedly thrown a dart at a map to name themselves after my town; the Bay City on the now defunct soap opera *Another World* was somewhere in Illinois.

Even saying I'm from Bay City is a bit of a stretch. I actually lived in a neighboring farm town on a dead-end street in the middle of a cornfield. In the early 1980s, Hampton Township was a haze of tractor rows, Little League diamonds, and the undersides of bleachers, where I'd scheme while my older siblings played ball. So I was left with Madonna as my elementary school beacon of hope. Hope that a girl—me—who spent hours doing back flips on abandoned track mats could one day be a bona fide material girl.

But early Madonna was all wrong for early me. Sure, I was sassy and outspoken—but not when it came to sex or anything near it. This was especially true at home, where I refused to gender my stuffed animals, avoided discussing boys (whether friend or boyfriend), and waited years to tell my mom I'd gotten my period. Years! You could point to any number of explanations. I was the headstrong youngest child of four. I harbored both a dogged sense of equity and an ingrained mistrust of my own body: Why did I think like an adult but look like a kid? And why did I have to physically mature beyond a childhood I'd never mentally inhabited?

Unlike me, preteen Madonna thought like an adult and aspired to look like one, too. "Don't tell me I can't be sexual and intelligent at the same time," she once told *People* magazine when discussing her adolescence. According to biographer Andrew Morton, in junior high she wrapped herself in a trench coat and danced onstage to the music of the TV show *Secret Agent*. A finale with the sound of gunshots was planned; her flashing the audience to reveal her black leotard was not. Madonna's father grounded her for two weeks.

Despite her precociousness, one of Madonna's musical narratives is of childhood lost. After her mother died of breast cancer when she was five, Madonna, as the oldest girl in the family, assumed child-care and housekeeping duties that she later admitted resenting. She struggled when her father remarried, and her adult recollections of growing up sound like the fable of Cinderella and her evil stepmother. It's one of many flash points where Madonna and her media coverage enmesh so seamlessly that one wonders, where lies the truth? Fortunately, I had no such burdens beyond a cunning imagination and strong will.

So it came as a shock when my mom came home from fourth-grade parent/teacher conferences with the report that I was "boy crazy." Okay, I had sharpened my already-sharp pencil near Von Schafer to pass him notes about roller skating at Metro on Thursday afternoon—this was how kids communicated in 1985. I knew I wasn't bad in the rosary-and-ripped-tights kind of way; Madonna's lacy undergarments and virginal corruption frightened me to no end. But take one step from Mary toward Madonna, from Jackie O toward Marilyn, from white to black swan, and you're sentenced: bad.

If anything, I rejected Madonna's antics and camped with the skeptics who tossed her off as a one-hit or—at a stretch—one-album wonder. C'mon, she was from Bay City, Michigan; how high could her lucky star possibly rise?

If only I'd been paying closer attention. In sixth grade I moved to northern Michigan, where, among the rolling hills and pretty beaches, lurked a surprisingly upstart little town. "Like a Virgin" overtook the charts, and I learned the hard way that pinstriped Lee jeans from Meijer Thrifty Acres—a hot commodity in Bay City—wouldn't suffice for the social order of my new school. Every morning, the class bully, who for a few weeks played the veiled role of being my friend, asked me "What brand is your shirt?" When I hesitated or didn't say the brand Guess, she grabbed my collar to see for herself. It was 1986, and Madonna and I both wanted new identities. Of course, she was eons ahead of trend, spinning retro-personas for the songs on *True Blue*. I just wanted to raise my hand in math class and get asked to a school dance. It took years to learn that a girl rarely gets it both ways.

By high school I'd matured enough to bring my boyfriends home (even the bad apples), and to appreciate Madonna for the game-changing entertainer she'd become. One ho-hum Friday night I rented *Truth or Dare* to rouse the "mixed company" at the unchaperoned party at my house. By Monday, word got round: *Truth or Dare* had caused a stir. My reputation took a hit. Ridiculous! I'm sure I either shook a fist or rolled my eyes.

At this point, I could see the absurdity of what Madonna knew all along: that most social expectations are suffocating, or desperately old-fashioned. Yet in my years of growing up, I don't recall her making a point of coming back to Michigan to perform. She wasn't one to call out to her girls this side of 8 Mile. And though I later figured out she didn't exactly grow up in Bay City—she was born during a visit to her grandparents' house, and returned often to visit them—she didn't grow up in "real" Detroit either, with its industrial grit and stronghold on music legend. No, Madonna grew up in its tony suburb, Rochester Hills. A cheerleader and straight-A student. Full scholarship to the University of Michigan. Teen Madonna, it turns out, may have behaved better than I did; I was a straight-A student who only earned partial scholarships. But that's like saying cake isn't cake unless it's frosted. Because let me be clear: No amount of good behavior would have been enough for either Madonna or me. Generations before and since have faced the same limited mindset about how girls should behave. Madonna's grasp of this enabled her to embrace the idea of girls having it every way, whether the world was ready or not.

That's why, even as I left adolescence behind, I still felt connected to her as an adult. If ever asked which famous person I'd most like to meet, she topped my list—I would play the hometown card as an icebreaker, and we'd slap backs in recognition. For a long time she was the only celebrity to whom I could claim a vague personal connection beyond being born in the same town—one of my aunts was a counselor in her younger siblings' school. Another relative socialized with her father and stepmother, who had moved to northern Michigan and started a winery. For a while, they all sang in the same church choir. Maybe my dreams of meeting Madonna in the flesh weren't as far-fetched as I'd believed.

So I took note when she moved to England, around 2000, and donned that odd accent, erasing not only her home state but also her home nation. Her abandonment struck a chord. After all, when a gal has high hopes in almost any field, she doesn't picture a future in the Wolverine State. At least that's what I decided after high school, when I ventured beyond the state's borders for college, ultimately landing in Boston. For those who think Michigan is a depressing place to live—a stinky little state—I fashioned Madonna's ex-pat status into a sign of my own charmed potential.

I still feel like an outsider of sorts in New England, but I am convinced that my most recent iteration as a writer would not have been possible had I not pursued opportunities outside Michigan. Who would I have been if I'd stayed? What about Madonna?

★

A few summers ago, I visited Madonna's father's winery in Sutton's Bay with my sisters and a few aunts. I'll admit, we gawked. The tasting room had a wide wooden bar and garish old-world Italian wall decor. The winery had issued a special bottling to commemorate the *Confessions on a Dance Floor* album release. We sipped samples; the wine labels and marketing posters were far from what I'd expected. They weren't stylish or slick. I couldn't imagine Madonna had any part in their design. In fact, the artwork was downright cheesy—images of Madonna, two decades after her debut, retro again, in '70s dance-floor poses with airbrushed pastels on black. It felt familiar, like it had been done before. The Madonna I knew, even in her fifties, had always been far ahead of cool. I tried to like the wine, but I didn't.

I could feel my own creeping judgment, as if I, too, had copped an accent I hadn't earned.

More than once since that afternoon I've wondered: at what cost do I remain connected to home, and at what cost do I sever the ties? If I ever found myself at dinner with Madonna, how much would either of us have to say about Michigan, anyway?

★

It pleased me to read the press clippings my mom saved from the 2008 Traverse City Film Festival. Madonna had arrived by limo and walked the red carpet at the movie house of my adolescence, the State Theater. The *Traverse City Record Eagle* blazed with a full-color picture of her on the front page. But I most appreciated the story about her in the independent weekly *Northern Express*. Though the writer had socialized with Madonna before, she did not respond to his requests for an interview, so he'd had to pen it without her. He chronicled their missed meetings with a generous helping of forgiveness and a few thoughtful points about integrity, superstardom, and small-town life.

Forgive her, Father, for she knows not what she leaves, nor what she takes with her. But if anything's for certain, Madonna's just the sort to make an about-face at the drop of her cane and top hat. Tomorrow she could move in to the vacant home next to my mom and dad's house in Michigan—the one they emailed me about last week (and again today). I wouldn't put it past her.

TRACK 2

Like a Prayer

"I was raised a Catholic and was never encouraged to ask questions, or understand the deeper meanings or mystical implications of the New Testament or the history of Jesus . . . So I rejected that, because who wants to go through life being told you do things because you do things?"

—MADONNA

"I think they probably got it on, Jesus and Mary Magdalene."

—MADONNA

Madonna vs. the Virgin Mary

Maria Gagliano

WHEN I WAS ten years old, my most dedicated pastime was praying the rosary. I'd go to my room at 8:00 PM, an hour earlier than my bedtime, to make sure I got through the entire circle of beads before getting tired. Just one set of ten Hail Marys wouldn't do—a pulling paranoia insisted that I pray the whole loop every night. I had to concentrate on every word, consider its meaning, and I wouldn't move on to the next bead until I'd felt each line in earnest. I forced myself to picture Mary, full of grace, blessed among all women with a blessed boy in her womb. Mary in her signature blue and white robes; God off to the side, just out of focus; Mary glowing, all-knowing, quiet and understanding, but with an iron hold that would not let me put down those beads. Even if it meant I wouldn't go to sleep until ten o'clock. I didn't give myself any other choice.

My parents, God-fearing Sicilians that they were, didn't know what to do with me. Yes, Sunday mass was nonnegotiable, and they were proud parents of my brother, the altar boy, but that was the extent of their devotion. Walking by my bedroom door to see me chanting Hail Marys instead of watching TV or reading *The Babysitters' Club* confused them. It just wasn't something they expected to see from their little girl. They seemed relieved the few times they caught me in the living room watching Madonna videos—I guess they considered this normal for kids my age—but the rest of my behavior baffled them. They didn't dare disturb my bedroom prayers; they just nodded awkwardly and closed the door. Then I'd dart from bed, shoot across the room, and throw the door back open; I was terrified to be alone with my prayers.

My pious insanity emerged in fourth grade, when my religion teacher went on a stint of showing us videos of Virgin Mary apparitions. Our Lady of Fátima appearing to three shepherd children; Our Lady of Guadalupe appearing before Saint Juan Diego in the early morning; Our Lady of Lourdes showing herself to fourteen-year-old Saint Bernadette Soubirous.

Saint Bernadette threw me over the edge. I still remember the video: A French shepherd girl, going about her business in the fields, saw the Blessed Virgin near a rock. She was glowing, holding rosary beads, and talking. Bernadette was never the same after that. She was forced to convince everyone of her sighting, urge priests to build a chapel, endure *even more* sightings. It completely freaked me out. She was so ordinary, such a nobody, so much like me. What would stop the Holy Mother from interrupting *my* suburban New Jersey afternoon, *my* anonymous little-girl life, to assign me the burden of convincing the world that she really existed?

My nightly rosary ritual began shortly thereafter. I'd follow it with an installment of Bible reading before going to sleep. My goal was to eventually finish the whole thing, cover to cover, in hopes of figuring it all out. I'd read and read until I could understand God, feel close enough to look him in the eye without trembling. On some days, I was prepping for Mary's arrival: Maybe if I knew enough about her and the heaven she came from, I wouldn't mind seeing her. Perhaps I could even ask her a few things I couldn't find answers to in the Bible. Like whether she'd had sex with Joseph *after* Jesus was born, or if she was doomed to be a virgin forever. And how was she able to ascend to heaven, body and soul, without her body dying or eventually rotting? I'd ask if dead people could read my thoughts—if my grandmother could hear everything I was thinking. And if so, was she mad at me?

Other times I prayed, hoping that if I did it hard enough, God would leave me alone. I didn't want to be among his holy chosen few; I wanted to be normal. Plain. Invisible. But the more I prayed, the more scared I became of possibly seeing Mary. So I took it further. *Maybe if I show God how dedicated I am in my actions . . .* I vowed to never have sex until I was married and, if I could help it, not even kiss a boy until I was at the altar. The Ten Commandments ruled my every action. Even white lies were forbidden, and I obsessed over not even *thinking* the Lord's name in vain—let alone saying it. If I did, I had to say a Hail Mary and Our Father on the spot. I allowed myself to say the prayers silently, but I had to do an actual sign of the cross when I was done, so God could see me. This meant sneaking behind the bleachers at gym for a quick Father-Son-Holy-Spirit. I'd dart to the bathroom at lunch or duck my head in the coat closet during class if a quick prayer was necessary. It was okay for God to see me, but if I could help it, I'd spare myself the peer humiliation.

I did have a few false alarms. I swore I saw the Blessed Virgin's silhouette in our hallway light fixture for a whole week. This was a real problem, since I insisted on sleeping with my door open and the hall light on. After four nights of not sleeping, I knocked on my parents' door at 3:00 AM in tears.

"Mom, I can't sleep," I said when she appeared, barefooted and night-gowned.

"Why, what's wrong?"

"Well, um, come here. Sit on my bed." She actually followed my instructions, confused and hazy, but ready for my confession. "Now look up at the light. What do you see?" I asked.

"Huh? Nothing. Is the light bulb out? Do you need more light?"

"You don't see Mary?" I was terrified even uttering the word.

"*Mary*? Mary who?"

"Like, the Virgin Mary. You know how she comes to people sometimes, like in a vision? Is that her?"

"Oh, God! I'm going to call your teacher if she doesn't stop showing you those videos. You're not even sleeping! No, honey, that's not Mary. She doesn't come to people anymore. That was hundreds of years ago. You don't have to worry. Please, just go to sleep. You were dreaming."

I feigned relief and scuttled under the covers. Her "reassuring" words freaked me out even more. Didn't she see? It'd been *hundreds of years*! The Holy Mother was just waiting to strike. In the end, the fact that my vision lacked a halo and rosary beads and didn't talk convinced me that the light fixture did not host our Blessed Virgin, but the incident refueled my devotion. That night, I said two rounds of Hail Marys—once for myself and once for my mom. She'd said God's name in vain while talking falsely about Mary. *Lord, help her!*

Sleep did not come easily that year. My grades slipped to Bs and Cs because I spent most of my time praying in the bathroom or hiding in the coat closet. When I wasn't praying, I was analyzing my actions to determine if I *should* be praying. I got an A in religion, but my parents still grounded me for the declining grades in my other classes. No TV in my room, and my homework had to be done right after school.

Without a TV in my room, I had nothing to do besides pray and read. It got exhausting. So I started venturing to the living room TV to get out of my head. My two brothers seized the remote when they got sick of the sitcoms I watched, which was often. One night after dinner, my brother Sal snapped after a particularly corny *Full House* moment. He snatched the remote and switched it to MTV.

"It's staying here. Permanently," he said. "There's such crap on tonight," he muttered. "Call me if Pearl Jam comes on."

As Sal left the room, I turned to see a burning cross on the screen. *What is this? Is this even allowed on TV?* I wondered. *Is this Pay-Per-View?* I looked around for someone to ask. But my dad had gone to bed, and my mom and brothers were down in the basement. I was alone. And I couldn't stop watching.

A woman was lying on the ground; a second later she began singing and I realized I was watching the video for Madonna's "Like a Prayer." Though the song had been on the radio for years by that point in 1992, I had never before seen the video. Madonna was in a church now, her dress's spaghetti strap falling off her shoulder, her bra straps in full view, and her cleavage even more so. I was pretty sure God wouldn't have approved. *Wow,* I thought. *How did she get away with that?* Then it got worse. The painted statue was crying; then he came to life and kissed Madonna. In the church! I could safely guess that Madonna and the statue weren't married; they had no excuse for kissing in church. I knew I was in serious trouble for watching this. *Mary's probably sitting on my bed waiting for me,* I thought. *I'm really going to pay for this.* But I couldn't change the channel.

As I watched, I became crippled with worry over what was waiting for me in my room. It felt like I'd undone a year's worth of getting on God's good side. He was going to send Mary—not because I was a chosen one, but to punish me because he knew it was everything I didn't want. I was going to have to pay for Madonna's filthy mess.

My fears only escalated as the video unfolded. I felt my throat swell when Madonna dropped a knife to reveal a stigmata in her palms. I didn't understand whether I should be happy that she was exposing our MTV Generation to Jesus or upset that she was making a show of him. Was she celebrating or mocking? All confusion aside, I couldn't stop staring at her toned, pale body as she sang in that nothing dress on a field of burning crosses. She was beautiful, sexual, and unapologetic about whatever chaos she was creating. It almost hurt to watch someone with such confidence, knowing I'd never figure out where to find it or what to do with it if I did. Even if the wrath of God were to strike down on her, she didn't seem to care. I hated her for that.

When the video ended, I decided to face my punishment and get it over with. I went upstairs, fully expecting to see Mary pissed off and ready to uproot my anonymous little life. But no one was there. I sat on the bed. *They're just deciding their plan of attack,* I thought. I waited patiently, accepting my fate, prepared for their decision. But still nothing. I watched my Jesus and Mary pictures on the walls, expecting their eyes to move like paintings in an old haunted castle. Nothing. I looked in the mirror, wondering if she was hiding deep beneath that dimension. Nothing. I even stared straight into the hallway light, begging Mary to show up. *Let's just be done with it,* I thought. *Let's end this war. I'm ready.* Only I wasn't. My courage deflated around two in the morning, when I said my prayers more quickly than usual and hurried to bed. I didn't want to call more attention to myself with thoughtful prayers.

After that night, I spent more time in the living room. My bedroom started feeling like a punishment chamber, ready to combust at any moment. And I came to realize that "Like a Prayer" was a popular video. MTV played it constantly—even more than Pearl Jam, much to my brother's dismay.

I decided to conduct a test. Each time it played and no one was around to change the channel, I'd watch it. I knew I was doing something bad. I couldn't put my finger on exactly which commandment I was breaking, but I felt guilty by association. Like I was approving of—even supporting—Madonna's blasphemy. But I was also angry. Why did *she* get to do what she wanted without consequence? Burn crosses as she pleased, kiss saints, play in churches like they were her bedroom, show her bra and boobs in front of God and not think twice about it? I was sure she didn't stay up at night wondering what the holy family thought of it, worrying whether they'd strike down and ruin her stupid boring life. Then I wondered if she knew something I didn't. Perhaps Madonna had actually talked to God and gotten his okay. Whatever the case, I watched it every time just to see what happened. Nothing ever did.

"Like a Prayer" started to feel like my secret weapon. Each time I watched it without consequence, I worried about apparitions a little less. It was thrilling to play with such fire, especially when one could argue that I wasn't the one doing the actual sinning. I bopped a little more each time I watched her dance with the church choir. I sang and clapped in sync with Madonna, pretending everything was going to be all right. She *was* all right, after all. She'd made this video years prior and she was still alive, making music and seeming not at all as though she'd suffered a Godly punishment. If she didn't get zapped for making the video, I'd probably be forgiven for merely watching it. My courage was feeble, though. I still said my prayers and read the requisite Bible passages each night. But as my confidence grew, I got through those beads a little more quickly. I could feel my soul loosening up, like maybe I actually had a choice in all this.

Then I took my tests further. On a gray Monday morning, after a rainy weekend of MTV stalking and four "Like a Prayer" sightings, I dared myself to use God's name in vain. Out loud. In front of people. No one knew of my pious insanity, but still, saying it among witnesses would prove it really happened. I'd do it in casual conversation during recess—nothing malicious. No one would notice. I'd just slip it in between jumping rope with the girls. I'd do it and force myself to just keep going. No hiding behind a tree to confess my sin, no coatroom meltdown when we got inside. I'd just act like a normal, sane kid. It was a lot to ask of myself.

It all went as planned. It was 12:17 PM on a Monday afternoon in April. Lenore kept the Double Dutch going for a full forty-five seconds, and when she hit a complete minute, I struck.

"Oh my God, Lenore, you did it! Awesome!"

I thought I'd immediately tense up and want to hide, but I didn't. In fact, it felt pretty good. Something about it was strangely liberating. I couldn't remember the last time I'd felt so light; so simply okay. I was so energized by the rush of relief that I called dibs on the next turn to jump rope. Until then, I'd only ever watched on the sidelines.

All I could think of for the rest of the day was how much I wanted to hug Madonna, maybe even tell her everything I'd been putting myself through. I'd never told anyone before; it was just me and my self-inflicted rules bullying my every move. Something told me Madonna would understand. She'd be like a cool big sister who wouldn't flinch at my ridiculous stories. I'd let it out and she'd laugh. And I'd know she wasn't laughing at me.

I still prayed, but worked my way around the beads a bit more quickly as each night passed. Then I decided the whole round of fifty Hail Marys wasn't necessary. A batch of ten would do. That soon turned to one Hail Mary and one Our Father. God seemed to understand. I stopped worrying about Mary sightings. Not because I didn't think it was possible, but because I was sure that if she wanted to visit, she would. No amount of praying or sinning would stop that. The few prayers I had left were more of a nod to God; a talisman of everything we'd been through. And a gentle reminder that I hadn't forgotten what he was capable of. I just needed him to let me be.

Are You There God? It's Me, Madonna

Jamia Wilson

WHEN I WAS nine, I read Judy Blume's *Are You There God? It's Me, Margaret*, a stunning bildungsroman about a sixth-grade girl's contemplations on God, her changing body, and her sexuality. I read the book while splashing in the bathtub, listening to Madonna and Salt-N-Pepa grooves, and painting my nails with pink peel-off nail polish. My copy of the book became dog-eared and worn from my many late-night readings with a flashlight. It resonated with me because I liked talking to God, too. I prayed every night before bed, then later asked forgiveness when I stayed up past bedtime (which I did often, reading my Blume book), and when I woke, I gave thanks for the new day. The end of the book struck me most. Instead of participating in a singular religious tradition, she finds comfort in the personal relationship she has developed with God, beyond doctrine, dogma, temples, or churches. Even though I was raised a Baptist with progressive sensibilities, I didn't know there were other people whose personal relationships with God went beyond praying in a temple, mosque, or a church. Everyone around me defined themselves as strictly Christian, Muslim, or Jewish. At that point in my life, I didn't completely comprehend that even though I was passionate about my religion, it was possible for me to define spirituality on my own terms.

Around this time, I was also a blossoming Madonna fan. Even though I didn't have a clear understanding of the meaning of the religious imagery in her videos, her bold exploration of religious themes impacted my perception of spirituality later on. I was completely fascinated with her. I would play *Like a Virgin* on my canary yellow Fisher-Price record player, dancing to "Material Girl," and singing along to lyrics that I didn't understand. I only knew that this mesmerizing creature I'd seen on MTV had a sublime presence—she commanded my attention and seduced me into moving my body until it felt freedom. As a child, I wasn't aware of what a "virgin" was—beyond what we called Mary when we sang "Silent Night" in Sunday school and caroling at Christmas—but I understood that Madonna's force was both worldly and divine.

★

Over the years, I became increasingly enamored with Madonna's enduring spirit and her rabble-rousing. She revered and re-appropriated religious imagery in "Like a Virgin," dancing suggestively while donning a crucifix and sexy lace. I was entranced by her use of song to express her own spiritual experience, revealing an alternative approach to restrictive and patriarchal traditions. For Madonna, religion was fun—it was about celebration rather than condemnation.

And she's made it fun for almost thirty years, rebelling against Catholic guilt and rejecting the tired association of sex with shame. She reveled in her own definition of feminine sexuality, exhibiting vulnerability and submission to a saintly figure in "Like a Prayer," and wielding a dominatrix's whip as she kicked off her Confessions Tour in 2006. As a teenager, I appreciated these contradictions. I viewed Madonna as a sort of pop culture Mary Magdalene, unafraid to express herself in the face of controversy or even condemnation from the highest Catholic judge himself: the pope.

Associating spiritual communion with sacred sexuality, in "Like a Prayer" Madonna equated holy redemption with the freedom of sexual ecstasy. She celebrated both God and sexuality, blurring the lines between the two, rejoicing in the power of both her body *and* her soul.

I first viewed this controversial video when I was entering my teens, before I understood much about my sexuality. I recall being drawn in by Madonna's fearless expression of raw sensuality in tandem with images and icons that signified God's grace. In contrast to what I learned from my church's interpretation of dogma, Madonna informed my belief that sex and the spirit are married, and the tension that exists between the two is man-made. Madge taught me that sex and spiritual devotion are often about the sweetness of learning to surrender, not about shame.

Madonna's evolution as a spiritual seeker has remained constant throughout a career fueled by reinvention. For almost three decades I've watched Madonna mature musically and spiritually. She has positioned herself as a spiritual icon that the public can buy, leveraging her celebrity to attract consumers to her music and to Kabbalah. But it wasn't just me taking note of her spiritual openness. She profoundly influenced the culture at large—she was one of the first celebrities to encourage the MTV generation to try yoga, calling it not only a powerful spiritual and physical practice, but "a metaphor for life." She was on to something. Not only did yoga become uber-trendy, but I blossomed under its teachings and practice as well. I realized that the quest for the alignment of mind, body, and spirit was imperative on my path to enlightenment. Before I discovered Sri Swami Satchidananda's mantra, "one truth, many paths" during a yoga class in college, I only knew Margaret's and Madonna's no-apology approaches to spiritual curiosity. When I found Satchidananda's mantra, I immediately experienced a connection with a sense of oneness that I instinctively understood but could not name.

Did this same sense of openness, I wondered, inspire Madonna's next spiritual evolution, when she devoted herself to Kabbalah, once again inspiring countless others to seek the same? I remember meeting two young men in graduate school who joined the New York City Kabbalah Center with the not-particularly-spiritual mission of getting a glimpse of Madonna herself. But months after they finally spotted her, they continued going, energized and enthralled by the beauty of the faith.

I am in awe of Madonna's transformative power, and her ability to expand our collective mindset about the limits of spirituality. I connect most with her message of self-love and of seeking a sense of authenticity through experimentation. Madonna makes the rules herself, rejecting the constraints of strict dogma to decide what nourishes her spiritually at any given moment. And if her videos and live shows are any indication, part of what has always nourished her most is dancing.

In her "Ray of Light" and "Frozen" videos, Madonna's performance, to me, seemed like one of transcendent spirituality through movement. And I related to this almost as much as her self-expression through singing, because it was an equally rich outlet for me in high school and college, whether I was performing in school recitals, belly-dancing with my Lebanese and Egyptian friends, or simply boogying with friends at our monthly Prince-inspired dance party. I discovered the beautiful solace that dance provided me, a sacred clearing of my consciousness that I couldn't find any other way. And I sensed that Madonna reached some similar place when she performed.

A pop-culture shaman, her intoxicating beats appealed to my primal energy, inviting me to leave my mind and simply enjoy my essential nature. She exposed her own truths in a way that inspired me to relate to her authentically, to the idea that we can evolve and reinvent ourselves, too.

But with evolution and wisdom comes personal insight, and while I love how Madonna seems to embody both Catholicism's Mary and Hinduism's Kali (she possesses both a calming and destructive energy) my relationship with Madonna today is complicated. As a faith-loving feminist, I respect her for challenging patriarchal dominance in both the music industry and the political church. But at the same time, I'm disturbed by her subscription to a brand of limitless capitalism that first emerged with her hit song "Material Girl." Her celebrity and financial success sometimes thrives on the selling of the exoticism and fetishization of women of color—as demonstrated in her geisha-inspired Drowned World tour.

I loathed her when I read her racist comments about dating "disrespectful" black men in a 1991 issue of *Spin* magazine, years after my initial love affair with her began. Truthfully, I am still working on getting over this betrayal by a woman who has both celebrated and co-opted elements of African American culture.

Though I still define myself as a Christian (with openness to many truths), I stand by Madonna's free speech and her individual interpretation and expression of her Catholic beliefs. I adored her when she kissed a beautiful black saint in the "Like a Prayer" video, rejecting historical racial and religious constructions. Still, I despised her hypocrisy when she turned against powerful feminist musician Sinead O'Connor, attacking her in the press for tearing up a picture of the pope.

Despite my mixed feelings, I condemn the attacks she continues to receive from Catholic organizations and family groups for simulating masturbation, using erotic iconography, kissing saint figures in her videos, and displaying glittery crosses during her tours. These critics attempt to crucify Madonna because she embodies an unruly brand of the "free will" they preach about but also fear.

Most of all, I respect the way she has transformed our culture and changed our conversation about the inextricable linkage of religion, sexuality, and the feminine divine. Madonna's rebellious border-crossing both titillates and infuriates us. She is a saint and a sinner, a mirror of us all.

Our Lady of the Hot Pants

Kristin McGonigle

I HEREBY NOMINATE Madonna, by virtue of my tangential connection to the Roman Catholic Church, for sainthood. Yes, I realize saints are supposed to be dead first. Hear me out.

Sainthood is usually reserved for the purest of heart among us, the holiest of souls, those who sacrificed their lives in the name of God, or charity, or hanging out with animals, like Saint Francis. But there are saints for everything: Saint Blaise is the patron saint of throats. You can pray to Saint Anthony when you lose your keys, as he is in charge of lost things, but not lost causes, because Saint Jude is the go-to guy for those. Madonna already is, in my opinion, the patron saint of the dance floor. I say we start the process of making it official.

The first saints were among the many that died at the hands of the Romans, martyred for their beliefs. This was during the dawn of Christianity, and anyone who died defending his or her faith instantly became a saint. Those who followed were known for their piety as well as their beliefs, but the club was becoming more exclusive. By the seventeenth century, the Vatican started setting up guidelines and making up rules. Dying was no longer enough; there had to be posthumous miracles and spontaneous healing. Then they created official steps in the sainthood process: beatification and canonization. People who were alive had to vouch for you; it was like getting into the Harvard of heaven. By the twentieth century, modern civilization had cemented itself and it was pretty easy to differentiate the possible candidates for sainthood. Catholics started streamlining the process for their favorites. Pope John Paul II himself was filling out the paperwork on Mother Theresa before they got her body on the stretcher. When he died in 2005, he got the EZ Pass treatment as well.

So I'm taking it upon myself to get the ball rolling for Madonna, whose selection may seem a both controversial and nonsensical choice. Madonna has certainly been persecuted for her faith, both in the beginning of her career and now, as she seeks God in a very public way. But when examining her contribution to the twentieth and twenty-first century religious experience, it is clear that her infusion of spirituality into modern music and her concept of religious ecstasy is a reflection of the ancient traditions of Catholicism, in a society where the pious are hard to come by.

I became familiar with Madonna in 1983, due to the television program *Solid Gold,* the video for "Borderline," and the fact that she was an actual person called Madonna—a name I had only known previously as belonging solely to the mother of Jesus. Even at a tender age, I thought, "Who names their kid 'Madonna?'"

It was a big deal, and with such a big name, it's no wonder she became the icon she is. It is common to name your daughter Mary in honor of the Virgin Mother, but to be christened "Madonna" is different. It's like naming your son "Jesus," but not the Hispanic version.

When "Like a Virgin" exploded onto the scene, Madonna had already established herself as a purveyor of street culture and dance hits. She was known for uniqueness and took pride in it. Her name itself was enough to get her in the door and to shock some listeners initially, but it was her incorporation of religious iconography and symbolism that made her a scandal star. Talking about feeling "like a virgin" while wearing crosses and rosaries as accessories, Madonna pissed off a lot of people.

Though most just assumed she was shirking authority and thumbing her nose at the Catholic Church, Madonna's use of religious imagery was actually a natural extension of what we Catholics were raised to do. We all wore crosses around our necks; Madonna just wore a bigger one, and often without a shirt. And whether or not it was her intention, Madonna's sexualized view of Catholicism, which debuted in "Like a Virgin" and crested with "Like a Prayer," held a mirror to the latent eroticism that simmers below the surface of Roman Catholic culture. Madonna is not the first person to fantasize about making out with Jesus; she's just the first one who did it on television.

As a parochial school student, plaid jumper and all, the dawn of Madonna blew my little mind. Because of—or despite—her name, I was drawn to her music, much like others of my age and gender. In 1984, Madonna released the album *Like a Virgin* and its titular single. That was the first time I realized that the word "virgin" could apply to people other than Jesus's mom.

In the "Like A Virgin" video, it was not the dancing and writhing on Venice's grand canals, or the "Boy Toy" belt buckle, or the unaccountable appearance of a lion (seriously, was that ever explained?) that was taboo or titillating. It was the appearance of Madonna in the virginal white gown. White dresses are a staple in the Catholic experience, used in the celebration of sacraments when rites are given at various stages of life to commemorate your commitment to the church. Their procurement and employment is taken very seriously. You receive your first sacrament as a baby, at baptism, when you are cleansed of original sin. Girls get their second fancy white dress (and second big party) when they celebrate the sacrament of Holy Communion. It's a rite of passage for girls in the second grade, but no one really talks about the symbolism behind it. These seven- and eight-year-old girls are trotted out in white gowns, veils, and gloves, like tiny little brides in tiny little wedding dresses. Boys wear tuxedoes. It looks like they are marrying God. There is commonly a giant party afterwards where guests bring money and gifts.

Marriage is the last big sacrament, so fun that many people do it numerous times (unless you become a priest or a nun—though that is, in a sense, a marriage to Christ; the dresses aren't nearly as nice.) For their weddings, Catholic women are expected to get the biggest, puffiest, whitest dresses they can find as a proclamation of their awesomely big, puffy purity.

In the video for "Like a Virgin," Madonna was role-playing. Her too-short wedding dress (which kind of looked like a communion dress, which is kind of awesome) was a caricature—no longer a symbol of sanctity, but of sex. People were pissed off because she was singing about virginity in the past tense. And, let's face it, because she's a woman. Women aren't supposed to talk about sex openly, and Catholic women aren't supposed to talk about sex at all, unless it is in relation to baby-making magic. Women are defined by their relationship and sexual choices, but sex is only discussed in relation to the creation of a family.

Let's take a minute here to think about how our conversations and perceptions about sex have changed significantly for the better within the last two decades. How the chasm between taboo and candid has gotten smaller. You know who helped make that happen? Madonna.

There is an undercurrent of sex that occupies everything, but it is rarely discussed. When it comes to the forefront explosively, like when Madonna shows up, there is a surprising amount of shock, but few sit back and ask, "Um, isn't this what everyone was thinking about anyway?"

The uproar over another religious-themed Madonna song, "Like a Prayer," was outdone by the cacophony generated by the accompanying video. But the song itself can be read as an homage to the Song of Solomon (or its street name, "that sexy part of the Bible.") It is familiar to most as the go-to passage for couples in Catholic wedding ceremonies:

> "My Beloved is like a gazelle or young stag. Behold, there he stands behind our wall, gazing through the windows, looking through the lattice."
>
> —SONG OF SOLOMON 2:9

It's a beautiful image, and the entire "song" is an eight-chapter poem that purports to be a conversation between two lovers (presumably Solomon in the male role), but most scholars read it as an allegory. "My beloved" is God, or for Christians, Jesus. It's a 117-line love letter to Jesus. It begins thusly:

> "Let him kiss me with the kisses of his mouth! For your love is better than wine."
>
> —SONG OF SOLOMON 1:2

When read from this perspective, it's not only romantic, but also kind of endearing. It's not hard to imagine having deep and profound feelings of affection for one's Messiah. It's kind of like the way little kids want to kiss their parents; there is sweetness to this desired level of intimacy.

And yet, we don't really talk about love that way. We talk about it in relationship to a man and a woman coming together in the sacrament of marriage. Much like everything fun and cool in life, namely sex and affection, Christianity has managed to put its own buzz-kill spin on it.

In the song "Like a Prayer," Madonna offers this: "Life is a mystery/Everyone must stand alone/I hear you call my name/And it feels like home." It is the first line of the song and repeated as the refrain therein, and Madonna's voice begins bare and choral. It's an incantation in the same vein as the Song of Solomon, a church song: "When you call my name/It's like a little prayer/I'm down on my knees/I want to take you there."

Granted, it's a little more direct than "For your love is better than wine," but it's the Madonna version of guileless affection.

In the video for "Like a Prayer," the narrative element supersedes the biblical allusion. The setting is a church, as well as a field where Madonna sings among burning crosses. A black man is unjustly charged of a crime, and his image is also similar to a statue of Jesus, which Madonna kisses, bringing it to life. One may argue that the images used to convey the song's themes are a bit heavy-handed, thus losing the message in the medium, but the essence is conveyed. We all want a human connection to our God. It is right and sweet to want to show affection to the divine. It is the human reaction, and our form of grace.

As a fan of her music and of her womanhood, I have always felt a kinship with Madonna. We both came from a Catholic upbringing where sexuality was oppressed, where women came into adulthood with a confused, shameful sense of their relationship to their bodies and sex. Of course, my experience was different, because I had Madonna to show me the way.

She may not have been chased by lions in Rome (though there was that one in the Venice castle) and she may not have sacrificed her life to service, animals, or helping people find their keys, but as we evolve as a society, maybe our concept of sainthood should evolve as well. Maybe we need our saints to understand sin as well as the divine; to be a little Mary Magdalene and a little Mary, Mother of God; to know the grace in the sweat and sweetness of the human condition. And to dance like someone who knows God is watching and just doesn't give a damn. Amen.

The Black Madonna

J. Victoria Sanders

IN A 1989 interview with *Rolling Stone* magazine, Madonna was asked if she ever felt African American. Her response: "Oh, yes, all the time . . . When I was a little girl, I wished I was black. All my girlfriends were black . . . If being black is synonymous with having soul, then yes, I feel that I am."

Somehow I knew that Madonna had a thing for black folks even before I read that passage. Her soulful presence connected me to her more than any other white female star of the 1980s and 1990s. She was down without trying to be. She was a sister in white-girl skin. More than her music, her movies, the *Sex* book, or her love life (except for the Sean Penn part, which I overtly envied), she kept my attention because of her interactions with people of color in her videos and concerts. Aside from the Run DMC "Walk This Way" collaboration, Madonna was the first non-black artist of my generation to really place herself in the center of blackness and black art without mocking it or trying to supplant it. She even moved a little like a sister, maybe because of her Alvin Ailey training.

In the video for "Like a Prayer," Madonna kisses the feet of a black saint who is imprisoned behind bars as she dances to a black choir with a circle of black children dressed in white. Even now, about twenty years later, watching the video moves me in a way that few other music videos have. Madonna had power and clout to spare, and she chose to subvert the idea that blackness was something white women should stay as far away from as possible.

Also, as far as I could tell from "Like a Prayer," she was either a former Catholic or someone who didn't like Catholics all that much. This was a no-no in my Catholic house, so naturally I wanted to find out more about her.

I eyed Madonna obsessively from around age eight until I turned eighteen—roughly from *True Blue* in 1986 until she told her *Bedtime Stories* in 1994. But I never quite understood what made her so compelling until I became a woman myself. Part of what endeared her to me was the way she wielded power in business, on stage, and in her own life as a badass bitch (in the best sense of the word). But it was also her connection to black women I admired. It made sense that Madonna signed one of my favorite artists of all time, the beautiful bisexual black woman Meshell Ndegeocello, to her Maverick record label. Another thing that made sense: The only other multiplatform female mogul in her league, business-wise, was Oprah. These two have a lot in common: a dramatic rise to fame, shrewd business tactics, and the ability to flip the world off just by basking in their own extreme success.

And they are both unlikely trendsetters. Oprah became an almost accidental arbiter of literary taste while Madonna made adopting African children chic for hot celebrity white women. She shook those brown-then-blonde curls and licked at the gap between her teeth like she was devouring life itself. Madonna offered little girls and young women swagger without all the testosterone-infused bravado.

This was big stuff to me, and it set the stage for this self-help geek to become mesmerized by a woman who helped herself to living vividly and unapologetically, no matter what the haters had to say. Her position in my world as a powerful pop culture figure was almost entirely separate from the quality of her music, which was never really my thing. I loved her because to me she signaled elements of who and what I could become if I dropped my doubt and self-consciousness.

That self-consciousness wasn't necessarily about race—I knew I was never going to be white, and I didn't want to be. I didn't see Madonna and cry Pecola Breedlove-of-*The Bluest Eye* tears, though I did grow up Catholic with my reference for Madonna, the mother of God, as a white woman. I believed, for a time, that white women had more heavenly DNA than black women, the same way I believed Mary heard me when I prayed her name using borrowed rosaries. But in the communities of color where I grew up, the most prized beauties had brown skin. Being affirmed culturally seemed separate from whether a woman was angelic, pure, or godly.

Religious life, like most things I experienced as a little girl, was a segregated sphere. White families, a la the ones on *Family Ties* and *Small Wonder*, existed on one side, with the black families of *The Cosby Show*, *A Different World*, and *Family Matters* existing on another. At Catholic Mass, Mom and I were usually one of the only black families in attendance.

And in the early 1980s, my music world was also segregated. The physical world around me was largely black and Latino, and it competed with the media I consumed. And media was everything to me—being poor meant not having money to travel, see a Broadway show, or do anything that wasn't free or requiring a "suggested donation." Music, movies, and TV were free, or pretty damn close, so they encapsulated my whole idea of culture.

"White" music was rock. Phil Collins, George Michael, and Taylor Dayne made up the fare I was exposed to via my mother's affinity for the soft-rock radio station on our alarm clock. "Black" music was what spoke to my heart. We claimed Michael Jackson, even when he started to look less like us and more like someone beyond racial classification; Whitney Houston, Prince, Tina Turner, and Marvin Gaye were other favorites.

As a rule, I was not a fan of white-girl music. Cyndi Lauper was okay, but I needed an image of someone like me—someone with brown skin. I got lucky that Whitney did some Cyndi-like punky stuff with her hair and her voice in the video for "I Wanna Dance With Somebody." If I weren't made to sing her song "The Greatest Love of All" repeatedly throughout elementary school, which made me sort of sick of her, I might have put Whitney on the virtual pedestal Madonna took up. As it was, Whitney was the sweet girl next door. Skinny, brown like me, with a wild wig and a big voice, and a breath capacity that I could only dream of. She was having fun—the daughter of a gospel singer with a "safe" image for singing ballads about love and broken hearts. Madonna was bigger, riskier, and it seemed like she had less to lose as she wore corsets while singing about sex and seduction.

In the absence of anyone else like her, Madonna became my standard for female sexuality, despite the fact that different rules apply to black women in the public sphere. Janet Jackson would come into her own later, but even her iconography was tamer. Her lewd expressions were more memorable for their suggestiveness ("That's the Way Love Goes") and for the unscripted Hottentot Venus-like performance (the Super Bowl flash) than for any purposeful expression of her sexuality. (See: "Let's Wait Awhile," "Velvet Rope," and "Anytime, Anyplace.") And Tina Turner was rugged and raw, tough and able, gritty and beautiful in her strength. But she was not saucy. She was not compelling. She was not scandalous.

I loved Madonna because she spoke to the part of me that didn't quite fit any of the sexual, racial, or religious scripts from which I was supposed to take my cues. It might have been the soul of feminism I was gravitating toward, though I didn't know any feminists in my Bronx hometown or in the shelters where we sometimes lived. There was a race- and class-neutral part of me that wanted to do whatever the fuck I wanted. I knew nice girls weren't supposed to curse and that, at least in my house, they were supposed to go to Mass once a week and confess their sins. But the way Madonna sang, the way she had fun, and the fact that she kept on keeping on even as she was derided for it, has always inspired a different part of me.

I can't say for sure how big this part of me was, really, but it was significant enough that at age ten I pulled a Punky Brewster. For no reason at all, I cut three pairs of holes in the thighs of my jeans and laced fluorescent green shoelaces through them. To her credit, my mother did not tamp down these horrid attempts at defining my own style. Thankfully, she also didn't take many pictures.

With that one homemade attempt to change my physical image, I was trying to be free of definitions of womanhood that I wasn't even fully aware of yet. Madonna circumvented those definitions. Despite the fact that she couldn't sing that well and wasn't that strong of a dancer, she seemed ultimately cool to me because she was disavowing herself of all the things I'd thought white women were supposed to do and be. She was outside all the pre-existing scripts—she hung out with hot Latino and black gay boys, mostly. She made "vogueing," the popular practice in which predominantly African American and Latino gay men dressed in drag and froze in model-like poses, a worldwide sensation (even though it was made moderately famous by the documentary "Paris Is Burning" a year before her song came out). And she wore, well, hardly anything.

Her skimpy outfits (or lack of them) stood out to me as I slowly, painfully grew out of being a tomboy. At that age, my awareness of my body and other women's bodies became more like an obsession. I wanted breasts, but I was flat-chested. I had no curves to speak of. I could sing, but I couldn't dance. I was better at reading, writing, and school than just about anything else I'd attempted.

These days, the list of black women artists who have Madonna-esque elements is long: Lil' Kim, Eve, and Nicki Minaj are just a few who embody the essence of her swagger. As a white artist who was unafraid to express her affinity for black culture in a time before it was cool, Madonna set the stage for a new generation of women—celebrities and regular folks alike—to express themselves outside of racial classifications. What was then taboo turned out to be just one more way that Madonna was a visionary, embracing the best parts of black culture before our generation caught up and followed her lead.

Mad Mensch

Wendy Shanker

AFTER HALF A century on this planet, Madonna has creative expression and power, intellectual curiosity, beautiful children, financial security (and then some), and a team of friends and colleagues who she can love and trust. Only one thing is missing.

Madonna needs a mensch. A good man, a stand-up guy with means and influence. "Mensch" is a Yiddish word meaning "a person of integrity and honor." Yiddish lexicologist Leo Rosten says a mensch is "someone to admire and emulate, someone of noble character. The key to being a real mensch is nothing less than a sense of what is right, responsible, decorous."

I'm thinking that since Madonna got such a life-affirming boost from Kabbalah, maybe she would be equally inspired by a Jewish connection in her love life.

She may have gotten fleeting pleasure from guys like A-Rod (emphasis on the *rod*) and 22-year old Brazilian DJ Jesus Luz, but they can't match her cerebral and artistic maturity. I know she's drawn to

Latino men. I know she is attracted to fiery figures. I know she's got a libido that made her ex-boyfriend Warren Beatty look like a prude. But clearly this kind of Renaissance woman requires more than orgasms and mix tapes to fulfill her romantic needs.

Sean Penn may have been a soul mate, but he was not a mensch. Mensches don't ball up their Versace suits and leave them on the floor. Mensches don't tie their wives to chairs (without asking nicely first).

Warren Beatty may have been a Lothario, but he was not a mensch. Mensches don't sleep with more than one woman at the same time. Mensches don't worry about their younger girlfriends stealing their spotlight.

Carlos Leon may have been a good sperminator, but he was not a mensch. You'd never confuse a mensch with a personal trainer.

Guy Ritchie may have been a . . . well, as far as I can tell, he was pretty much just an asshole. Or an arsehole, if you prefer.

In my head, I picture Madonna with a guy her age or older. He's been a success in life in both appearances (money, taste, looks, philanthropy) and on more subtle levels (intelligence, influence, self-confidence). He's a man who has already had a wife and children and is not seeking more. A man who is not, I repeat, *not* in the entertainment business. He may find showbiz amusing, but his ego is not affected by media whims. His investment in the relationship isn't about being attached to "Madonna," the icon, but connecting to Madonna, the woman. The activist. The artist. The mother.

And he definitely needs to be a Jew.

Some of Madonna's most successful relationships in life have been with Jewish men: Seymour Stein, who signed her to Warner Bros. Freddy DeMann, her pre-Maverick manager. Liz Rosenberg, her publicist and defender for decades (fine, she's not a man, but she's as tough as one). Guy Oseary, her longtime partner in crime. And Michael Berg, the rabbi who taught her Kabbalah.

I'm not talking about a neurotic Jew, like Woody Allen or Larry David, or a power-hungry Napoleon type, like Michael Bloomberg or

Ron Perelman. I'm picturing a Thomas Friedman, a Rahm Emmanuel, a Guggenheim, an Annenberg—a thoughtful, strong-willed Jewish man who is more impressed by her brain than her resume or connections. A man who can offer her stability, security, and a nice pair of diamond studs. A man who makes reservations, vacations in Miami Beach, and respects his mother, God rest her soul. A father figure who is not her father.

I'm not saying that Madonna (or any woman) is incomplete without a man. Far from it. But since she's always indicated that she wants a relationship, why not have one with a mensch? Granted, they're in short supply. I'm in the mensch market myself, and I'm not exactly striking gold. I can tell you that when a Jewish girl gets serious about finding a real relationship and not just a fling, a *b'sheart* (meant-to-be) instead of a one-night stand, there's only one place to go. So I hope she won't mind, but I signed Madonna up on J-Date.

Believe me, Madonna wasn't the first shiksa trolling the site. Plenty of non-Jewish women who want to strike gold with a NJB (Nice Jewish Boy) lurk around on there. No one knew it was Madonna who signed on, anyway. If they recognized her stats, they probably weren't straight. I didn't put pictures up, because everyone would identify Madonna. My point wasn't to lure men in—even if someone tried to initiate contact based on her profile, I didn't respond. I wasn't trying to impersonate her, just profile her. Plus, it was probably illegal.

First I had to choose a sign-on name. Since she used it in Kabbalah, I went with "EstherC." The "C" is for Ciccone, but I also thought it was a good play on Ester-C, the vitamin, because Madonna is such a health nut. Then I began to fill in the rest . . .

Name

EstherC

Your Birthdate

AUGUST 16, 1958

What is your current relationship status?
DIVORCED

Do you have children?
3 OR MORE (Lourdes, Rocco, David & Mercy)

Your Zodiac sign
LEO (Very important in finding the right partner. We want a Leo-appreciative man, not a conflicting sign.)

Describe yourself and your personality. What are you passionate about? Are you a political junkie, a Ph.D. in archaeology, a tennis fanatic? We all have something that makes us unique; this is your chance to tell about yourself and the things that get you excited. Don't be shy—dare to bare it all!

I thought I'd let Madonna handle that one herself. So I borrowed a few lines from her essay about her Kabbalah-inspired awakening from Israel's leading paper, *Yediot Ahronot*:

"I had traveled the world many times over, performed in soccer stadiums, appeared in films, dined with state leaders, collaborated with great artists and achieved what most people would view as a high level of success but I still felt something was missing in my life. Suddenly Life no longer seemed like a series of Random events. I started to see patterns in life. I woke up. I began to be conscious of my words and my actions and to really see the results of them . . . I also began to see that being Rich and Famous wasn't going to bring me lasting fulfillment and that it was not the end of the journey; that it was the beginning of the journey."

Well said, Madonna. I moved on to physical information: *Height?* Five-foot-four (but debatable). *Weight?* Let's say 102. *Body style:* Athletic?

Muscular? Ripped? Yes, but I didn't want to scare people. I went with FIRM & TONED. Hair BLONDE, eyes BLUE.

I grew up in . . .
MICHIGAN

Languages you speak?
I wasn't sure about that one. I checked off ENGLISH, ITALIAN, and OTHER in honor of Chichewa, the local dialect in Malawi.

Religious background?
Catholic was clearly not an option on J-Date. So I checked off CULTURALLY JEWISH BUT NOT PRACTICING.

Education level?
SOME COLLEGE (She never graduated from my alma mater, the University of Michigan. Hey, that might be a good gift for the girl who's got everything—a college degree!).

Describe what you do:
World dominator? Most famous woman on the planet? How about ENTERTAINER.

Off to the next section, "Personality and Interests." I just clicked on boxes for this part.

My personality is best described as . . .
Adventurous/Wild/Spontaneous, Argumentative, Artistic, Compulsive, Flamboyant, Flirtatious/Playful, High Energy, High Maintenance, Humorous/Witty, Intellectual, Sensitive/Nurturing/Loving, Outgoing, Practical, Romantic, Self-Confident, Serious/Responsible, Sophisticated/Worldly, Spiritual, Stubborn, Talkative, Unconventional/Free-Spirited.

What didn't make the list? Conservative. Easy-going. Procrastinator.

In my free time, I enjoy . . .
Antiquing, Collecting, Dining Out, Entertaining, Hanging Out with Friends, Home Improvement/Decorating, Intimate Conversations, Investing, Listening to/Playing Music, Partying, People Watching, Photography, Reading/Writing, Shopping, Surfing the Web/Chatting Online, Traveling/Weekend Trips/Adventure Travel, Movies/TV.

What didn't Madonna enjoy? I left out Board Games, Card Games, Video Games. The woman does not seem to enjoy activities where you have to sit down.

In my free time, I like to go to . . .
Antique Stores/Flea Markets/Garage Sales, Art Galleries, Bars/Nightclubs, Bookstores, Charity Events, Concerts, Dances (Line, Ballroom, Tango), Live Theater, Movies, Museums, Opera, Political Events, Raves/Underground Parties, Restaurants, Symphony, Volunteer Events.

Where didn't Madonna like to go, in my estimation? I skipped Comedy Clubs, Shopping Malls, Sporting Events (her bullfighting era is over).

My favorite physical activities:
Aerobics, Biking, Working Out/Weightlifting, Dancing, Hiking/Walking, Horseback Riding, Martial Arts, Yoga/Meditation.

I left out cricket, hunting, and rugby. Hey, Guy . . . *snap!*

My favorite food(s):
Does she actually eat food? This is a stumper. I stuck with VEGETARIAN/ORGANIC and VEGAN. And KOSHER, naturally.

My favorite music:

All of 'em. I checked off every kind they offered.

Now this is where I really had to stop and think: the "Relationship" section. Again, I didn't want to put words in her mouth, so I let Madonna speak for herself. I went back through those revealing 1991 Carrie Fisher interviews from *Rolling Stone*, along with a few other choice interview snippets, to compile the answers for this section.

My ideal relationship:

"I'm dying to meet someone who knows more than me. I keep meeting guys who know less. I suppose looks are important, but I've certainly found myself attracted to men who aren't conventionally attractive. Painters are good, too. There are two things that I can't do and wish I could—write and paint. Smart, confident, smells good, sense of humor, likes to write letters, likes antique jewelry."

My past relationships:

"I'm not with any of the people I'm not with for a much larger reason: We just weren't meant to be. If I had changed and given in, or what I conceived to be giving in, to certain concessions that people had asked of me, maybe the relationships would have been successful on the one hand, but then I would have had to give up other things in my career. And then I would have been miserable."

I am looking for:

"A male image that I'm really moved by is somewhere between an Oscar Wilde type of a male: the fop, the long hair, the suits, too witty for his own good, incredibly smart, scathingly funny—all that. But then my other ideal is more like the Buddhist monk—the shaved head, actually someone who sublimates their sexuality. I am attracted to a thug. I like that quality, but I like the other side of it, too. Because all guys who go around behaving in macho ways are really scared little girls. So you have to look beneath the surface. There's a difference between my ideal man and a man that I'm sexually attracted to, believe me. Therein lies the rub."

My perfect first date:
"Dinner is really good. Where they have good margaritas."

Done. Madonna's J-Date profile was now complete. It was kind of creepy how much I knew about Madonna, but at the same time, it was totally fun to fill out. I finally understood why J-Date claims that 22 percent of their subscriptions are paid for by parents who want to marry off their kids. And why my married friends are always so anxious to help me with my dating search. It's wish fulfillment for them. Though I still don't understand why people push so hard for marriage when so many fall apart. Even Madonna told Carrie Fisher, post-Sean Penn, that she wouldn't get married again. Yet she did. I guess love changes everything. *Sigh.*

Now, with that information set up in "EstherC's" profile, I did a search to see who might be a good match for her. *Ooh, 360 hits!* One for every day of the year (not including Rosh Hashanah, Yom Kippur, and let's say . . . *Tu B'Shevat*). One of the first selections: BIALYBOY247. A handsome sonovabitch, and he was wearing a tux, holding a violin. Sixty-three years old. Divorced, six-foot-two. He described himself this way:

"Played music all over the world (orchestral, festivals, Broadway, etc.), and would enjoy it even more with someone who adds fuel to the fire of the usual chemistry."

A professional, worldly musician! That would be a nice fit for Madonna. He's a Scorpio. Could be kind of devious, but they're also pretty sexy. Plus, no kids of his own, so he could treasure Madonna's children without any distraction! I added him to her J-Date "Hot List."

Next in the search results: BONAPPETIT1. A native Frenchman! A brilliant cook! But he was only five-foot-five! Forget it. How about TAKEACHANCE? He was sixty-seven and divorced. His picture looked kind of dated, but the guy could write with tongue firmly in cheek:

"Seeking a rich, sexy dame with a mansion in Miami, an atelier in Paris, and a winter home in Monaco where we can snuggle in front of a roaring fire, gazing into each other's eyes. Did I mention you should have blue eyes, blonde hair, and a perfect body? And it's essential you be high maintenance. Very high maintenance."

A rich, sexy, high-maintenance, blue-eyed blonde? This had Madge's name all over it! TAKEACHANCE had a PhD and had studied psychology, philosophy, and comparative religion. Here's what he said about past relationships:

"What I want in a "Relationship Kit": a sense of humor, to keep things in perspective; a shovel, to leave no stone unturned when trying to make a relationship work; and a towel to throw in when it really ain't working."

TAKEACHANCE was funny! Liked him! Put him on the Hot List!

Okay, back to the Search Results. MICHAELMAN. Wait—I *knew* that guy! He'd hit on a million of my friends. One girl who went home with him said he had a kinky side—based on *Erotica*, that's not necessarily a bad thing for Madonna. His fetishes went unmentioned in his well-written (and grammatically correct, always a turn-on) profile. But he was looking for someone way younger than Madonna. Good luck with that, buddy. Same went for SPANKY. Whether his user name was a naughty thing or a goofy thing, I wasn't feeling it.

YOUNGATHEART lived in Queens. Nope.

HAPPYHAROLD used a headshot. Nope.

MUSIKLOVE was watching TV in his photo. Nope.

321SHELDON had a photo so old it was probably taken with a Kodak Disc camera. Nope.

MATZO MAN . . . He was handsome, had kind of a Frank Langella look, but . . . an actor. Forget it.

DEEPWATERU. That guy was hot. Would never have guessed he was over fifty! Dirty blond hair, blue eyes, six-foot-four, looked like a surfer. Okay, so he meant "love at first sight" but spelled it "love at first site." We all make mistakes when it comes to homonyms. He'd never been married, but said he had two kids—that's interesting. A single dad?

My babies are a pug (Luke) and a French bulldog (Leia). They are the best little people in the world.

Star Wars dogs as stand-ins for actual human children? Deal breaker. We're out.

Check this one out! MILESAWAY is a black dude! I knew there were non-Jewish women crawling around the site, but I'd never seen a black guy on J-Date . . . oh, he was a biracial Jew. Like Lenny Kravitz! He had kind of a jazzy, light-radio way of writing, and he used the phrase "my woman" with too much frequency. But on the plus side:

My woman is intelligent, insightful, worldly, sexy, playful, mindful, and happy. She's warm, romantic, emotionally stable, and spiritually evolved. Soft and talented lips are a plus.

Madonna always said she was a great kisser! Remember—kissing, thumbs up; hummers, thumbs down?

What about HOLYHUNK212! Total man meat, he looked like that

Italian guy from the first *Sex and the City* movie . . . wait, the picture wasn't him. HOLYHUNK212 was actually a husky nerd, luring Jewesses in with a fake photo. But I found that hilarious. He wrote:

"I AM A FUN LOVING DIVORCED MAN WHO WAS MARRIED FOR TWENTY SIX YEARS AND HAVE HAD A CRAZY TIME MEETING MANY WOMEN BUT AM NOW READY TO SETTLE DOWN AND FIND THE RIGHT WOMEN WHO WILL MAKE ME FEEL WHOLE AND SOMEONE I CAN SETTLE DOWN WITH AND ENJOY THE INTAMACY I HAD WITH MY FIRST WIFE."

Okay, he had a caps issue and a run-on sentence problem, plus he lived in Jersey, but at least HOLYHUNK212 spoke from the heart. Too bad he was looking for a thirty-year old. Oy! Lots of guys available, but where were the sleek and sophisticated professionals? Did they not go on J-Date? Did they have their own boutique site, CEO-Date? Hey, was this one? Nah, he spelled ENTERPRENER wrong, so forget it.

All this made me wonder why hunting down men on J-Date was so much fun when I was doing it for Madonna, but so agonizing when I did it for myself. I guess it's that strange phenomenon where you can look so ugly to yourself in a picture, but in someone else's eyes, you're beautiful. Or how you can fix other people's problems so easily when your own seem impossible to solve. When it comes to finding true love, everyone can tell you how it's supposed to be done, but you don't really know until you get your heart broken yourself.

But . . . one final scan . . . Look! NYCMENSCH! An actual mensch by name! He wrote:

"I was the youngest son of nine in a loving, orthodox Moroccan family. I have a master's of law in economics, I consider myself a businessman with a lawyer's edge. Several years ago a tragedy struck my life, when I lost the three most important women a man could ever love in a one-year period: my wife, my mother, and most importantly, my daughter. Nonetheless, I am a very happy person. I have tried to go on with my life, by giving back to the Jewish community and by living life as fully as possible."

Heartbreaking, genuine, and so sweet. We've found our man, Madonna: NYCMENSCH. Let me know if you want your password.

Burning Up

"Your sexual identity is so important. The more you pay attention to it, the more you realize that just about everything in the world is centered around sexual attraction and sexual power."

—MADONNA

Madonna Is Down With the Swirl

Tamara Lynch

MADONNA'S BOOK WAS large and black, with *SEX* embossed on the front. The coffee-table book of all coffee-table books was an enigma to me, sort of like Madonna herself. One day she was telling you to "Open Your Heart" and the next she was telling you to open your legs, but whatever her message, people were listening. To Brad, my new gay friend, Madonna's book was the Holy Grail. To me, a tough biracial girl from a small town in Pennsylvania, it wasn't that big of a deal. Hadn't we seen her naked already? But I stood next to him in his freshman dorm room itching for a glimpse; there were rumors of bestiality and naked pictures of Vanilla Ice. Cradling the book on his forearm, Brad opened it to a random page and the words "I like my pussy. Sometimes I stare at it in the mirror" burned up my retinas. My face got hot and I smoothed a hand over my brittle straightened hair.

Reaching across Brad, I turned the pages for more.

"Dude, this is porn," I said, transfixed.

"It's not porn, it's *art*," Brad shot back. "I waited in line for hours at the record store downtown to buy it."

I thought this was extreme for naked pictures and a CD, but Brad loved her, wanted to be her. A magical spell glued us to each lust-filled scene as we flipped through depictions of S&M, prostitution, and orgies. I was about to walk away when he literally squealed.

"Look at this!" He held up the book.

I blinked; then blinked again. There was Big Daddy Kane, one of my favorite rappers, in a threesome with a black woman and a fully naked Madonna. It was a Madonna sandwich, giving new meaning to the word "Oreo."

"What is *he* doing in there?" I barked.

"*Girrrrl*, you know she likes the chocolate."

Grabbing the book, I brought it to my chest for a closer look. Kane was cupping Madonna's vagina and giving her a "I'm gonna fuck the shit out of you" look, while her upper body twisted to give the black goddess behind her some tongue. I went from mortified, to intrigued, to kind of turned-on.

It wasn't the sex that gripped me, it was the *interracial* sex. I was raised by my white grandmother in a dominantly white town and had endured years of racial taunts for being half-black. The worst of them was being called an "abomination" by my high school humanities teacher, who had preached to my class that mixing races was wrong. My defense was to straighten my curly hair in an attempt to look like everyone else, but my tan skin was like a permanent smudge on the Caucasian canvas of my high school class. The only other kid who was tortured more than me was Reggie Johnson, a black kid adopted by our town's white reverend. If I had wanted a date, he was my only option, but he was two grades below me, and I didn't want him. I wanted Jeremy, a blonde-haired, blue-eyed basketball player in my class, but that crush stayed a secret. By the time I was a freshman in college, my hair was fried from straightening it every day, my self-esteem was bruised, and I was ready to go from blending in to being invisible.

Closing the book, I handed it back to Brad.

"I didn't know Madonna was down with the swirl," I said.

"The swirl?"

"Yeah, black and white love; like a chocolate and vanilla ice cream cone."

"Well, then she's the *Dairy Queen*," Brad laughed. "You remember 'Like a Prayer?'"

"Yes, I do," I said with a sigh. I remembered it well—controversy about Madonna's "Like a Prayer" video had roared through the halls of my high school. She was kissing a black Jesus. To me this was major—and totally unexpected from a pop star. Although I had appreciated Madonna as an artist and could sing along to several of her songs, I had none of her albums. N.W.A, Janet Jackson, and L.L. Cool J had dominated my boom box. Madonna was blonde, boy crazy, and did everything she could to stand out from the crowd. I was brown, shy, and did my best to blend in.

To catch the video one night, my grandmother and I had assumed our living-room positions: me curled up on the Lazy Boy while she sat knitting in her rocking chair.

"Tsk," my grandmother sucked her teeth. "Why is she kissing him like that?"

"Like what? It was a peck. You watch simulated sex on *Days of Our Lives*," I said, thinking it was the kiss she objected to.

"She shouldn't be kissing a black man."

My eyebrows shot up.

"Gram, you do realize I'm half black . . . ? Your daughter did more than *kiss* a black man."

Her knitting needles raced.

"Well, you're half white too," she'd said.

★

Hours after I left Brad and the *SEX* book, I couldn't get Madonna's scenes with Big Daddy Kane out of my head. I found myself questioning what she was trying to say with those pictures. Sure, they were shocking, but I didn't think it was just about sex. The pictures of her crawling from the ocean with wavy, golden extensions trailing over her breasts made me think of Aphrodite, offering mortals a taste of enchanted love. Could she be healing the gap between black and white through her vagina? She was a pop sensation and an advocate for homosexuals and women's sexual freedom. He was a lyrical genius and a hip-hop icon. Maybe she was melding not only race, but also cultures. Whatever it was, she was giving herself freely, gender and race be damned.

Later that night at a popular off-campus bar, I spotted Billy, the six-foot-two, 220-pound senior wide receiver I had been hooking up with for a few weeks. We were both mixed, which made me think he was the perfect guy for me, so I stuck around even though he treated me like a booty call. He winked at me as I squeezed through the crowd, but he didn't talk to me. His arrogance was exasperating. Moving past him, I glimpsed a cute white guy wearing a driver's cap in the corner. His eyes caught mine and he smiled, but I quickly looked away and found my friends.

With Billy across the room ignoring me, it was hard to enjoy myself, and my beer went down too quickly. I walked to the bar for another.

"Hi," I heard behind me.

From over my shoulder, I saw the white guy in the driver's cap leaning toward me. My gaze set on his wide chest before locking onto his green eyes.

"Oh, hi, sorry . . . am I in your way?"

"No, but it would be okay if you were." He had a deep voice and a nice smile. My skin tingled, but I clamped it down. White guys didn't flirt with me. *He probably has a blonde girlfriend somewhere*, I thought.

I grinned and turned toward the bar.

"I'm Hank," he said over my shoulder. "I've seen you here before."

"Yeah, I come here sometimes with my friends," I said, sliding a glance at Billy, who was frowning at Hank and me. I gave Hank a full smile.

"You're cute."

"Actually . . . I'm Tamara," I said nervously.

When my beer appeared on the bar, I grabbed it, waved a goodbye, and ran back to my friends. But as I sipped my beer and snuck glances at Hank, I had a nagging feeling that I had missed out on something. *Could he have been flirting with me? Should I have stayed and talked to him?* My high school hang-ups drowned me. I remembered my constant senior-year daydream of having sex with the blonde basketball captain, Jeremy. I'd wanted him to take me to prom, but he had asked a redheaded cheerleader with milky white skin and freckles instead. As the prom had grown closer with no invitation, I'd started a list of guys to ask.

"Are you going to ask Reggie Johnson?" my best friend Nici had asked me during chemistry lab. Nici had dyed her hair blonde and hair-sprayed her bangs into stiff ringlets. I had straightened my hair that morning and donned a black T-shirt over my black acid wash jeans.

"Ewww. Are you serious?"

Reggie was fifty pounds overweight, wore Coke-bottle glasses, and had a lisp. Contrary to stereotypes about black people's natural abilities in sports and music, Reggie rode the bench in football and his rendition of Run DMC's "Walk This Way" during our talent show was God-awful.

"Well, he's black," she'd said.

My head snapped up.

"So I can't ask a white guy, Nici?" I'd tried to study her face, but she wouldn't look at me. She just shrugged and dipped her litmus paper in a beaker. I didn't pursue an answer.

★

As I finished my beer at the bar, Kane and Madonna came to mind, and I imagined Hank and I in the same positions—sans the extra woman. The dream me was a caramel-colored goddess enveloping a white knight with green eyes. *Madonna would have made that guy her bitch, not run away like a scared rabbit.*

I had let fear keep me dateless in high school; I couldn't let it happen again. I knew what I needed to do. It was time to "express myself."

Penning my number on a napkin, I gathered my bag, hugged my friends, and walked up behind Hank. Shoving my napkin in his back pocket, I held my breath as he turned and grabbed at his butt.

"My number," I smiled as I started to move past him.

"Wait, where are you going?"

"I gotta be up early," I lied. I just wanted to seize the moment and get the hell out of there. "Give me a call," I said, with more confidence than I felt, and then I jetted without a backward glance.

Instead of going back to the dorm, I wandered the campus, hoping I hadn't made a jerk of myself, hoping I'd read his signals right, and hoping he was as interested in me as I was him. Arriving at my dorm an hour later, I read a message from my roommate scrawled on our dry erase board.

"Hank called. Call him when you get home. Any time." His number was written just beneath it.

It worked! As I read and reread the message, a confidence I had never felt before shot through me. That's when Madonna's photographs all made sense; I didn't have to live by anyone's rules but my own. It was time to *be* whoever I wanted, *with* whoever I wanted. I didn't need to be white *or* black. I just needed to be me.

Hank and I ended up dating for the rest of the semester, then I moved on to a Latin guy, then a Filipino guy, another black guy . . . my swirls were endless. Finally feeling free, I let my naturally curly hair go wild; no more straightening. No longer was I invisible or trying to blend in. Whoever wasn't down with my swirl really wasn't down at all.

Madonna Speaks Sexual Truth to Power

Gloria Feldt

FESS UP, LADIES. Is there anyone among us who has *not* used the power of her sexuality to get something she's wanted? From the time we discovered around age one that flashing an adorable smile got us that extra cookie, or when we learned at, oh, age three, that showing the neighbor boys how a girl peed got us our preferred sandbox toys, we were off and running.

My father used to call me a prima donna, but I'm so *pre*-Madonna it isn't funny. As a girl from the so-called "ungeneration"—the small cohort born during World War II who grew up among all the Rosies who'd Riveted during the war and then returned to kitchen and kinder of their own volition—I experienced adolescence in the no-choice and low-aspirations (for women, that is) 1950s. There was little or no sex education—no one even said the word "sex" aloud in polite company, and polite company was a rather important concept at the time. It was pre–birth-control pill, too, and according to the British poet Phil Larkin, "Sexual intercourse began in 1963."

But I have a secret: Sex and its power were around even then. I'm pretty sure that's how I became pregnant at fifteen, married to my high school sweetheart, and genuinely thinking I'd be living happily ever after behind our neatly painted white picket fence.

In 1958, the year Madonna Louise Veronica Ciccone, the third of six children in her fairly traditional 1950s Catholic family, was born in Michigan, my eldest daughter, Tammy, was born a few thousand miles away in west Texas.

Madonna was just a kid during my early years of marriage and motherhood, but I think her essence was there as a nascent but gestating metaphor for the social ferment of the times, when women were just beginning to break out of our girdled, socially prescribed post-war roles.

I was not the first of the second-wave feminists, but I did become an early adopter in the 1960s. There were several triggers that pushed me in that direction. First were the practical ones: those "Help Wanted: Female" ads that kept me from applying for the higher-paying "men's" jobs I wanted, and how I found that even after I was gainfully employed, I couldn't get a credit card without a man's co-signature. I was ticked off! Like many in the burgeoning feminist movement, my "click" moment came when the personal experience of injustice converged with popular culture, such as the new *Ms.* magazine and the television sitcom *That Girl*, which illustrated another way.

Initially, I experienced my indignation alone. Then other young wives timidly whispered similar thoughts. When I saw emerging feminist leaders like Gloria Steinem and Florynce Kennedy on the evening news protesting the status quo, I felt they were giving political voice to our inchoate personal desires to break free of the old molds. Women began shedding more than girdles in our quest to live less constricted lives. I searched out the five other at-large members of the new National Organization for Women who lived within a one-hundred-mile radius of my Odessa, Texas, home. And I became fueled with a passion to make sure my daughters would have more options and more opportunities than my peers and I had.

Sex and sexual power played a central role in my newfound activism, too. First of all, the average age of marriage for women then was nineteen. Like me, most women married young, either so we could have sex "legitimately" or because we'd already had sex. We realized *en masse*—and a little late—that this wasn't the healthiest way to start a lifelong relationship. The divorce rate shot up. Though my ex-husband and I made a brave eighteen-year try, we simply didn't have the emotional maturity to sustain a marriage during those times of roiling social change; we split in 1976.

I was like many other women who joined the 1970s sexual revolution after a divorce. We were chafing against the long-held cultural archetypes—still in place today—that viewed women only along a sex-saturated continuum that incorporated:

- *The whore*, who needs no definition. Like Mary Magdalene, she sometimes has a heart of gold despite her morally fallen state. Hers is the most straightforward power transaction, and if she's a smart businesswoman, she makes sure to get paid before delivering the goods.
- *The evil temptress*, like the iconic character Matty, as played by a sultry-voiced Kathleen Turner in the 1981 film *Body Heat*. Her lover Ned, played by William Hurt, says that Matty "shouldn't wear that body," by which he excuses the intensity of his desire (he smashes windows to get to her and murders her unwanted husband at her behest).
- *The eyelash-batting manipulator*, who might even be noble if her manipulations were in the service of others, such as the Biblical Esther who saved her people through her feminine wiles. Another example is Scheherazade, who kept her king

mesmerized night after night to save other women's lives and end his brutal practice of getting a fresh wife every night and then killing her the next morning.

- *The clueless incompetent,* personified as the dumb blonde hyper-sexualized Marilyn Monroe model that seemed to define most of womanhood in most men's eyes most of the time. "In men's eyes" are the operative words. The Barbie doll was born in 1959, a year after Madonna; her tiny waist, big boobs, and long shapely legs represented the objectified feminine ideal—sexy but not too overtly sexual.

- *The virgin,* a.k.a., Mary, the original Madonna, morally pure because she is sexually untouched. The paradox of the very concept of virginity, as authors like Hanne Blank (*Virgin*) and Jessica Valenti (*The Purity Myth*) have demonstrated convincingly in their books, is that the idea of virginity itself is socially constructed, with no objective meaning of its own. If you think about it, the belief that a woman's hymen is what gives her value to a man is among the most ridiculous in human history. I think that's why I have always loved how the ironic humor in Madonna's lyrics: "Like a virgin . . . touched for the very first time" punctures such ancient notions.

Madonna challenged every one of those female archetypes, complete with shocking costumes. She did it by taking on elements of each character at various times and twisting the stereotypes into ironic pretzels. For example, her signature bullet bra seems to me a perfect caricature of those chastely sweatered pointy breasts that bedecked 1950s movie stars—the ones who were never filmed sleeping in the same bed with their on-screen husbands. And the fact that she broke out with such a blatantly aggressive sexual persona during conservative Ronald Reagan's presidency in the 1980s, when the political right wing was beginning to mount its crusade for sex-negative abstinence-only education, made me love her all the more.

The song "Like a Virgin" exposed the hypocrisy of American attitudes toward sex, especially about women's sexuality and sexual pleasure. "Sex is nasty and dirty; save it for the one you love," we were told in messages both overt and subtle, much as today's abstinence-only zealots still give to youth. Madonna seemed to retort, "Sex is beautiful and fun; love the one you're with, and make damn sure you get your fair share of pleasure while you're at it. Oh, and if he (or she) doesn't give it to you, give it to yourself. Ha, so there!"

As "Jbnyc" on the blog Madonnatribe.com writes, "Madonna sings of sex making her stronger, bolder, as opposed to sex . . . making her a possession of the man in question . . . [She] has publicly said that she was interested in holding up a mirror to society to show them that a woman can be intelligent, powerful, and sexual." You can't get more feminist than that.

Sexual power has always been the universal engine that drives human activity, whether we have been able to acknowledge it or not. Madonna is universal and timeless in that same way, a throbbing life force that makes powerful men fear the loss of control over everything they've held sway over for centuries.

Like many other women, I feel a kinship with her, despite the gulf between our eras. While she was producing sexually boundary-breaking music that encouraged women to embrace their sexual power and pleasure, I was busy breaking boundaries—both sexually and socially—that had enslaved women for millennia. Separating sex from childbearing and biology from destiny—to free women and give them the power to be whomever they choose—became my life's mission. That includes Madonna's freedom to be her amazing, authentic self.

While Madonna worked through the medium of pop culture, my work took me from political campaigning to three decades of leading Planned Parenthood, which provides essential reproductive health services for women, from pap smears to birth control to abortion and prenatal care. For nine years I was its national president, during one of its most politically challenging times. And that led me to study, write, and teach about women's still-complicated relationship with power in this unfinished revolution, for few of us walk as comfortably in our own power as does Madonna.

The quest for power—for agency over our own bodies and, by extension, our lives—is essential to human development. We all use whatever gifts we've got. When women haven't had formal power (which has been throughout most of the long arc of history), we've found other, informal ways to extract mastery, however small, over our lives. And if men are gifted with greater brute force than women and have, through most of recorded time, been in the ruler's seat, women have used their sexual attractiveness to effect the results they desire.

Only when you already have some formal or political power can you challenge the entire system and expect to live to tell the tale. Madonna could speak sexual truth to power because of how far the women's movement had already come. When "Like a Virgin" debuted in 1984, birth control had separated procreation from recreation. It was just a short step from there to women demanding the right to sexual pleasure, and to flaunting their sexual power to get what they wanted—"shiny and new."

It's also not surprising, considering the era I grew up in, that my own inner life's work has paralleled my professional career, and that although she is much younger than me, I learned a great deal from Madonna.

By the way, back as a child in my grandmother's backyard, a girl-friend and I actually got the three-year-old boys to show *us* how they peed. And we didn't have to give them anything in exchange, except promise that we wouldn't tell their parents. Sometimes speaking sexual truth to power just takes a big bluster.

My Pocket Madonna

Laura Barcella

MY FIRST LOVE, John, was a Holocaust denier. Of course, I didn't know this at the time we were together. If I had, I never would have dated him. What can I say, I was blinded by college naiveté, his Buddy Holly glasses, and his well-worn Smiths T-shirt. I only discovered his penchant for bigoted delusion many years after our breakup. Looking back, I should have known something was off. Why? Because he never liked Madonna.

Not that most straight men I know *do* like Madonna. They just don't seem to "get" the Material Girl—her mercurial style changes, her outspoken nature and penchant for weird sexual power dynamics, and her enduring resonance with modern women. But John was much more vehement in his distaste; he seemed to downright resent her, calling her nasty names and making ludicrous proclamations about her "setting feminism back hundreds of years."

Whenever we'd "talk" about Madonna, we'd inevitably end up in a fight. Of course, I was twenty and desperately in love for the first time. Back then, love meant drama (underlined, italicized, with a capital D): roiling, over-the-top passion, fire, and . . . fighting. Lots and lots of drunken fighting, about the state of us, the world, other people—and Madonna.

★

When I first met John, I was a college junior and a recently self-proclaimed feminist. I was immersed in writing, literature, and women's studies. I screamed along to riot grrrl mix tapes my friend Karen had made me as I tooled around Amherst, Massachusetts, in my little white Honda Civic.

I'd dabbled in pro-choice activism since I was twelve or thirteen, attending rallies and sending the occasional $25 membership check to NARAL (I loved their cool purple bumper stickers). But this—*this* was different. Those riot grrrl bands, like Bikini Kill and Bratmobile, reached my rawest places, offering a direct retort to all the shitty cultural messages I'd internalized: that I was nothing without a guy; that I could never be too pretty or too thin; that sex was a sinister, scary forest where every woman was forced to play either Virgin or Whore. Add those crappy cultural cues to the fact that I'd been clinically depressed since I was a teenager, and the message I got was that I had no agency over my own life. That I would never be happy, serene, or free from the bondage of my own mind. Riot grrrl rhetoric spoke to my angst, dismantled the negative messaging, and fed me empowering ideas in their place. Music gave me hope—suddenly I wanted to reclaim my sexuality, scream about systemic oppression from the nearest Berkshire mountaintop, make zines, and write letters to the editor.

If riot grrrl was the AP course, Madonna had been the 101. My obsession with her started young; I was age six when she first flounced onto MTV, and I latched onto her instantly. I was a burgeoning music junkie, into everything from Tears for Fears and Samantha Fox, to Lisa Lisa and Cult Jam, but there was something about this twenty-six-year-old new girl on the block that hooked me in a different way. After hearing my very first Madonna song ("Borderline"), I became a bona fide wannabe. She was just so . . . *cool*. (And supposedly she had a genius IQ! Not only was she cool, she was smart as hell.) It was love.

I memorized every lyric to every song, and I used my friends' birthday parties as an excuse to dress like her. (I still can't believe my mom let me out of the house in some of those outfits: black lace headbands, fingerless gloves, mesh tank tops, neon socks; I was a full-fledged Madonna mini-me). My obsession faded a bit as I grew up and my musical tastes changed, but I continued to follow her career and her personal life. I kept her in my back pocket like a little guardian angel, and I turned to her for hits of strength and inspiration when I needed them. She always delivered. When I felt scared or anxious, I'd think, *What would Madonna do?* She seemed to handle life with such assurance, swagger, and self-respect. Of course there were insecurities in there somewhere (there must have been) but she never showed them; she maintained a perpetual air of invincibility, and I admired her for it. Whenever I felt weak or depressed, she radiated strength and self-reliance. Particularly in high school, when I was not only swamped by insecurity, but drawing little to no attention from quality guys. I constantly fought off feelings of inferiority because of my sheer lack of experience in the dude department. Like lots of teenage girls, I'd given the idea of romantic love too much weight, too much power (aren't American girls taught, even encouraged, to think this way?). By the time I hit college—Madonna still in my back pocket—I understood intellectually that a woman didn't require a romantic relationship to be happy, but I found it difficult to apply that notion to myself. I believed *other* women were fine on their own, that their single status indicated nothing lacking about them, but it was different when it came to me and my perpetual single status: I felt lost and unlovable.

And so it was that when I first saw John standing outside a bodega on St. Mark's Place one muggy summer night in New York City, I was ready. I'd waited a long fucking time to fall in love. It was his Smiths T-shirt that first sold me—I was a longtime lover of the Smiths and Morrissey, and I was attracted to fellow fans. They tended to be like me: a bit socially awkward, maybe, but also tender-hearted misanthropes who thought too much, analyzed everything, and wanted love but had absolutely no effing clue where to find it (or even how to flirt).

Something tugged me toward him. I liked him immediately—his lankiness, his pasty blondness and his blue eyes behind hip glasses. (I was pasty and blond and wore glasses, too.) I got his number and called him two days later. Within a few dates, I was falling for him; it was mutual and heady and beautiful. We looked like brother and sister, which felt somehow sick and sexy at the same time.

Speaking of sex, that aspect of our relationship was . . . interesting. John was a virgin, for all intents and purposes, and had a long-standing aversion to masturbation (yes, really). Hence, he knew very little about, well, anything when it came to pleasure—his own or other people's. This made things a bit tricky (to say the least), but I also found his bedroom inexperience weirdly exciting. I liked the idea of being his first, and of helping guide him through the dark and delightful world of naughty exploration.

My memories of that summer are vivid but spotty snapshots. I remember making fun of the way he organized his CDs—they were all displayed face-out on his shelf, like he was showing them off. I remember the heavy, ornate bright-red door of his apartment building on St. Mark's. I remember the swelter and humidity, drops of sweat rolling down my chest, down my stomach, as we walked the streets hand in hand. I remember sleeping over at his dark, cramped railroad apartment, how my fine hair would tangle up into crazy bed-headed knots overnight, and how in the morning I'd sit in front of him on the bed while he brushed the tangles from my hair, so gently I could have cried. I remember when we held each other one night and his face broke out in a sudden swath of giddy happiness, and he squeezed me and murmured "you're mine." I'd never felt truly wanted or protected before; not like this. It felt innocent and perfect, like words I'd been waiting to hear all my life.

I didn't need my pocket Madonna; she wasn't even the *spark* of a flashpoint in the new-couple bubble we inhabited. Instead, we were full to bursting with inside jokes and stupid pet names. At the end of the summer, I returned to college in Massachusetts. He stayed in New York, where he was raised, and we continued our relationship long-distance.

But things changed, as they tend to. The fighting started. It would usually happen when we were drinking together (which happened frequently during our monthly visits). I'd watched one too many artsy foreign films, and I thought real love brought constant pain and turmoil. So I picked fights. About *everything*. I was young and dramatic, craving—no, demanding—more reassurance than one person could ever be reasonably expected to give me. But in those fights, I learned some things. Things about John, things about me, things that weren't always pretty.

I began to glean that beneath his goofy Morrissey-loving shell there lurked a darker John—insensitive, intolerant, possibly even bigoted. I learned this when he began to mock the riot grrrl music I loved as "bratty chatter." When he said that every nail-salon owner was an aging Korean woman who couldn't speak English. (Yes, we once fought about nail salons.) When he described, during our eventual breakup phone-call, "not knowing how to tell his girlfriend"— um, *me*—"that her butt was getting big." (Those times he read my diary, went through my computer files, and hid my makeup from me didn't help, either.)

But oddly, I learned about our differences most glaringly from John's outright, unabashed loathing for Madonna. We probably fought about her more than anything else—more than about our own relationship, even. I'm not sure why, but there was something about the venom he reserved for her, his cruelty in dissecting what he perceived as her "slut factor." In saying she set feminism back hundreds of years (which he enjoyed saying often), he was dismissing everything I loved and admired most about her: not just her sexual agency, but her ballsiness, her self-possession, her boundary-pushing, and her never, ever giving a crap what anyone thought of her. She was the golden rebel-girl icon of my childhood, a shining example of everything I wasn't (yet), but wanted to be. Seeing her do all the things she did (strike a pose, lash a whip, wear corsets and collars and bustiers—oh my!—change her hair color, publish books, have babies, find God) showed me that if I wanted to, I could do those things. Watching her live without shame allowed me to believe that I, too, could live without shame.

John's rejection of Madonna felt much deeper than just some petty distaste for a pop star. OK, I might have been a smidge biased—she *had* been my idol. But his perspective on Madonna felt like nothing short of derision—for her, for me, for women as a whole. His inability to accept Madge for all the complicated intricacies of who she was indicated that when it came down to it, he couldn't accept me, either (hello, big-butt comment). And it did us in, just shy of a year together.

Now it's been thirteen years, and I can't lie—I still feel a twinge when I think of him. It's probably just rose-tinted memories of our early days, getting sweetened by time; that impossible nostalgia many of us inadvertently hold onto for the intensity of our first loves (which may have been all wrong, but felt so Big, so Irreplaceable). I don't think John and I should have ended up together, and I don't envy the woman he's married to now. In fact, it was just last year that I realized the full extent of his issues (I found, buried in my Gmail archives, a paper he'd written that asserted his strident belief that the Holocaust never happened). But the early days of our relationship were some of the happiest times of my life. For an anti-Semitic Madonna-hater, he sure had a hold on me.

I'm still single. I'm still a feminist. And I still crave a romantic relationship (I'm human!), while knowing, deep down, that it won't cure my struggles with depression and self-doubt. Love won't magically "fix" me. It won't make me serene or content or self-confident. Only I can do that. I realize now, more clearly than ever, that I owe it to myself to practice patience. I owe it to myself to wait for someone who accepts me wholeheartedly, variable butt size and all; someone who looks at women's self-expression as what it is: self-expression, not "bratty chatter." Someone who respects women with swagger, drive, and adamant sexuality.

And if I feel lonely during the wait, I can still turn to the Madonna in my pocket to remind me to keep my head up and keep moving. She grins defiantly and reminds me—my childhood idol, my shining beacon—"absolutely no regrets."

Safe Harbor

Stacey May Fowles

I WAS PROBABLY about six years old when I first displayed an interest in domination and submission.

Of course, at the time it wasn't about sex. I didn't know anything about sex or how it worked, other than what the tomboy down the street had sloppily taught me about kissing boys on our brown corduroy couch. A lonely only child with an overactive imagination, I was the puppet master of bizarre and complex Barbie-land scenarios in our suburban rec-room. While my stay-at-home mother was busy with household chores, Ken would kidnap an unwitting Barbie and tie her plastic wrists and ankles with ponytail elastics. Blindfolded and gagged, Barbie would be driven aimlessly around in her pink Corvette for Ken's (and my) amusement and pleasure.

When I was old enough to have bath time by myself behind a closed door, I was again mentally enacting an elaborate kidnapping fantasy. In the midst of my bathing, pirates would sail though the soapy water and savagely abduct me from the tub. They would then force me to choose—what part of my body would I conceal with the square foot of terry washcloth available to me? I never questioned my need to be their imaginary captive.

When playtime was over—in and out of the bath—the pirates would sail off, Barbie's clothes would go back on, and I'd have a bowl of chicken noodle soup and clean my room, just like any other kid. You could blame this sort of imaginative storytelling on the seeds of a writing life, but an interest in "surrender" that roots early is impossible to remove entirely. These memories are now a comfort to me in a world (both progressive and traditional) that occasionally looks upon my desires with disdain and judgment.

My childhood was healthy, normal, and supportive, and yet still, I turned out "wrong."

Those first juvenile inklings of submission were completely harmless, but writing them still fills me with a twinge of embarrassment and a compulsion to explain. It would never have occurred to me to think they were anything but innocuous fun until the world of adulthood rushed in with judgment, disappointment, and the notion that "nice girls *don't.*" With age comes a desperate need to define desires, catalogue them, compartmentalize them, and sometimes even forbid them. With age comes shame. We learn that our sexuality is only acceptable when it's in a quiet, culturally sanctioned form. Certainly never when desire asks our lover to hurt us.

★

In American television broadcasting there is a specific term for the late-night hours during which broadcasters are allowed to transmit material deemed indecent. Referred to as "the safe harbor," it is a time slot generally reserved for material that falls outside the sexual norm. Subsequently, a large part of Madonna's music video canon was slotted to air here. In a culture where we are so often asked to hide our fringe desires, I find this term strangely reassuring. Those of us with a secret identity and a compulsion to hide it, those of us who engage in something forbidden, can find reassurance and protection from storm or attack.

My awareness of the forbidden began to coalesce around the time of the 1989 release of "Like a Prayer," a song and video that, at its core, contradicts any doubt that sexuality can be sacred and sublime. While I was a preteen learning how to be complicit in a culture of shame, Madonna delivered a triumphant pop anthem that success-fully brought sickly sweet romantic love and euphoric lust to holy status. The video literally sent a scantily clad, confident, and self-sexualized Madonna to church, and the controversy that followed was my first mainstream taste of a woman's sexuality being relegated to the realm of the forbidden. When Madonna is "down on her knees" promising to "take you there," she's providing a lyrical ambi-guity that forces us to question whether or not she's articulating holy devotion or sexual satisfaction. The reality is that she's coyly articu-lating both, gleefully spitting in the face of those who would question that they can't be one and the same.

The true art of the music video is, much like Barbie bound and gagged in that pink Corvette, fantasy reenactment. Madonna videos were my earliest exposure to BDSM imagery and the tran-scendent possibilities of power exchange, however watered down and MTV-friendly those early nods were. When I was no more than ten, Madonna was urging her listeners to "express themselves" in a glossy, uncomplicated version of sex-positive feminism. Visually that expression was dressed in nothing but white bed sheets and a metal collar on the end of a chain, making Madonna a consenting "pet" to the sweaty, hulking object of her desire. "Express Yourself" was, at the time, the most expensive music video ever made, and Madonna's feminism put her in both a pinstriped suit and black lingerie crawling cat-like under a dining room table to lap up milk from a bowl on the floor. The conclusion? Her paramour, a well-built steelworker oppressed by "the man" and fresh from a fistfight, comes to her and takes immediate control before falling to his manly knees in front of her. It was the first visual representation that I, a sexually confused preteen, had of the statement that "the submissive has all the power."

A year later, *The Immaculate Collection* brought with it "Justify My Love." The grainy art-house–style video, now laughably tame compared to Christina Aguilera's assless chaps and Britney Spears nude in the steam room, features a distressed Madonna breathlessly wandering the halls of an "alternative lifestyle," partner-swapping hotel. Every open door reveals gender-ambiguous couples exploring fetish, clad in leather and latex. Madonna proceeds to have a tryst with a mysterious and presumably recent acquaintance in a flurry of voyeuristic, gender-bending, and general gleeful eroticism. "Justify My Love" sparked international controversy and was banned by MTV, outraging Madonna and provoking her to publicly defend it. The mainstream's rejection of the video confirmed that fringe sexuality was thoroughly unwelcome. Although nudity was cited as the reason, the only actual nudity in the video is a topless dominatrix with suspenders strategically covering her breasts (an obvious homage to *The Night Porter*'s Charlotte Rampling.) It is far more likely that the dominatrix's rough treatment of a bound man, among other Dominant/submissive (D/s) and androgynous imagery, was responsible for the argument that it was unsuitable for public consumption.

With every bold step in Madonna's career, the mainstream reaction made it clear that any sexuality that fell outside the sanctioned norm—like mine—would be forced into hiding if it reared its "ugly" head. Though that knowledge is difficult to swallow for someone coming into their first desires, Madonna had a bestselling video single driven by the hand-wringing and slut-shaming of public curiosity. In a *Nightline* interview about censorship, it was suggested that Madonna was set to earn more money from the video being banned than if it hadn't.

Her response? "Yeah, so? Lucky me."

★

When I was thirteen, and sexuality was delivered to me via cable television's midnight blue movies when my parents were out for the night, Madonna donned a mask, raised a riding crop, and proclaimed that "only the one who hurts you can make you feel better." While I was accustomed only to boisterous, bawdy, and generally misinformed schoolyard talks of sex acts, her "Erotica" video is five glossy minutes of unadulterated BDSM bliss, a collection of images I'd never seen before but was immediately drawn to. Mainstream entertainment showed featured clips of the video in prime time while proclaiming it obscene and again banned it from the airways.

Whatever this was, it was wrong—and I desperately wanted to be a part of it.

The mainstream condemnation of the "Erotica" video, "Justify My Love," and the *Sex* book were the first times I realized that my desires—the very same ones that had sprouted innocently from play and bath-time—were contraband. Depictions of consensual sexual practices by empowered women were censored and relegated to "safe harbor," while news of Canada's Scarborough rapist, Paul Bernardo, and his countless female victims screamed from local dinnertime airwaves. At the same time, a reluctant female teacher took me and the other girls at school aside to explain, in a stern voice, how afraid we should be of sex, and the inevitable disease and pregnancy that came with it. While Madonna and her nearly naked friends cavorted around fearless in blissful black-and-white bondage, celebrating their capacity for pleasure and pain, I was being indoctrinated into a post-AIDS sexual education that taught me that pleasurable urges led to death, and that the possibility of sexual violence lurked in every bush and at every bus stop.

For these reasons, the teenager with sexual inclinations outside of the mainstream is rarely a happy creature. Sexual awakening coincides with indoctrination into shame and fear, young women in particular bearing the burden of their potential victimhood (and sluthood). This reality was emphasized to me once I started writing openly about sexual submission. I received letters from teenage girls lamenting not only a puritanical status quo, but an oft-judgmental school of feminism that looked down its nose at any woman's desire to consensually subjugate herself. We find our fearless heroes where we can, and for those whose puberty coincided with Madonna's fierce challenging of sexual norms, her defiance was an obvious choice.

For me, those teenage years devolved into the kind of relationships one might blame on a penchant for submission. Date rapists and domestic abusers littered the landscape—a shiner here and the questionable consent of a drunk fuck there. By the time I was legal to drink and vote, I had latched firmly on to feminism, which made me feel a desperate need to shelve the submission in order to "pass" and carry the card. Third-wave feminism promised sex-positivity, as long as the focus was female pleasure and not pain, even the consensual variety. I hid my private daydreams and dramatic reenactments while I fumbled fruitlessly with cautious men raised on antisex rhetoric. The desire to be dominated needed to be relegated to a metaphoric "safe harbor," a place in the dark where it was understood that these things weren't discussed in daylight.

Madonna didn't seem to feel the same need for that "either/or" scenario I felt suffocated by every day. When it came to female empowerment and sexually submitting, her words and imagery suggested the two could coexist peacefully and powerfully. When I was sixteen and on the cusp of losing my virginity, she was unapologetic about her behavior in "Erotica" and Sex, quite literally saying "I'm not sorry" while raising that signature riding crop in the video for "Human Behavior." Clad in black leather and latex, she was more jovial, playful, and defiant than ever before. She even went as far as to ask, "Would it sound better if I were a man?" and it became impossible not to wonder.

For all its good intentions, "express yourself, don't repress yourself" was liberating in theory but proved to be difficult in practice. When I finally escaped suburban expectations of acceptable femininity and sexuality by going to university, I desperately tried to liberate myself from the same judgment that banned Madonna's videos from "good society." I met a very nice boy who tied me up with silk scarves and called me a "cunt" when I asked him to. His love for me grew until it bordered on obsession, and his need to dominate me bled outside our playtime until it was intolerable. He eventually ended up on my doorstep, brandishing a scalpel and yelling "you fucking bitch."

While hiding your sexual self is damaging, sometimes yanking it out of the closet and subjecting it to experimentation can be even more painful. My desire to be demeaned by my lovers grew with every new sexual discovery, but the idea that "nice girls don't" con- tinued with every disappointed look I received when I asked to be tied up and called a whore. Those early filmic representations of un- abashed BDSM celebration and the holy nature of submission were all the more clear to me, but the possibility of enacting them seemed further and further away. It turned out that the fantasy reenactment was just that: fantasy. It failed to translate well into real life and left a loneliness within me that refused to leave regardless of how hard I tried to fake "normal." Coming out as submissive is difficult in both the white-bread normalcy of suburban culture and the faux-progres- sive siren song of modern feminism.

I failed to fit anywhere.

★

The 2001 video for "What It Feels Like for a Girl" also failed to fit the rules of daytime programming, relegated to "safe harbor" by the fear that its violence would offend. Unlike previous controversies, the Guy Ritchie-directed creation is largely sexless, depicting Madonna and an elderly companion on a reckless crime spree in a stolen Camaro. Its "violent" content is almost laughable when compared to the vio- lence and sexist torture-porn of modern prime time. Madonna herself called the contents of the video "fantasy and doing things that girls are not allowed to do," and having it banned only furthered her point.

The song itself is a condemnation of double standards, the extreme burdens women are forced to carry via their sexuality, the quiet suffering they endure while balancing expectations and personal authenticity. It is an anthem for frustrated dismay, delivered sweetly.

At the time I first heard the song, my post-university boyfriend was telling me how "nice girls" were allowed to act, and I was complicit in that burden of inauthenticity by desperately attempting to be "normal." I was doing all of the things good girls were supposed to do, baking pies in false domestic bliss and polishing my exterior in an effort to pass. The video was an extreme representation of what I longed for; something unexpected, something denied to me, something outside the false norm—Madonna's character is a victim who suddenly, gloriously, refuses to be victimized.

Most importantly, the release of "What It Feels Like for a Girl" marked a time of personal realization that my desire for submission was not about sex. It wasn't about sex when Ken practiced bondage techniques on Barbie and it wasn't when a boy tied me up with silk scarves in his dorm room. Of course the acts included sex, but the need for it was more about disposing of an artifice that was suffocating me—the binaries of what good girls can and can't do, want and can't want. Submission was Holy Communion with my authentic self, a self that the rest of the world had tried to keep me from, a self that was relegated to "safe harbor" by social moral obligation. Submission was a moment where my identity, and the necessary armor that comes from a life lived female, was stripped bare. In private submissive moments exist a real yearning free of cultural projection, a moment that subsequently terrifies mainstream mores. The ability to share that vulnerability with another person and strip it of supposed shame was, for me, the only real way to transcend sanctioned and restrained sexuality.

For someone grappling with the notion that submission can reflect our authentic selves, watching a very public icon play so fearlessly and defiantly with the roles thrust upon her can bring a sigh of relief. Whether it be her dancing exuberantly in front of a gospel choir, or embarking on a crime spree that defies the norms of what "good girls" do, Madonna strategically does what she wants and raises a middle finger to those who condemn her.

When it comes to the many depictions of subversive desire that Madonna has constructed over the years, I would argue that it's not really about sex for her either. I realize that statement is laughable, given how sexuality infuses almost everything she does, that the imagery she puts into the world is dripping with it, but submission and dominance are just items in the unlimited toolkit of her persona. Much like the submissive sexual act, the sexually charged music video is her way of saying "Here I am, stripped bare, and I'm sharing it with you," even if that vulnerability is nothing more than temporary performance.

After twenty years of Madonna videos, I am now in a place where I am open about and even proud of my private desires. In so many ways, over so many years, it was Madonna that gave us a mainstream window to a place where we could feel comfortable with ourselves, a safe harbor to explore those desires we most feared being exposed. Perhaps her greatest cultural contribution is her ability to make us feel normal.

And I Feel

Laura M. André

MADONNA HIT ME in the gut every time I stepped into the women's bathroom at Pepper's Pizza in Chapel Hill, North Carolina. Given my early graduate school dining and drinking habits, this happened frequently. She instilled a certain fear in me, so at first I tried to ignore her. I knew she'd bring up the same old nagging issues I didn't want to acknowledge. But (especially if I was alone) I'd eventually be drawn to her, so I stopped and reluctantly met her gaze. And in those fleeting moments, my hands started to sweat, my knees weakened, my heart pounded, and I'd once again have to acknowledge the fact that I was a depressed, emotionally cut off, deeply-closeted lesbian who was living a lie and paying the price for it.

The "Pepper's Madonna," as I like to call it, is a life-sized poster featuring Patrick Demarchelier's well-known photograph of Madonna dressed in a black leather biker vest, with a chauffeur's cap perched on her head and a lit cigarette hanging from her lips. Her crossed arms indicate a pose that is slightly protective, but more emphatically intimidating. While the cap shades one eye, the other is narrowed almost completely, rendering her gaze either languid or piercing, depending on how one interprets it. I prefer the latter, since I've never considered Madonna to be passive. For me, the Pepper's Madonna is an icon in the truest sense of the word: an image that not only pictorially represents an important figure but also possesses symbolic power as an object. Like the icons popular in Eastern Orthodox churches, the Pepper's Madonna instilled in me equal measures of fear and reverence for the looming issue that was my sexuality. *Truth or dare?* Madonna pulled both out of me, just like an icon should.

The placement of the Pepper's Madonna was brilliant. In the dingy women's bathroom, the BDSM-inspired, Tom of Finland–style image suggested illicit homoerotic encounters between Madonna and every woman who entered that room. In that guise, Madonna's confrontational pose and gaze pointed explicitly to my own coming-to-terms with my sexuality. It wasn't that I desired Madonna sexually, and it wasn't that I desired to be her. What I found to be irresistible was her sexuality itself, and the easy way she seemed to express it. I wanted that confidence, that sense of power that comes from not giving a shit about what people might think of you. It seems ironic that the queen of reinvention would have prompted me to become more real and to live my own truth, but over the course of several years, that's exactly what she did.

★

I was in high school when Madonna first hit the music and fashion scenes—her first single, "Borderline," is still one of my favorites. I was at the perfect age to fully appreciate her—old enough to understand her savvy brilliance, and yet young enough to go childishly crazy over her particular brand of pop. I was never a wannabe Madonna; she never influenced my sense of style (I was, and still am, a strict prepster), yet she provided the soundtrack of my teens and college years. But as much as I loved her then, it's the later Madonna who really influenced me.

Beginning with 1989's *Like a Prayer*, Madonna shifted toward becoming the mature artist that she is today. Alongside her, I was transitioning out of college and into a more grown-up phase in my own life. I had graduated from college with one degree (in art history), but was embarking on another, more serious, career-minded degree in architecture. And I was slowly coming to terms with my sexuality. I never seriously dated anyone in high school, and by my early twenties I still hadn't had a sexual relationship. It was beginning to dawn on me that part of the reason for this was that I just wasn't attracted to guys. Women were much more appealing, both physically and emotionally, yet growing up in the conservative Midwest I had few role models of alternative sexualities and a strong cultural bias against homosexuality. My crushes on women were secret and forbidden—in a few cases I was truly in love—and I was miserably depressed as a result. Madonna, on the other hand, was exhorting me to express myself, and echoing my deepest wishes in the songs "Like a Prayer" and "Cherish."

The Pepper's Madonna photograph was used for the cover of the notorious single "Justify My Love," which caused quite a lot of controversy when it was released in 1990. I remember how MTV banned the video, mostly due to nudity (one shot reveals a woman's nipples—*gasp!*), but also because of its (oh-so-fleeting) portrayal of homoeroticism between both men and women. Watching the video today, it's hard to imagine what all the fuss was about—a couple of frames reveal two shirtless men snuggling on a sofa, and two androgynous women draw mustaches on one another (while Madonna giggles in the background). The song's rather benign lyrics were also inexplicably slapped with a warning label. I clearly remember the first time I heard the song, though—it aroused in me the same feelings the Pepper's Madonna would incite several years later: the promise of erotic potential mixed with an undeniable desperation. I was a sexually repressed twenty-four-year-old woman who had never so much as gone to second base with anyone, boy or girl.

Those feelings also surfaced when Madonna was on her Blonde Ambition tour. I was living in Italy, participating in a study abroad program through my university. I had developed a deep attraction to a woman back in the States who seemed to have similar feelings toward me, and we were exchanging increasingly suggestive letters. I was sexually ready to burst, but had no outlet. I spent that summer fantasizing about her and rebuffing a guy who kept making passes at me. Meanwhile, the Italian newspapers were full of front-page headlines about how the Pope called for a boycott of Madonna's appearance in Rome, but I was obsessed with the possibility of traveling to Turin to see her perform. Ultimately, I couldn't convince any of my friends to go with me, and I was running out of money, so at the last minute I decided not to make the trip, which I regret to this day. I was able to watch the HBO broadcast of the tour's final night in Nice when I returned to the States in August. While the show horrified my conservative mother and sister-in-law, I was riveted. The athleticism of the performance amazed me; I was enthralled with the spectacular Gaultier costumes, impressed by the art direction, and most of all, intrigued by Madonna exuding such raw sexuality dancing and cavorting around suggestively with her female dancers, Niki and Donna, as well as the male dancers.

I could no longer resist or deny my sexuality to myself, and it was time to take the leap. The woman I was in lust/love with and I moved to Los Angeles that month and began a serious, committed, and sexual relationship. For a brief period (maybe a year), I felt like my problems were solved. However, I was still closeted to my family, friends, and coworkers. Again, Madonna was way ahead of me, carousing with Sandra Bernhard and Jennifer Grey, hanging out at lesbian bars, and generally stoking the gossip about her sexuality. Publicity stunt or not, Madonna's Sapphic flirtations in the early 1990s gave rise to an unprecedented wave of lesbian chic that started to make it more acceptable, socio-culturally, to be gay. That meant something to me, and helped crack open the closet door, if just a little.

By the time I entered graduate school in 1995, my first girlfriend and I had broken up, and a brief rebound relationship was on its last legs. By this time I was out to a few friends and to my parents, who were not at all supportive, and I was mostly unhappy. It all began to change after I embarked on my third relationship. It lasted almost ten years, and during that time I fully embraced my sexuality, my parents grew to accept and love me for who I was, and I earned a PhD. After that relationship ended in 2006, I became depressed again.

Then, in 2008, I met the love of my life, and I found that even on my darkest days, it was impossible not to dance to "Music." I healed. It's only in retrospect that I have gained insight into the significant influence Madonna has had on my life, especially my growth over the past few years. I think I'm finally catching up to *Ray of Light*—I now live my life to the fullest, I am completely open about my sexuality, I am in touch with my spiritual side, and I'm happier than I've ever been—and I know I owe a debt of gratitude to Madonna.

Although I've worshipped the Pepper's Madonna, I can't call myself the world's biggest Madonna fan. I've never seen her perform live and there are entire albums I've never heard, but she's been a constant source of inspiration, as an artist and an entrepreneur, over the course of my life from high school on. I have a tremendous amount of respect for her, and as she gets older—as I get older—I look forward to the ways that she will model what it means to be a vibrant, sexual, spiritual, strong woman over fifty. She's come a long way from the curvy, under-depilated, post-Punk, East Village *Italiana* she was back in the day. I've come a long way, too.

And I feel like I just got home.

Keep It Together

"Family is everything. Family comes first. It's not what
I expected it to be, but nothing ever is."

—MADONNA

In the Name of a Mother

Kelly Keenan Trumpbour

EVERY LITTLE GIRL wants to know what her name means. After I mastered writing the five letters that made up "Kelly" in kindergarten, I learned that my name meant "warrior maiden." I tucked this information into my back pocket, and when life called for an extra shot of bravado—whether I was asking a boy to dance with me, taking the bar exam, or giving my first lecture in front of a crowded room—I could muster a silent whoop of a warrior cry, plunge in, and hope that through my name, the universe had given me better than even odds of coming out the other side.

Twenty years before I knew what "Kelly" meant, let alone how to spell it, Madonna was learning to write her own name. While the meaning behind my name stayed hidden, a fun tidbit I could share at my pleasure, hers wore its meaning like a vestment: the Virgin Mary, Mother of Christ. Those seven letters didn't just identify her, they represented one of the most famous mothers of all time. Imagine being a little girl, and before you have even set foot in the neighborhood of imagining what motherhood might mean to you as a woman, your name holds you to the highest standard of maternity that Western Civilization has to offer.

In the Catholic faith, "Madonna" is a term the devout use when praying with reverence and endearment to "my lady," or the mother of Christ. When little-girl Madonna walked into her family's Catholic Church, she would have seen people kneeling and praying, asking for the religious Madonna's intercession as they passed small beads through their fingers and meditated on her virtues: grace, favor, fertility, and mercy. The people in her pew would hear her name and think of the mother of Jesus before they would think of the little girl sitting next to them. In Catechism class, she would have learned that this other Madonna, though mortal, was the only woman who didn't need a man to reproduce.

Now consider what it would be like for five-year-old Madonna to grow up in the Ciccone household. When she hears "Madonna," she doesn't just think of Christ's mother, she thinks of her own mother, an attentive, loving woman named Madonna Louise Fortin Ciccone. Any awe or pressure little Madonna might have felt from her name was likely softened by the knowledge that she was named for her own mother—not Christ's. Now imagine if this flesh-and-blood mother, who must have been more comforting to little Madonna than any rosary or marble statue could ever be, dies of breast cancer the same year Madonna learns to write her name.

Madonna's family was Catholic, and her mother's funeral Mass would have taken place in a church where a statue, a stained glass window, or a station of the cross would have depicted a scene from the life of Madonna, the religious icon. Months earlier, perhaps on Mary's feast day, the priest's sermon might have mentioned something about how the biblical Madonna was spared death, literally lifted up into heaven by her divine son, because he loved her too much to see her body fail.

How does a five-year-old reconcile this teaching with the loss she has just suffered? In Andrew Morton's biography *Madonna*, the pop star recalls, "I saw my mother, looking very beautiful and lying as if she were asleep in an open casket. Then I noticed that my mother's mouth looked funny. It took me some time to realize that it had been sewn up. In that awful moment, I began to understand what I had lost forever. The final image of my mother, at once peaceful yet grotesque, haunts me today . . ."

Madonna's faith taught her that, in at least one case, a mother can be saved from death by the love of her child. Combine that understanding with the memory of her mother lying in a casket with her lips literally sealed forever, and perhaps Madonna made sense of the world by relying on the power of her own voice to ensure everyone remembered not just her name, but her mother's name. In this way at least, she could keep her alive.

With so much meaning and memory associated with her first name, it's no wonder that just one year before she starred as Eva Peron in *Evita*, Madonna told an interviewer that she was absolutely certain she wanted children. Why wouldn't she want to recreate the mother-daughter relationship after grieving it for so long? Nonetheless, her self-awareness surprised me for its clarity. Despite having an already full and busy life, here was a woman who *clearly* knew she wanted children. Why did this knock me for a loop? Perhaps because when I held that mirror to my own life, the desire to have children wasn't that clear. Yet I found myself walking a very deliberate and difficult path to do just that.

When I discovered that my husband and I weren't likely to get pregnant on our own, the faint sense I had that motherhood might be "nice" became poor consolation. Maybe that's because I had grown up hearing about my parents' struggle with infertility. For six excruciating years, they waited for me. From their stories, I learned to fear infertility, not just because I might never have a baby, but because hoping could wear me down. Still, I went forward with infertility treatments believing the life I painted for myself was just around the corner. The "warrior maiden" in me also wanted the chance to defeat what had been a road block for two generations in my family. I would win, infertility would lose, and my life would continue without the same agonizing interruption my mother had endured. What I failed to realize was that I could not battle my way through an experience that has no real enemy lines, and pick up again where I had left off.

Before I stepped foot into a fertility clinic, I don't think I was very different from women who imagined they would enjoy raising a child, would begin the adventure by waking up pregnant, feeling both a little nervous and a little excited to start rolling with the punches of motherhood. But when I started in vitro fertilization (IVF) treatments, I had to give up the idea of falling into parenthood. Every injection, sonogram, and blood test felt like I was verifying that yes, in fact, I *really, really, really* wanted to be a mother. If I didn't know that for sure, why on earth would I be there? But I didn't know anything for sure. To tell you the truth, I don't know what motherhood is about. I'm an only child. I've had pets, and I wave to the friendly neighbor kids across the street—there's my maternal instinct for you. Yes, I wanted to recreate the loving relationship I had with my own mother, but I also wanted to vindicate her struggle by loving the life she had helped win for me, as it existed, with or without children. I could spend my time trying to get pregnant, or I could be out living my life. Even if my own existence is proof that staying in the game can give you a happy ending, the more treatments I needed, the less I understood why I kept coming back.

When the hormones gave my thoughts the jagged edges of anxiety and depression, and when my body fought off rare reactions like "ovarian hyperstimulation syndrome," a condition that almost landed me in the emergency room, I had to remove myself from treatments to assess what I was doing. I had only attempted three cycles and spent less than sixty days as an IVF patient. Taking a break was the right thing to do, but it felt early, and I was used to confronting obstacles, not walking away from them. I knew women who'd suffered multiple miscarriages during IVF, and they showed up for as many as ten cycles because they knew how much having a child meant to them. "Just remember what you are doing it for," they would say, not to dismiss the physical pain and heartache but to help catapult me over it. But where they could push forward without flinching, I hesitated. For a moment, that hesitation begged the question: Did I even want children?

The answer, I finally realized, was a qualified yes. When my mind painted pictures of my future, I noticed that despite everything I'd gone through, a child with my husband's dark hair and my blue eyes was still somewhere in the frame. However, no matter how hard I tried, no one could guarantee this child would ever exist. Without that real infant in my arms to make me slip into the heady cocktail of motherhood, I didn't know if the struggle was worth it. I found myself trying to hang on to who I was as Kelly, the person beyond the blue exam gown, while the desire to be called "Mom" started to lose its hold on me. Some women suffering through infertility envy women who can get pregnant easily. That has never been my problem. I envied women who wanted motherhood without a doubt. It turns out I was a little too successful at convincing myself that I didn't "need" a child. But I also never imagined walking away from parenthood forever. My warrior maiden was vexed, and I was left with a tattered war cry caught in my throat.

★

I have always appreciated Madonna's ability to play among the gray tones rather than choose black or white, especially as it relates to motherhood. If you take a sampling of her work from 1985 until her daughter Lourdes's birth in 1996, you will find both the subtle and the obvious attempts of a woman teasing out the mingling identities of Madonna the religious icon, Madonna the departed mother, and Madonna the girl who became a powerhouse on stage, eventually contemplating her own shot at motherhood. For most women, including me, it's harder to distinguish between the images of motherhood we cling to in our heads, and the reality we are offered.

It's telling that Madonna, the woman who would go on to become known as "the mother of reinvention," would not choose a stage name to launch her career. No one would have blamed her if she ran as fast as hell away from the memories and expectations that came with her birth name. Instead, she self-titled her first album and faced a wave of criticism. The controversy suggested it was blasphemous to invoke a divine figure's name on a pop album, and not just any divine name—the virgin mother's. I was seven years old when *Madonna* came out, and I remember many adults around me were shocked by her moniker. Who uses that name and sings about losing her virginity?

On her third album, *True Blue,* the song "Papa Don't Preach" describes a young girl who is very similar to a modern-day Virgin Mary. She's a teenager, she's pregnant out of wedlock, and she is going to keep her child no matter how scandalous it seems to the outside world. Madonna didn't write this song, but she chose to include it on the album, and she chose to answer the wave of criticism that came after it. Some listeners thought she was advocating that teenage girls go out and become mothers. She was also attacked for alluding to abortion. It's never mentioned explicitly in the song; instead, people latched on to what was implied in the lyrics, "But I've made up my mind, I'm keeping my baby." In a 1986 *New York Times* article, Madonna commented on the song and its meaning:

"'Papa Don't Preach' is a message song that everyone is going to take the wrong way. Immediately they're going to say I am advising every young girl to go out and get pregnant. When I first heard the song, I thought it was silly. But then I thought, wait a minute, this song is really about a girl who is making a decision in her life. She has a very close relationship with her father and wants to maintain that closeness. To me it's a celebration of life. It says, 'I love you, father, and

I love this man and this child that is growing inside me.' Of course, who knows how it will end? But at least it starts off positive."

Four years later, Madonna released the album *Like a Prayer*. The slow, bittersweet track "Promise to Try" ("Will she see me cry when I stumble and fall/Does she hear my voice in the night when I call?") was a departure from her usual up-tempo pop beats and was written to honor her mother. Twelve years and a stream of hits later, Madonna took on the role of Eva Peron. Known as the "Mother of Argentina" to a devoutly Catholic people, Evita was revered in a way that's very similar to the Virgin Mary. She was a woman who carved out a place for herself in politics, not content to merely be the wife of the man in power. Evita died of uterine cancer after refusing a hysterectomy because it might have interrupted her political work.

Before shooting began on *Evita*, Madonna was interviewed by Forrest Sawyer for ABC's *Primetime Live*. It was an introspective and moving interview. The conversation began with Sawyer asking Madonna about the life of Evita Peron. At first she replied in a slightly aloof, even sarcastic tone, mocking Sawyer's attempts to psychoanalyze her character, but when the discussion turned to the similarities she shared with Peron, the interview grew serious. Asked if, like Evita, Madonna had been hurt by life, Madonna gave a poignant answer: "Losing my mother at a very young age was a devastating experience, and I really did feel completely abandoned . . . I'm sure that has influenced every decision I have made, and left me with a feeling, a hunger, a longing, a feeling of emptiness . . . afraid to love things because they are going to leave you."

The interviewer pressed on, asking if there was any place she felt safe at all. Tears welled up and Madonna answered quickly, "No, not really."

I am fortunate that my mother is still alive. I've never felt abandoned the way Madonna must have felt. But when she talked about a hunger, a feeling of emptiness, and a fear of loving things you can't hold onto, my heart ached. I have gone through enough IVF cycles to know the grief of loss. The bruising reality of a negative pregnancy test has stayed with me even as I try to pick myself up and hope again for something I barely understand. I don't want to say goodbye to the beautiful mystery of having a baby, but I don't want to cling so tightly to that idea that I wear down my body and spirit.

Eventually, the *Primetime Live* interview turned to whether Madonna wanted children of her own, and her answers were emphatic. "Absolutely," "definitely," and "it's time" came without hesitation as her porcelain face lit up with a beaming smile. For those who wonder if Madonna was trying to one-up Angelina Jolie by adopting two children from Malawi, it's interesting to note that in this interview, she mentioned the possibility of starting her family by adopting one or two children. The interview took place on December 6, 1995—when Angelina was barely an adult, burning up the screen as the crop-haired computer whiz in *Hackers*. Madonna's first daughter, Lourdes, was born less than a year later, followed by Rocco in 2000, and her two adopted children, David and Mercy, in 2006 and 2009. By then, Angelina Jolie was an active humanitarian, and Madonna's struggles to adopt from a foreign country brought awareness to the odyssey hopeful parents experience as they try to find their family.

I take comfort in the fact that this woman, who started life with a name intractably tied to her own mom's tragic death, found a way to not just accept and understand the idea of motherhood, but to rush toward it with open arms. Early in her career, Madonna told *The New York Times*, "I think people are named names for certain reasons, and I feel that I was given a special name for a reason. In a way, maybe I wanted to live up to my name."

I hope for a similar type of resolution: to live up to my name as a warrior maiden, soldiering on through frustration to get my baby, whether biological or adopted; or, equally brave, to walk away from motherhood all together.

Mother Madonna

Sarah Sweeney

I TOSSED MY pink felt coat across my unmade bed and took off my pajamas. Nude, I slid into a pair of leather pumps I'd sneaked from our front closet. It housed the '80s glamazon wardrobe my Aunt Gayle had left behind when she died of breast cancer. Aunt Gayle was my mother's sister, and unlike her, she'd been a fashionable head-turner. I would open the closet late at night when my parents were getting stoned in their room and my brother was hooked to cartoons. I would be wide awake, bursting with wanderlust, as I rifled through Aunt Gayle's old business suits, shoulder-padded blouses, lingerie, and shoes.

My tiny feet swam inside her size-9 ostrich heels, and I stumbled a bit as I shrugged the coat around my shoulders. I stood in front of my dresser mirror and stared at my tiny breasts. I touched the soft domes of skin and then hit rewind on my portable tape player. Inside was my secret weapon: a cracked cassette of *Like a Virgin*, its holographic spool twirling out my pre-pubescent dreams of escape, stardom, and happily ever after. I was eight. It was a ritual, this: dressing up in my dead aunt's clothes. It was the closest thing I had to glamour, and I would dance in the mirror, half nude, to "Dress You Up," singing over Madonna's whale-sized voice, our house quaking as I posed and pretended, my bedroom door locked behind me.

It was 1989. Madonna was busy promoting "Like a Prayer," and everywhere I looked there she was—blonde and writhing in fishnets, black eyeliner, and makeshift Marilyn-mole; the next day brunette, muscular and bustier-clad, part dominatrix, part drug addict. I wasn't sure which incarnation I liked best, only that she was the most beautiful woman I had ever seen, and everything I wanted to be.

★

I lived in North Carolina in a brick house with a maple tree in front and a white cement driveway. My father sold electrical equipment and my mother was an x-ray technician. Both were ex-hippies still grappling with their lives of responsibility and childrearing, and our upbringing was loose, strange, and embedded with music, the soundtrack of my parents' glory days. When my mother cooked dinner she played Fleetwood Mac and Steely Dan's *Aja*; my father loved Led Zeppelin and the Allman Brothers Band. We were what most people might call dysfunctional—my parents loathed each other and my brother and I were heathens. We stole from nearby stores, snuck out at night, and took to drinking early, raiding the poorly hidden liquor cabinet during Saturday's after-midnight extravaganza, when we had no bedtime and our parents slept.

My father was sick with Crohn's disease and my mother was bitter about how her life had turned out. They were so busy sparring that my brother and I became lone renegades in a house with no government or structure. When my father did make a play for power, putting his foot down, we were often shocked and fearful of his demands. His maniacal moods and heavy drinking led to bizarre outbursts of Puritanism, nothing at all like how he ran his own life—like the night at dinner when he informed me that my new idol, Madonna, worshipped the devil. I was eight.

"She worships the devil," he said, forcefully chopping my steak into bite-size pieces. He was angry, looking at my mother for input on his wish to ban MTV from our household.

"The devil?" I asked.

"And little girls who worship Madonna worship the devil, too," he said. "She's a whore. And what you're doing is idolatry."

"What's a whore?" I asked.

"Someone who has sex with a lot of people."

This was a lot to process at the dinner table. "What's idolatry?" I asked.

"When you love someone more than you love God," my father answered.

We never went to church, never said grace before meals, and Christmas held no mention of Christ in our home. With his comments, my father had introduced the immense gulf between my terrestrial life and heaven, which could never be paved as long as I cherished Madonna.

I had seen the video for "Like a Prayer" at least a hundred times and though there was something about it that told me I shouldn't be watching, I didn't dare look away.

I had no idea at the time what the song or video meant—the tonguing with a black man (something I had been told was taboo, especially in the South) and the symbolism. So each time it aired, I studied it for clues: the stigmata, the inmate-turned-Jesus, Jesus sexualized, the crosses flaming as Madonna danced down a grassy knoll. These images floated in my mind like the huge question marks I had toward the world—especially at night, when my father's words echoed and my shadowed room held me, and I feared the devil was closing in.

Madonna's religious fixation and my father's veiled comments and successful ban of MTV sparked something inside me that lasted for years. During late 1989 and early 1990, I watched news segments about religious groups persecuting Madonna for cross burning, as well as some more farfetched reports that claimed she had AIDS.

One afternoon, I asked my father if Madonna did indeed have AIDS.

"Probably," he answered, and tears welled in my eyes. This was my father speaking, and I took his word as gospel. How could I have known any better?

It was another assault against Madonna, but I couldn't manage to un-love her. I was an idolater, and my love for her thrust my life into limbo with both my parents and a God I was now so acutely aware of. I believed I'd volunteered myself into the world's relentless witch hunt against Madonna, and we were in it together.

When my father wasn't around, I watched MTV as much as I could. Madonna was on every fifteen minutes and my clandestine viewing made me even more guilty and anxious.

I had asked my father what kind of name "Madonna" was. I had never heard it before and it seemed bewildering to me.

"That's another name for the Virgin Mary," he told me.

"The who?" I asked.

"The Virgin Mary—Jesus's mother."

Madonna exuded all things religious and yet she worshipped the devil, I thought. I knew this was complex stuff. In my unkempt room at night I hardly slept. Instead, I propped my battery-powered tape player on my pillow, played *Like a Virgin,* and succumbed to deep bouts of prayer. I asked God to save Madonna, to save me, and for nearly two years I prayed fanatically—for freedom from the world, from the devil. I really did believe he was chasing me: that Madonna had been his entryway into my life, that he was gnawing at my soul, and only consistent prayer would rid me of him. On my worst days, I prayed tens of times in my bedroom. Sometimes during playtime with my brother or friends, I'd be overcome with worry and obsession and slink off to the bathroom for a meeting with God. I prayed for my family, for Madonna, for the other girls out there obsessed with her and tormented by the devil—"Free us all!" I begged, my voice a muffled cry into my pillow.

During these years, while I prayed and grew older, I led my double life of dancing that rattled the windowpanes at night as I leapt around my room and twisted in the mirror, lip-syncing into a hairbrush. I posed seductively in Aunt Gayle's satin chemises and tripped in her four-inch heels as they pierced our dingy carpet. I was leading Madonna's life, I told myself, a life of sexuality and expression. I was only a provocateur in my bedroom, alone, caressing my body the way I'd seen Madonna do, her hands sliding down her breasts and hips.

Sometimes I stared out my window facing the backyard and watched our neighbor Russ wash his car in the hazy evening as smoke from our grill wafted up through my room. I don't know what drew me to Russ, but he became a short-lived figure of my veneration. I knew that in order to be more like Madonna, I needed a *boy toy*, and Russ fit the bill. He was late thirties, early forties, not particularly attractive, but in my fantasy world I was a performing diva and not a little girl. Outside of my fantasies, I was not in love with Russ; but inside them, we admired each other from afar, watching, waiting.

I could see Russ in his kitchen window some nights, washing dishes underneath a halo of light. When the sky was grey, I'd flick on a lamp and parade in front of my window, stark nude as the moon that streaked yellow beams through the lawn. I don't know if Russ ever saw me there, but it was my first exercise in being a seductress, a woman of zero inhibition.

I spritzed myself with Love's Baby Soft, the pink perfume my parents had bought me that Christmas, and sometimes sneaked a spray of my mother's sultry Nina Ricci inside my cotton nightgown, the spicy scent burning my nose.

I lay down in my bed and touched my body, the soft hairless spot between my legs that Madonna grabbed during performances, a move that prompted my mother to make noises of disgust.

"What? What is it?" I remember asking her.

"Look at her," she said, shaking her head, "grabbing her crotch like that."

I had a name for it—a crotch. Nothing particularly romantic about the harsh sounds it made leaving my mother's mouth, but I knew Madonna was as close with her crotch as a girl could be and that I had catching up to do.

I touched my crotch and looked in the mirror and dreamed of bleaching my hair blonde and shaving my legs. I asked my mother if I could do both and she said I could not, that I was a kid, and there was plenty of time for that.

I felt stifled by time, unmoved by her suggestion that my life had just begun and there was a swath of endless highway ahead of me. Madonna was living my life, the life I wanted that was incubating inside of me, and I was trapped. I watched Madonna and begged my mother to move me to Los Angeles; I had become enamored with the idea of making it on *Star Search*. I practiced night after night in the mirror to all of Madonna's songs; I knew the words by heart, every additional *ooh* and *ahh,* every backing harmony. I had no fear of dancing, of exposing myself to neighbors; I was ready to grow up, to be an outspoken woman and make my own decisions the way Madonna had, as though she had pioneered those two very things. The more Madonna accomplished, the more enthralled I was, and the more left behind I felt.

Before I was banned from watching MTV, I viewed the "Justify My Love" video during its brief airtime in 1990. It was late at night and everyone was asleep but me. I sat on our living room carpet, stunned and paralyzed by what I was witnessing. I had viewed the soft-core porn highlights of HBO after dark, but nothing like this. It was erotic and dangerous and real and so typically Madonna and I loved it. My crotch tingled like it never had before. Something was happening, and I knew this was the reaction Madonna lived for. Madonna tingled nonstop.

From our local drug store I pilfered razors, hair dye, lipstick, mascara, magazines, tampons, and sultry summer paperbacks from the magazine aisle. I scrolled through the pages looking for standout words that would give me a tingle: breasts, thighs, desire, climax.

★

In the summer of 1991, my mother divorced my father. We stayed in the brick house and he moved into an apartment not far away. After he left, my mother reinstated MTV. I could watch all the music videos and Madonna I wanted.

"Mom," I asked her one night. "Dad said Madonna has AIDS."

She paused over a fry pan to look at me in horror. "He told you that?"

"And that she worships the devil, too."

My mother heaved and sighed and, visibly angry, took this as evidence that divorcing my father had been the correct thing to do.

"Honey," she said, turning once more to the stove. "Your father is crazy. Now go watch TV."

And I did. My mother's response signaled that my father had been untruthful all along, and I was vindicated and relieved. I could finally stop praying.

In the fall of 1992 I turned 10. My breasts were swelling, and in the eyes of the mirror I could envision the years ahead of me; I might've even seen my childhood evaporating.

During that time, Madonna's book *Sex* was also released. I'd heard the press surrounding its publication and wondered where I might steal a look. It was promised to be some unholy tome, largely criticized, which made its secrets all the more compelling to me. I was ignorant and thirsty; I had to see the book somehow.

My mother's foray into a sex talk was, simply, "You won't do it until you're married." One command, and I knew nothing else for years. Early on, I believed sex was sleeping part-to-part all night, a meticulously constructed act that resulted in a child being born sometime in the future.

A summer after *Sex*'s release, another of my aunts drove me to a bookstore and let me wander around alone. On a display table in the back of the store were sealed copies of the book. I sneaked one away and opened it on an empty aisle. The iconic photograph of a nude, hitchhiking Madonna resembling Marilyn Monroe was the first image that seared into my brain: Madonna cheekily smoking a cigarette with a thumb lifted to traffic. I slammed the book shut, the slick pages heavy and thudding, and began to cry. I felt suddenly blinded by self-awareness. My heart pounded, and all at once I knew that I was a child, would be a child for a while, and that becoming Madonna was impossible.

★

In the 1992 film *A League of Their Own*, Madonna played the streetwise and sexy ballplayer Mae Mordabito, a character much like herself then, but her character also showed a softer, more human side by falling in love with a G.I. in the movie. This role provided a dimension to Madonna I'd never seen before: Even if it was just acting, she could be womanly, coquettish; not just brazen, but rounded and complex. It was a critical turning point for how I wanted to be as a woman. I wanted to have it all, while being it all.

As I grew older, Madonna did too. And my Madonna religion waned. I loved her but didn't need her as much. I was still with her in 1993 when she released "Rain." My cousins stayed with us that summer and we snuck out to the neighborhood cemetery at night and smoked cigarettes in the woods. It was my favorite song of the 1990s, a powerful ballad about catharsis and letting go of love.

Madonna's music videos were instruction manuals, and in so many ways Madonna was my true protector, best friend, confidante; I listened to her when nothing made sense and crucial relationships and beliefs in my life dissolved at a rapid pace. Always untouchable, Madonna withstood years of condemnation, but I believed I understood her the way no one else did. Madonna emblemized happiness, a life without limits, and I knew I wanted that and not my parents' humdrum version of living: their tired bodies dragged out of the house each morning, the gruff churning of the engine, the invisible desire to flee.

Even more of a quandary for me than Madonna's supposed pact with Satan was that she only had one name. I was blithely naive to the idea that Madonna was anyone's child, that she was birthed as routinely as any infant in a local hospital. Before Madonna, I had never envisioned myself without my parents; we were one body, an entity, but with just her name Madonna showed me independence; she was whole and alone and was seemingly born that way.

She was with me in 1994, when the blood pierced my panties on a Sunday morning and I called to my mother for assistance. I knew something had finally happened, and I was finally transitioning into a woman.

And as I aged and changed and began crafting my own life, my feelings toward Madonna changed. Where I had once worshipped an idealized version of her—youthful, sexual, beautiful—I now see much more, even fault. How I now view her is entirely unlike my childhood idol. I look back at those years with a sad fondness for us both, the struggling girl and the female on top, both bemused, giddy, exasperated; and I think of her as a mother of sorts, the person who taught me not *everything* I needed to know about being a woman, just a lot of the important stuff.

Marrying Madonna

Christine Bachman

I WAS SEVEN years old, dressed in sparkly plastic heels, my mother's slip, my father's fake boobs (yes, that's right), and makeup clumsily caked on my face: It was my wedding day.

Actually, it was my wedding day almost every afternoon when I played "house" with my next-door neighbor, Lucy. We would solemnly hum "Here Comes the Bride" as we walked slowly down the red-carpeted hallway and approached my stuffed monkey, Coco, who would momentarily join us—Madonna and Michael Jackson—in holy matrimony. And while the focus was on the ceremony itself, the game didn't end there. We would play on, simulating the consummation of our marriage, which would then result in the birth of the couple's first child. And as we, Madonna and Michael Jackson, managed our successful careers, we also found happiness in all the mundane chores of a "normal" middle-class life: cooking dinner, tidying the house, and teaching our children proper table manners.

Years later, as I look back on this well-rehearsed performance of my childhood, I attempt to make sense of the freakish union of the King and Queen of Pop, two of the biggest queer icons in pop culture. Why was *this* union—with marriage being the epitome of heteronormativity—which places heterosexuality as the foundation of normalcy and all that is socially acceptable—such a focus of my young life, and why was Madonna, in particular, my leading lady?

As my father's fake boobs suggest, my childhood was a little unusual. I was raised by a German mother and a gay father; one parent uprooted from her country, never to fit into the cookie-cutter suburbs of America, and the other an escapee of Salt Lake City, who ultimately ended up living among a chosen family of gay men. I was the product of their marriage (and later, when my father came out, their divorce), and believed for years that *everyone's* father must be gay, and that all mothers revert to speaking German whenever they are counting or cooking. I grew up in an impossible family, a family that made no sense compared to the heterosexual, two-parented families around me, but I felt loved, supported, safe, and happy. Maybe that's why, when constructing my fantasy family, I chose another impossible couple. The make-believe romance of Madonna and Michael—the parents of my idealized world—married the normative and the queer, allowing my seven-year-old brain to make sense of the contradictions that I experienced in my everyday life.

My youthful obsession with Madonna herself, however, was a much more superficial idolization. I was surrounded by gay men who knew her songs, her dances, her history, and her gossip. Through Madonna, they shared a language and a borrowed identity—one Madonna appropriated, in part, from gay and black culture—to express their own. To be part of their world, I learned this language and grew to identify with the perspective of my gay adult role models, who looked up to this icon of "fabulousness." Yet I also grew to identify with Madonna *herself*, as the only woman in the room, the model of idealized femininity, whose performances simultaneously glorified enforced, and then *destroyed* the rules of gender and sexuality. In this way, my make-believe games blurred into my reality and the creation of my own identity, shaping the way I would understand my place in a world of gay men.

There is a growing community of children and adults that have been raised by queer parents. Some of us call ourselves "queerspawn." We queerspawn are familiar with living between the dominant heterosexual world and the often less conventional world of our parents. We inhabit both of these worlds as insiders *and* outsiders. It's quite a powerful position to occupy, having access to the safety of socially acceptable rules and codes, and also to a universe that transcends traditional boundaries, giving us a passport by birth to explore a more radical and imaginative territory.

Unlike me, Madonna was not lucky enough to have a queer parent, though a community of gay male fans adopted her early in her career. And as a gay icon, a sexually provocative pop star, a rule-breaker, *and* a privileged white woman from a traditional Catholic family, Madonna has also spent most of her life straddling both worlds as an insider and an outsider. This "hybridity" permeates her work, merging elements of both worlds into her performances, as she evokes Marilyn Monroe (the iconic heterosexual ideal of feminine allure), while indulging in a variety of illicit sexualities and ambiguous genders in her banned 1990 music video "Justify My Love." In this video, and in so many of her performances that borrow themes from the mainstream and the queer worlds, Madonna exploits both realms to gain access to new levels of cultural relevance and power.

By the time I entered young adulthood, power was much more interesting than sparkly plastic heels and pretend weddings, though Madonna was still my leading lady. As an undergraduate, I chose to write my senior thesis on Madonna and her successes and failures in disrupting, or "queering," some of our most seemingly stable binaries: sexuality, gender, race, class, and age. My thesis provided me with a legitimate excuse to throw myself headfirst into a thorough examination of Madonna's career, and my academic quest to understand Madonna and her relationship to queerness and power became a fierce obsession.

Ultimately, I was in it to discover how this gay-male icon—this legend of pop-star greatness—claimed access to untethered power. Desperately I read between the lines, committing every Madonna lyric, movement, and performance to memory. What did these performances *mean*? How did Madonna, a character that had played such an integral role in my coming of age, move between traditional and queer spaces so successfully? And how could I, a queerspawn born in the age of Madonna, channel my insider/outsider status to question, resist, challenge, and ultimately *celebrate* access to both conventional power *and* queer power? Madonna was the key to understanding one more piece of this power puzzle.

As a college student, when I wasn't poring over hours of Madonna music videos, I was testing the new limits of my world as a young adult, discovering my passions and learning how to act on them: from coming out as a queer-identified straight woman, to creating an institutionally supported space for queer studies on my college campus. Madonna had guided me through my early childhood, providing me with the tools I needed to communicate with my world of gay men, while opening my eyes to the rigid rules of femininity as well as the strength she found in breaking them—seemingly just for the fun of it. As a college student, she guided me again, taking me through each of her performances until I was finally satisfied with the knowledge that I had had all along: Our real strength is our ability to move, adapt, change, grow, be part of and separate from the worlds which we inhabit. My childhood fantasy, in which I, Madonna, married Michael Jackson, was not just a mockery of a heterosexual ritual, it was also *exactly* where I felt most comfortable and powerful.

Thus, it is ironic, informative, and fitting that I am now recreating this duality in my real life as I prepare to get married. Though my partner is neither Michael Jackson nor the clueless neighbor that grew to know her part so well, he too understands the life of an insider/outsider. As a competitive triathlete, model, and all-around privileged white man, he is a poster boy (literally) of mainstream America; but as a feminist and queer-identified man committed to exploring the limits of gender-bending, he feels more at home at a drag show than at a football game, though he can easily pass in either arena. Our partnership has always balanced the thin line between the queer and mainstream worlds, and exists as an anomaly in both: We look like your typical heterosexual couple, but we subscribe to the ideologies and values of the queer world. Thus, as our relationship has grown, so has our shared commitment to challenge our conventional facade in order to identify with and reveal the radical, queer position we take in our communities, our politics, and our sexualities. To shake things up, as it were, Madonna-style. What would she think, I wonder, of our "Save the Date" cards, complete with a photo of me in a tuxedo and my blushing groom in a white wedding gown?

As a composite creation, I have much fear about this "next step" in the script of conventional heterosexual romance. Will I lose my membership to the queer world that has raised me? Will I gain permanent acceptance to a heteronormative world and *become* a straight girl? These thoughts terrify me. Struggling with the idea of entering—'til death do us part—a world of mainstream heterosexuality, I find myself trying to signal my disapproval and resistance. But doesn't Madonna teach us that the most effective way to change the rules is not to resent them or ignore them, but to upend them and make them your own?

Embracing her many contradictions, Madonna does not shy away from celebrating ambiguous genders and sexual identities, nor does she refuse to champion the myth of heterosexual romance. Rather, she marries elements of her queerness with traditional ideals of conventional sexuality, experimenting with drag and gender-bending, as she did during her 1993 tour The Girlie Show. Performing "Like a Virgin," Madonna mimicked Marlene Dietrich with a low voice and thick German accent, but also evoked *Cabaret*'s "Emcee," dressed sharply in a tuxedo and presenting the audience with a deliberately confused masculinity. Her ever-present bright-red lipstick undermined her claims to manhood, and as she slipped into the Detroit accent and persona of a working-class male in "Bye Bye Baby," her character was aroused by three androgynous dancing girls—exotic for their gender-bending as well as for their racial ambiguity. Madonna's performance throughout the piece emphasized the ways in which she borrows cultural cues from queer staples, and from traditional heterosexual scripts. And with this unexpected combination of the mainstream and the queer, Madonna brings something new to her audiences, tapping into a power not limited by conventional rules *or* the rules and expectations attached to carefully maintained queerness. I relate to that.

She reminds me to find strength in the insider/outsider identity that has defined me since my make-believe weddings to Michael Jackson. As a queer-identified woman with a queer-identified male partner, our marriage will be just as freakish and fun as my imagined childhood weddings. So, I owe her thanks, for reminding me from childhood onward, to always "express yourself, don't repress yourself!"

Come July, dancing down the aisle to Madonna, I will embrace the creation of my own impossible family, marrying the traditional and the queer in a perfectly imperfect union.

Into the Wilderness

Soniah Kamal

I WAS STANDING before my full-length mirror holding blood-stained cotton balls to my ears when my mother barged into my room and gazed at me in despair. Like all good Pakistani girls, getting my earlobes pierced was a traditional rite of passage, but I was seventeen years old and I had just plunged a sewing needle into my cartilage six times in each ear. It hurt, but I felt good.

"Do you think you are Madonna?!" my mother yelled.

I stood before her in fingerless blue lace gloves, black rubber bracelets, red leggings and a white shirt over a black bra. My mother eyed me with sorrow and worry. Good Pakistani girls did not dress this way, not if they wanted to fulfill their parents' dream of making a decent respectable marriage. I felt my mother's pain as she yelled again, "Do you think you are Madonna?!"

★

Madonna came into my life when I was fourteen years old. At the time, we lived in Jeddah, a hot, dusty, port city with a brilliant blue cornice alongside the Red Sea in Saudi Arabia. I attended an international school that apparently provided the best education. But because it was co-ed, my parents constantly reminded me that good Muslim girls did not speak to boys, under any circumstances. And as long as we were *good girls*, all was okay.

One afternoon I was visiting a school friend, Shannon. I was allowed to go to Shannon's house because she had no brothers and she was Irish Catholic. My mother believed Irish Catholics were just like Muslims: appropriately strict with their daughters. My mother would have been appalled if she'd seen Shannon prancing around her house in a skimpy tank top and underwear. The only Western clothes I was permitted to wear were loose, long shirts, jeans, and dresses and skirts, as long as they were paired with knee-high socks. I felt foolish and ugly in those socks. But I couldn't even take them off at school because I was not allowed to shave my desperately-in-need-of-a-shave legs. Nor was I allowed to grow my nails or wear makeup. I couldn't figure out what being a good Muslim or Pakistani had to do with hairy legs, short nails, and zero makeup.

On this particular afternoon, we lounged in Shannon's bedroom, sipping chilled cans of Vimto grape soda and listening to music. Shannon had bought a new audio cassette. The girl on the cover reminded me of Pakistani singer Nur Jehan. They shared a plump, sultry, victorious mien, as if they'd just eaten the creamiest pastry in the world.

"Tell me what you think?" Shannon said as she pressed play.

You may be my lucky star, but I'm the luckiest by far . . .

The tune: catchy. The beat: like bubbles popping. The rhythm: joyous, cheery. Before we knew it we were jumping on the bed through "Holiday" and "Everybody," yelling bits of the choruses we'd picked up. Finally we collapsed, and I passed my verdict: Madonna sounded like a squeaky mouse. Shannon laughed and agreed. Then she asked, "Do you want hear a really *sexy* song?"

"Okay," I said with false bravado—in my home, "sexy" was a bad word.

"Like a Virgin" throbbed through the speakers. If Shannon hadn't been sitting there, my mouth would have fallen open at hearing the word "virgin" out loud, but Shannon was belting it out as if it were no big deal. Perhaps it wasn't. Shannon's parents expected her to be a virgin until marriage, but dating, boyfriends, crushes, and first kisses were dinner-table fodder at her house. At my home, dating, boy-friends, crushes, and kisses were all *bad* words, and not only was I expected to be a virgin at marriage but woe betide I had *anything* to do with any male before my wedding night.

When the song was over, I said, "My parents think *virgin* is a bad word." I rolled my eyes even as I asked Allah to forgive me for saying "virgin" and for speaking ill about my parents.

Shannon popped her gum. "My dad would die if he heard this song."

"My dad would kill me if he even heard me hearing this song."

A few weeks later, my mother allowed me to attend Shannon's birthday party because she thought it was girls-only. Because I was the only Pakistani/Muslim at the party, I relaxed—my parents knew no one here, so nothing would get back to them. Streamers and bal-loons decorated the walls. Boys and girls stood at opposite ends of the room, finding refuge behind Pepsis and potato chips until Shan-non's mother shepherded us into the center and warned us to start having fun. "Material Girl" blasted through the room and everyone started to move.

"Who is this?" I asked Shannon.

"Madonna," she said.

"The Mouse?"

"Yep. The Mouse. I like her."

"Me too."

Our movements intensified through "Borderline," and by the time "Into the Groove" came on, we were all jiggling our butts off.

Then a slow song came on: "Crazy for You." Amid giggles equally shy and coy, everyone paired up and began to slow-dance. I had never been in such close proximity to a boy. My parents would be mortified. Not that B, with his black spectacles and knobby knees, qualified in my mind as a "boy"; he was simply a classmate who happened to not be a girl. I felt guilty even as I consoled myself that if Shannon could dance like this with her mother in the room, then surely it couldn't be such a crime.

Still, I felt I was letting down my parents and Allah. But if the Christian God and Muslim God were one and the same, then how could one religion deem slow-dancing all right and the other deem it bad? I squeezed my eyes shut and prayed for an answer.

The next day, I begged my father to drive me to a supermarket with a music department so I could purchase every Madonna song available. I winced as my father glanced at the cassette covers. Madonna's curls were unruly, eyebrows brash, mouth bold, nose absolutely beautiful, but most of all, I loved her defiant gaze: She resembled a tigress that'd spotted her favorite meal.

My parents were connoisseurs of *ghazals* (a form of poetry that could be put to music and sung), as well as Indian film songs. Their small collection of English music consisted of ABBA, Boney M., and the Bee Gees. My father, inspecting Madonna on the covers, asked me who she was. I told him: "A new singer I heard at Shannon's house." He pursed his lips. For a moment I feared he would screen the songs. I could just imagine his heart attack over "like a virgin touched for the very first time" or "crazy for you, touch me once and you'll know it's true."

As it was, my father presumed that all entertainers hailed from questionable stock. Whether this belief was unique to him or part of our culture, I had yet to discover. Either way, his disdain did not deter his own pleasure in listening to music or watching classical dances in Indian films. This dichotomy left me irritated and annoyed.

Eventually, my father handed me the bag. At home I whisked my mother's tape player into my room. Door shut, volume low, I crooned along with Madonna for the rest of the evening. Even though I still felt guilty for having slow-danced, I kept playing "Crazy for You."

At one point during the evening, my mother popped her head in to inquire if I'd prayed that day. I whipped out my prayer mat and a head covering (mandatory only while praying) before rushing through the ritual so I could return to the songs. I particularly liked "Live to Tell," despite not gleaning the secret that was burning inside of her. And "Like a Virgin" thrilled me. It really was the sexiest!

Madonna, everyone at school proclaimed, was the Queen of Sexiness. I agreed, even though I wasn't altogether sure what "sexy" meant. One day, B, the boy I'd danced with at Shannon's party, passed me a note in class: "U R Sexy." My face burned. I thought I was going to pass out. "Sexy" scared me. Sexy was in the same category as "shame-shame," our euphemism for genitals. I felt ashamed and dirty, as if I *had* done something sinful.

And I had: I had slow-danced with B, and had thus inadvertently invited him to say such a thing about me. Guilt gnawed at me. I loved my parents and didn't want to let them down no matter how annoying or unreasonable they could be. Red-faced, I crumpled B's note and did not even tell Shannon.

Instead, I decided to take my mother up on her constant assurances that I could ask her *anything*. I ambushed her in the kitchen just as she was pouring chickpeas into sautéed onions.

"What exactly does *sexy* mean?"

My mother turned off the stove, led me to the kitchen table, and held my gaze.

"Why exactly do you want to know?" she asked.

I told her I'd overheard a boy at school say it to a girl. My mother sighed, muttering that this was what came of sending girls to co-ed schools. Sexy, she proceeded to inform me, was a very, very bad thing—it was a girl who wanted boys to want her in a shameful way, that not only should I never say the word but I should also distance myself from those who did. She ended with a kiss to my forehead and an order to pray to Allah to instill in me the sense to know right from wrong.

So I got down on my mat and prayed. Afterward, I continued to sit and talk to Allah, as was my habit. "Allah-mian," I said, "if sexy is so bad and I am sexy then how is it my fault, since I have purposefully done nothing to be this way?" Allah did not answer, but rising from the prayer mat I decided to take a break from listening to the Queen of Sexy.

Perhaps Madonna would have truly disappeared from my life had another friend, Anya, not returned from her summer vacation in the United States with a VHS tape in tow: Madonna's Virgin Tour.

One afternoon, while my father was at work and my mother recuperated in her bedroom after being on-call (she was an anesthesiologist), Anya and Shannon and I congregated in my living room to watch the video. We were three excited girls perched on the edge of a green velvet sofa, waiting for a cassette to rewind, not knowing that when the world changes, this is how it happens, in ordinary living rooms on ordinary afternoons.

When the concert began, Madonna's silhouette appeared on the dark stage and she began to sing "Dress You Up." The visual quality may have been grainy and the audio not perfectly clear, but strobe lights pulsed, smoke billowed, the crowd cheered, and there was Madonna—gliding, pirouetting, gyrating across the stage like lightning come to life. I was mesmerized; a strange energy engulfed me, my shoulders were sprouting wings, my stomach birthing butterflies, my feet growing light. I felt I was readying for flight.

Madonna was hypnotic—her voice, her body, her daring moves and attire: high-heel ankle boots, leggings that ended midcalf, black bracelets engulfing her wrists in lieu of the glass bangles favored by Pakistanis, and Christian crosses worn as pendants and earrings. ("Madonna is Catholic just like me," Shannon informed us gleefully.)

Each time Madonna lifted her arms—and she lifted her arms plenty—her transparent top rode up to expose her midriff and bits of her bra. I was embarrassed for her, but because she wasn't embarrassed for herself, I felt stupid for being embarrassed.

I watched, riveted, as she went from costume to costume until she was dressed in wedding-style white lace with white leggings, white boots, crosses and rosaries galore, to sing "Like a Virgin." "Will you marry me?" she asked the audience, and they roared back. Madonna was immorality and morality entwined like stripes on a candy cane. Madonna was magic. Madonna was madness. The concert ended with a man—Madonna's real-life father—barreling on stage to drag her away as if she were a naughty girl. At that moment I felt akin to Madonna. *I was Madonna.* She understood my life, so I gave her my soul. No matter that it had been an act, and that she returned to the stage to do a curtsy.

When the concert was over, Anya, Shannon, and I peered bashfully at each other.

"That was great."

"Greater than great."

"It was the sexiest."

Breaking into giddy shrieks, we rewound the tape and watched it all over again. The third time around, we rose to copy Madonna's moves, and that was when my mother walked into the living room and found us awkwardly flailing about. We instantly stopped and sat down.

"It's a Madonna concert," I blurted out. And, as if sensing my nervousness, Shannon and Anya also began bombarding my mother with assurances.

"It's the latest thing in the States."

"She's huge there. Like Michael Jackson."

"Everyone's watching this video."

"And copying her dancing."

"She's Catholic," I added sheepishly.

To my surprise, my mother sat down with us and watched for a while before announcing that her moves were more gymnastics than dance. But she didn't tell me to turn it off. Instead my mother smiled and told me to move the glass coffee table to one side if we were going to dance. Then she left. I wonder if Madonna had mesmerized her too.

Before Anya left, I made a copy of the video. Each day, as soon as I returned from school, I'd switch it on for my daily dose. It was not long before the word "virgin" became routine and Madonna's undergarments ceased to embarrass. They had metamorphosed into a symbol of conventional morality and tradition turned on its head. Her use of religious jewelry was particularly alluring to me. In wearing her religion, she included God in her sexiness. Either that, or God was sanctioning her himself.

Madonna's name fascinated me, too. Madonna, Mother Mary: a good, virtuous woman. For Madonna, there seemed to be no schism between religion and sexiness, and I was a student eager to learn the same. To break the schism between my religion and my body and the bizarre moral codes of my parents, I shaved my legs, grew my nails, and applied whatever shade of lipstick a friend would share, once I'd arrived at school.

I finally understood what it meant to be sexy—it was only a four-letter word if you allowed it to be. Sexy was neither good nor bad; it just was. Sexy did not mean sleazy or slutty or of questionable stock. Sexy just meant that people found you sexually desirable. The fact that I was growing more comfortable with this idea, as well as the ability to say "sexy, virgin, crushes, kisses" no longer filled me with dread.

Madonna made my young heart flutter with endless possibility. I would listen to her on my newly acquired Walkman—a reward for earning stellar grades—on our frequent weekend drives to Mecca or Medina, holy cities for Muslims. When we'd arrive there, I would switch off my Walkman, don a hair covering, and joyously worship Allah; then, on our drive back, I'd remove the hair covering, put my earphones back in, and return peacefully to Madonna. I would happily lip sync to "Papa Don't Preach," not at all shocked by the song's message. Mothers loved their kids, I concluded, whether unwed in the West, or like Hajra/Hagar in Islamic lore, desperately running in the barren desert in search of water for her thirsty infant. Incorporating Madonna into my Muslim self was beginning to feel as effortless as my being bilingual. I could balance revolving around Madonna one minute, and circling the *Kaaba* the next. The two didn't seem at all contradictory. I had entered a dual universe, one I still live in, and Madonna was instrumental in my learning to create a symbiotic existence.

Ironically it was in Mecca, during ablutions before prayers, that my mother discovered my shaved legs. I had rolled up the long pant-leg of my *shalwar* and was merrily pouring water over my feet and ankles, when she yelped, "Are your legs shaved?"

I shrugged.

"Who gave you permission?"

My mother remained silent on our return drive. I figured it was to spare my father news of my fall. But once we arrived home, she cornered me in my bedroom, enraged and even more upset when she learned I'd filched the razor from her own stash.

"You did it to attract boys, didn't you? You did it to attract *boys*."

I was shocked and angry that she refused to believe I'd shaved my legs only to avoid the girls laughing at my hairy limbs.

The shaving caused enough bad friction between us, but my mother found my expanding style of dress even more abhorrent. As the Jeddah stores began to stock Madonna-like clothing, we girls were fast transforming into mini-Madonnas, eager to rule the world in short skirts, leggings, and black bras.

My mother was lost as to how to discipline me. She kept saying I should pray for forgiveness. And pray I did, but only to complain to

Allah about how my parents were ruining my life. Finally my mother began to blame Madonna for my transgressions, as if it were Madonna's direct instruction rather than my own choice that had me questioning and discarding my mother's—and my culture's—principles.

In the end, it was my father who brought things to a head. One afternoon he arrived home early from work to find me glued to the concert—*of course* he walked in just as Madonna's two male backup dancers were thrusting their hips at her. He was livid. As I expected, he called Madonna a prostitute. Now I was livid. For the first time, I found myself defending an entertainer from his damning evaluation. Shame colored me red, but I stood my ground.

My father asked me through clenched teeth if my mother was aware of what I was watching.

"Yes," I said, "and anyway, there's nothing wrong with this; she's sexy and that's not *bad*."

My father immediately telephoned my mother at work and raged at her. I could hear my mother agree that I was no longer allowed to watch the tape. But I defied them both—I made it a point to keep watching the video, especially when my father was home. This went on until the day they told me we were returning to Pakistan.

I do not know how much of a role the Madonna tape played in our return to Pakistan, but when we got there we learned she had conquered that place, too. Posters of Madonna festooned video and music stores, bedroom walls, and even pencil cases. Her music and videos played everywhere, including at my aunt's house, where I first saw the video for "Like a Virgin" while my admittedly progressive aunt, much to my mother's chagrin, teased her for being old-fashioned. Indeed, if my parents brought me to Pakistan to take me away from Madonna, they'd miscalculated.

And so it was that one day my mother barged into my bedroom, found that I'd pierced my ears against her wishes, and asked me if I thought I was Madonna.

"No," I said quietly. "But apparently you do."

★

In the long run, Madonna did not inspire me to do any of the things my parents feared: become a prostitute or birth a child out of wedlock, become a drug addict or even an actress. In fact, to their relief, I ended up respectably married. Yet Madonna's physical bravado was my spiritual mother. In having to repeatedly defend everything she symbolized, I gradually became a person able to see shades of gray, as well as a person who knew her own mind and spoke it.

Over the years, Madonna's presence in my daily life has waned. But the fact is—will always remain—that Madonna made my "today" possible. Current musical acts are just that—acts—but Madonna was pure, unadulterated, raw sexual liberation.

What Madonna meant to me back then and even now: a guide through the wilderness, a soul mate, sexy, but beyond being sexy, she was Hope. Hope that sexy girls did not necessarily die bad deaths, hope that sexy girls lived to tell their tales, hope that sexy girls could rule the world. And do.

Ciccone Youth

Jen Hazen

PINK LEOTARD, PINK tights, ballet slippers. Since the age of five, I had wriggled into spandex after school two days a week to take dance lessons at Meeth Studio in Paw Paw, Michigan. My mother had trained for years when she was growing up, so even after her sudden death a couple of months after my eighth birthday, I chasséd in her footsteps with ballet, tap, and jazz classes.

After my lesson I usually stayed late to watch my teenage dance instructors, Miss Cindy and Miss Lisa, practice their modern dance routines. I recall a day when ten-year-old me leaned against the bar and watched in awe as the girls pirouetted and jetéd across the hardwood floor in black cigarette pants and frayed gray sweatshirts that hung off one shoulder à la *Flashdance*. Their synchronized movements refracted in the mirrored walls as they slid to their knees and fanned their legs into languid poses like *Solid Gold* dancers.

After the rehearsal, I asked Miss Cindy the name of the song they'd been dancing to. "It's 'Lucky Star' by Madonna. She's from

Detroit." She handed me the album cover, which had a full headshot of a woman with bleached blond hair and dark eyebrows, like Marilyn Monroe. Her hands touched her face with a heap of chain jewelry on her wrists and neck. I went home that night and mocked Madonna's cover pose in the bathroom mirror. *We're both from Michigan,* I thought.

We didn't have a turntable in my house, but we had MTV. The luxury of cable television magically arrived when my mom died. My dad, who'd worked second shift while my mother cared for me and my older brother, had no idea how to raise kids. I guess he decided that TV would be a good nanny. After the relentless rotation of Night Ranger's "Sister Christian" and Kurt Loder's music news, I finally caught what I had been waiting for: Madonna's "Lucky Star" video. I studied her dance steps: pas de bourrée, dig step, turn, dig step, roll on the floor, show your stomach. I scrutinized her outfit: capri pants, short skirt, lace everywhere, tons of bracelets, and a floppy bow headband.

That year, I asked for a ghetto blaster for my birthday, and when the "Lucky Star" video aired again, I held it up to the TV and recorded the song. I danced to that crappy cassette recording in our family room for a year, mimicking Madonna's moves in a getup consisting of torn black tights cut off at the knees, one of my dad's black T-shirts knotted on the side, and about twenty gummy bracelets I'd scored from a gumball machine. I didn't have a mom to tell me how to be, so Madonna would have to do. Besides, someone told me that she had lost her mom, too, and she turned out okay, right?

My idolization of Madonna ebbed and flowed as I grew up. My early teen years were tinged with the musical influences of my older brother, who had discovered leather pants, pierced ears, and "alternative" music. My dad was horrified and I was hooked. Cassettes of Siouxsie and the Banshees, New Order, The Cramps, and Sonic Youth ejected my homemade Madonna tapes straight into the garbage.

When all of the kids at school fell in love with Madonna thanks to "Like a Virgin," I snubbed her popularity. Yeah, I was alternative now. Madonna wasn't deep like Siouxsie Sioux, who used words like "lament" and "torpor" in her song lyrics. Besides, Madonna seemed tame, rolling around on concert stages faux-humping in a hacked-up bridal gown, while Lux Interior looked like a creature from *Night of the Living Dead*. Sadly, Madonna just wasn't the outcast that I'd hoped for, so I dismissed her.

Or at least until tenth grade, when I saw the "Like a Prayer" video.

The uproar over this scandalous little number ignited a shit storm in my tiny, homogeneous high school. In the halls, kids were squawking about "Madonna kissing a black guy," taking sides about whether that was acceptable, and probably regurgitating their parents' opinions on the matter, whether they realized it or not. The controversy even made the local news—Madonna kissed a black man! In a church! Burning crosses! Pepsi yanked its sponsorship! She'll burn in hell with the Devil!

My love for Madonna was rekindled with that kiss. It was the best "fuck your status quo" move by a woman that I had seen in my life. And she did it so stylishly—with wavy brunette locks, a strappy corset dress, and no shoes. Brilliant. I remember declaring to my gaggle of girlfriends at the lunch table, "Well, *I* loved it. So she kissed a black guy. Big deal."

But it *was* a big deal then, which, frankly, pissed me off and made me rebel even more. So much so, that I went out and bought the "Like a Prayer" tape. I remember reading the liner notes. Madonna mentioned her mom. *What would she think of her daughter doing all this?* I wondered. And then I wondered if my mom had been proud of me.

★

Being raised in a male household often felt like being reared by wolves. Supper consisted of TV dinners, cereal, or popsicles most of the time, and the day I told my dad that I had gotten my period, he nudged a box of tampons through a small crack in my bedroom door. On the other hand, he taught me that I was just as strong and capable as a boy. But I quickly learned that liberation only existed within the walls of our home.

When I stepped into the real world, I felt an indescribable undercurrent of inferiority and dismissal. I began dressing in baggy clothes for fear that I wouldn't be taken seriously, much like the girls in my class who prattled nonstop about clothes, boys, and prom. I studied to the point of exhaustion to prove my intelligence, with straight As and a high GPA.

Before long, I was dousing my baggy jeans with bleach for the "splatter" effect, ripping holes in my shirts and lining them with safety pins, and dyeing my hair every possible shade of red or black. I did it because I couldn't tolerate the small, close-minded town I was living in, and because my dad had been diagnosed with cancer. The color of my hair seemed to be the only thing I could control.

In my early twenties, I cared for my dad in our home along with the help of hospice. After battling various types of cancer for five years, he had a stroke and was partially paralyzed. I would occasionally leave the house to attend college classes part-time or work at a hair salon at the mall, but I rarely left his bedside. Although it felt like I was serving a prison term in a tiny town where everyone was on lockdown for life, I stayed in that house until my dad didn't need me anymore. When he died, I ran as fast as I could from that place with a population of less than two thousand, and I never looked back—"quicker than a ray of light."

I graduated from undergrad and moved to Chicago. Although it's been ten years since I left home, I still cry every time I hear "Ray of Light." Not tears of sadness, but tears for the good memories of my parents that I packed into a suitcase to schlep along with me. I felt free for the first time in my life. I wonder if that's how Madonna felt when she left Detroit?

I wonder how she felt when she lost her mom.

★

My mom had been fed up with my dad's affairs. He was sleeping with so many women in our small town when I was a kid that the neighbors didn't make eye contact when Mom and I went to the grocery store. I remember answering the rotary dial phone in the kitchen only to be hung up on, time and time again, by the woman of the week. I can only imagine how mortifying the ordeal was for my mom.

When she told Dad to get out of the house because she wanted a divorce, he refused to give her one, but he did move out. Mom had no idea that he would cut her off financially during their separation—no assistance with the mortgage, the bills, the expenses of raising two kids. How would she raise us on her meager secretary's salary? Mom called her parents in California to ask if she could move us to the West Coast, but they told her to "stick out her marriage."

She didn't last a week after that.

She committed suicide instead.

In those days, women didn't have the means to achieve financial independence as easily as we do today. And her heart was broken. And then rebroken. Over and over.

★

I was standing in a crowded Chicago bar the first time I heard Madonna's "What It Feels Like For a Girl" in 2001. I was starting a master's degree program, and I loved living in the city. As the song played, I listened to the lyrics. I thought of my mom, who wore a perfect poker face for me and my brother while my dad publicly humiliated her. I didn't know what that felt like. I thought about her cry for help to her family—a cry that fell on deaf ears. I didn't know what that felt like. I thought of how she felt so trapped that death seemed like the only way out. I didn't know what that felt like.

But I did know how it felt to be loved by her. The eight years that I shared with her taught me that I can do whatever I want. I can be whomever I want. Just like Madonna. Who lost her mom, too, and she turned out okay, right?

Lucky Star

"I won't be happy 'til I'm as famous as God."

—MADONNA

Our Lady of Perpetual Motion

Cintra Wilson

AT THE PEAK of the enormous popularity of the show *Britain's Got Talent,* when frowzy Susan Boyle temporarily wowed the world with her big unvarnished singing voice, Mike Luckovich, the great political cartoonist, drew a panel. On the left side was a caricature of Madonna: eyes blackened, face grimly determined, her body hard and stringy with over-exercised muscle, cramping under the squeeze of her cone-bra corset.

"Time to reinvent myself again," says Madonna's joyless thought-balloon.

On the right side of the panel was a depiction of Susan Boyle, warbling freely with her caterpillar eyebrows and dishtowel house dress: *"Li-ii-ike a vir-gin . . ."*

The subtext of this cartoon? That Susan Boyle is genuine and Madonna is fake—"Look how the innocent singing talent of Boyle so effortlessly outclasses the high-tech, overwrought fraud Madonna, whose only real talent is for fabulously overcompensating for the fact that she has no talent," he seems to be saying.

Apparently, Luckovich hasn't watched Madonna closely enough to get the point of Madonna, but then most people don't, and it doesn't matter. In the final tally, Madonna "got" Mike Luckovich. There she was, coexisting in a panel with Susan Boyle, at the zenith of Boyle's popularity, in Luckovich's mind. After some twenty-five years, Madonna is still at the forefront of our cultural consciousness, and that, as well as I can guess, is the point of Madonna: She always wins.

A Dirty Joke We Never Got Over

For all the criticisms one might make about her, it is unfair to say that Madonna has never legitimately revealed herself (apart from occasional bouts of artistic nudity). On the contrary: In an almost grotesque *commedia dell'arte* style, Madonna has overshared every phase of her own psychic development throughout her career, by exploding it outward into large spectacle. We have known exactly what her big, unsubtle feelings have been at nearly every phase—all of her joys and disappointments (marriages, births, divorces), her failures (acting), her voyages of self-discovery (S&M, bisexuality), her psychological breakthroughs, and even her embrace of religion. Madonna has always been the star of her own ongoing opera, and she has always compulsively performed it for us.

Coming of age as a female during the reign of Madonna was like pushing through the earth as a shoot from a seed, and at the completion of this terrible labor, shaking the dirt out of your eyes only to find yourself standing under a Stalin-sized statue of the Jolly Green Giantess. In some ways, she's a dirty joke we never got over. In other ways, she has always been God—a terrorizing example of everything a girl could be, if insatiably possessed by a drive toward enormity. She has exerted an old-school totalitarian command over my consciousness since adolescence. When you have lived your life under such dominant image-leadership, its pressures put a certain invisible English on the cue ball of your development: It influences all of your ideas about who you should be, all the ways in which you become yourself.

On a subconscious level, Madonna became a constant tension in my personal plotline. Her all-pervasive example (at least for a teenage bottle-blonde like me) simultaneously embodied a combination of hero, goal, and obstacle. She was infuriating, awe-inspiring, depressing, appalling, beguiling—and ultimately irresistible. She always got you in the end, whether you liked it or not. Madonna was never your friend—more like a bullying older sister whose moral character you questioned and whose opinions you despised for being too cynical—but who was always right.

As a teen, I saw concert footage of Madonna performing a forgettable song called "Gambler." I had been in dance classes for most of my life, so I could more or less intelligently judge that Madonna's cardiovascular stamina was near-superhuman. Her dance moves weren't difficult, but there were millions of them during a ninety-minute performance. They required impressive flexibility, and minute-blocking (spatial) intricacies. Plus, she had to sing at the same time (her voice was so imperfect, you knew she wasn't faking it.) I had sung and danced onstage, at a sub-microscopic suburban level, as a kid in musical theater performances, and I knew that there were weird energies you couldn't control during a performance. If you became too nervous or overexcited, you couldn't breathe normally. Irregular oxygen intake could be disorienting; it was easy to either botch the singing or forget the choreography, or even to just look sweaty, uncomfortable, and winded.

Madonna's mental game, however, was too tough for these variables, even at a stadium level. I realized that she must have a NASA-level of mechanical control over her own inner dashboard—reliable control switches for a staggering amount of physical and emotional factors—and undoubtedly four or five extra lungs.

I was once hired by local musicians to impersonate Madonna for a Naval Fleet Week gig. While doing my homework for this—learning how to mimic Madonna's pronunciation in "Material Girl"—I realized her sped-up voice was baby-talking and pouting through the whole track, like a three-year-old throwing a cute tantrum for daddy: "Coz evuh-boddy's living . . . in a materi-uhl wuhld/and I yum a mahteer-iuhl gull . . ."

I found it stunningly manipulative on a psychological-operations level, the only possible winning comeback being "Yes, baby, here's your diamonds." But then, she was playing to win the battle of the sexes, and there was a certain brazen ruthlessness about this that nobody seemed to mind. Brattiness, after all, is Madonna at her best: "nyah nyah nyah-nyah nyah," kicking walls in her pumps, rolling around looking sexily anguished, and seeking revenge for untold mistreatments by spray-painting guys' cars.

Vanity/Reality/Myth

Madonna once described her daily routine as something like this: Three hours workout. Three hours business/phone calls. Three hours of "being creative." Then she allowed herself the rest of the evening for "goofing off."

(Embarrassing confession: This quote was the primary motivating factor behind the fact that I have always worked out. Gyms, yoga, running, dance classes—whatever that bitch said she did to keep fit, I did too—and I owe my habit of regular exercise to her fearful example.)

Sir Laurence Olivier once credited physical strength as his most important asset as an actor. It is safe to say that strength has been a primary tool of Madonna's Will to Power, too. She's never been a real singer or a great dancer, but these deficits became invisible as she vastly overcompensated with outlandish personal style, a canny use of controversy, and the dedicated gym time of an Olympic contender . . . And this strategy *worked*.

"She does back-to back aerobic classes, with weights," said a friend of mine, a singer and fellow bleach-blonde who had actually witnessed Madonna's regimen in an L.A. fitness studio in the '90s. "It made me realize I could never *be* her," she sighed.

There is a special tar pit in my mind that has always been involuntarily designated to retain select unattributable fragments of worthless Madonna information. The impressions these little media droppings made are indelible, and fresh as the day they fell in.

Example 1: "I act out by being productive," Madonna once said in an interview, somewhere.

Example 2: In an article about her home in L.A., Madonna spoke with the interviewer about a Frida Kahlo painting in her foyer. She half-jokingly said that the painting was a litmus test for her: "If you don't like this painting, you can't be my friend." It was a relatively scary work of Kahlo's—a self-portrait of the artist giving birth to herself.

In his interview with Madonna for *Esquire* in 1994, Norman Mailer wrote:

> "There is nothing comparable to living with a phenomenon when the phenomenon is you and you observe yourself with a cool intelligence, your own, and yet are trapped in the cruelest pit of the narcissist—you not only are more interested in yourself than anyone else alive, but suffer from the likely suspicion that this might be justified. You could be more interesting than anyone you've encountered."

Mailer was always a sensible kind of jerk, but Madonna is no mere run-of-the-mill celebrity narcissist. Over the years, we've watched her walk straight into the looking glass, which yielded in concentric circles as a still pool yields to a diver, and we have witnessed her transformation into myth. Then, periodically, she gets sick of being a myth, and she wades back into reality and tries to put on a normal-looking human face—her stint as a children's author, for example. But she always goes back to the music and the mirror, and her own irresistible cycle: reality/vanity/myth/vanity/reality/vanity/myth.

Ray of Light

Madonna's mythological self traffics in pure ideals. It seems like she has tried to drag these ideals through the looking glass and impose them on reality. For instance, we have seen her suffer from touchingly childish efforts to assemble a perfect family life, something any nice Catholic girl would, naturally, dream of.

In her strangely moving old song "Oh Father" ("You can't hurt me now/I got away from you/I never thought I would") Madonna declares herself psychologically liberated from what, one presumes, was an unhappy childhood—what with her mother becoming ill and dying (memorably depicted on MTV in an open casket, with stitches across her mouth), and several artsy scenes suggesting her father was abusive.

What I can guess, from reading between the lines of twenty years of random quotes, is that Madonna felt her father never approved of her. When, following the success of "Hung Up"—her hit from her 2006 *Confessions on a Dance Floor* album—she was informed that she had finally achieved the same number of Top 10 hits as Elvis Presley, she remarked, "Me and Elvis? Are you kidding? I'm going to tell my dad. Maybe that will impress him."

This was a painful revelation, suggesting that her dad has never been overly impressed by her cute pouts and fake tantrums—and perhaps revealing some insight into her less-than-ideal love life. We've seen her in and out of relationships: all the affairs between husbands—models, boy toys, dancers on tour, Dennis Rodman, Warren Beatty. At times Madonna seemed genuinely infatuated; at others just lonely and grateful for any man who could actually remain standing on his hind legs while facing the white heat of her. "Make a

point of saying something disarming at least once on a date"—I remember her saying something like this to a magazine. But unarmed
moments came at a premium, and they were, possibly, quite rare
once she got serious about someone. She seemed to plunge into both
of her marriages with sincere high hopes, but made the same mistake: She thought both men were capable of being stronger than she
is. She proved to be indomitable, and she ate Sean Penn and Guy
Ritchie for breakfast . . . and we feel sorrier for them, somehow, even
though it is likely that Madonna suffered more. One suspects that
she doesn't really want to crush men under her boot heels, but for
some reason, that's where they always seem to end up.

Her first child was an experiment in pure eugenics, if not an actual
virgin birth or act of spontaneous generation: Madonna spotted the
right sperm taking a jog around Central Park, made the proper business arrangements—and *pow.* Daughter Lourdes was created, with
one perfect Frida Kahlo eyebrow.

One bit of genuine pleasure seems to have been captured thanks
to this act of parenthood: The *Ray of Light* album, which—dumb and
thumpy as the arrangements are—is clearly a portrait of the artist
shaken to her foundations by the overwhelming love attending motherhood. This ecstatic New Age sensibility wore off, however—Madonna's metabolism for pleasure seemed to grow only faster with
age. Subsequent albums seemed mainly to dwell on recapturing plea-
sures, either sexual or nostalgic.

One look at the cover of 2008's *Hard Candy* ought to be enough to
inform the aforementioned cartoonist Mike Luckovich of his error.
Madonna is shown, on the cover, in terrible candor. She is, I believe,
honestly revealing what she feels she has become: invulnerable, com-
bative, brittle, and difficult to love. She has successfully worked off
all the parts of herself she was insecure about—her ass is rock-tight
as any high-school track star's. But there is no more cushiness, vulnerability, or softness in her; all that remains is vanity and vexation
of the spirit. She still always wins, but it hurts, and it isn't fun

anymore. She has the heavyweight championship belt, the throne, and an expansive kingdom in a world with no king.

There she was, finally inducted into the Rock and Roll Hall of Fame in 2008, without her husband. It reminded me of the moment at the end of the movie *Elizabeth* when the queen cakes her face white, dons the starchy wig, assumes the corporeal majesty of England, and forsakes all hope of equality in companionship. Madonna was forced, as Elizabeth was, to publicly acknowledge that the reward for all her work is the terrible loneliness of being too singular.

These days, all the sex in Madonna seems predatory and praying-mantis–like—she's in it for the young blood; it's an age-reversal injection, like Botox or vitamin B-12. Fertility having abandoned Her Madgesty, the star now chases an expensive motherhood-high by adopting exotic infants, and attempting, like a good Catholic girl, to do a little good in bad places.

But there is no negative publicity for goddesses. A goddess is either powerful, compelling you to project your love or fear or hate on to her, or she is dead, because her followers have lost interest and forgotten her.

"Are You Having a Good Time?"

I was most impressed with Madonna in 2006, when I believed that the eleven-year-old daughter of a man I was dating detested me. The one place we were able to connect was dancing around the living room to *Confessions on a Dance Floor.* I had to hand it to Ms. Ciccone. I was only a couple years older than the daughter when I rocked out to Madonna's first album—and here she still was, still fascinating kids enough to give me a few tension-free, girl-power moments with a deeply resentful tween.

But operas rarely have happy endings. Madonna seems to be on the cusp of a certain Wagnerian third act; the Parthenon she has built as homage to her own realized potential is wobbling, despite her best-laid plans. Certain things have simply been beyond her control. Madonna has yet to realize, as Dolly Parton has, that for a performer to age gracefully, she can't just look sensational—she must also appear to be *happy*. Life's wisdom must seem to have enriched her in some beatific way, or there is no point—she has gained the world, but the price was too high.

"Are you having a good time?" Madonna asks her audience in a concert film. There is no joy in this inquiry—it doesn't sound like *she's* having a good time. She sounds weary and disappointed; one can hear what effort it costs to combust her way through yet another display of brute strength and rude will, alone in the middle of her eponymous industrial complex.

But this is the point of Madonna. She is working. She is undergoing labor for you. She is giving birth to herself again, and the baby is yours—the projection screens, the dancing boys, the lasers, the drum machines, the corsets, her ass, and her boots. Her id amplified. Her life, her pain, her joys, her sorrows, her indiscretions, her kinks, and her mistakes. This is the point of Madonna.

She is that untouchable object of desire: the beauty myth as *Wizard of Oz*.

Pay no attention to the woman behind the curtain, because there is no woman behind the curtain. She is, and always has been, in front of the curtain—she is the great flaming head. The soul working the levers is the lonely little girl in the center of the all-consuming fire, always out in front.

Desperately Seeking Stardom

Sarah Stodola

A MEN'S COAT happens to dominate this black-and-white photograph. Stained and grubby-beige, it very nearly engulfs Madonna as she poses in front of the old tenement buildings of St. Mark's Place; my best guess is she's standing between 1st and 2nd Avenue. Photographer Amy Arbus (Diane's daughter) ran into her by chance back one day "when she still had a last name." She holds a bowling bag for a purse. Her girlish white socks and black patent shoes sit so close together on the sidewalk that the heels touch a la Dorothy's ruby reds, though they in no way render her girlish. Rather, they emphasize the impenetrability of her tough exterior. She comes across as short yet looming. Her bleached hair is long on roots, hairspray, and volume. Heavy eyeliner, deep lipstick, and a fake mole above her mouth comprise the face she put on that day.

She remains resolutely stone-faced, wears a scarf tight around her neck, rests a hand in a coat pocket, and kind of looks like a bitch. Probably a month after the moment is captured, she will be famous.

The photograph was taken on the spot as part of a series Arbus was working on for the *Village Voice* in 1983. It is my favorite version of Madonna because it is her at her least forced: a rare captured moment when Madonna, not yet an object of universal interest but already a person desperate for attention, is merely walking down the New York City street, perhaps distracted, not hoping or expecting to be seen. It links her inextricably with the city that made her.

What you are seeing is a person, as opposed to the much more common persona. And in her case, especially, each persona was carefully—too carefully—cultivated. For all of Madonna's innovation as a performer, her successive public guises never managed to shake their contrived aura. But for the Madonna Ciccone who lived in New York circa 1983, this was not quite the case—yet. There were very real things about her then. For one, she didn't have enough money to manufacture a new look when the whim struck; having famously (albeit questionably) arrived in New York with a mere $35 to her name, she wouldn't have been capable of doing anything too polished. She had to work with what she had at her disposal, and the result was a mish mash of an image, not unlike many sartorial presentations by women of that age group, but also uniquely her own. Madonna was, like most creative and ambitious people in their early twenties, grasping, emulating, experimenting. Above all, she was looking to set herself apart, and to prove her independence. Independence, in fact, became a cornerstone of her career.

And yet, one wishes she didn't have to be quite so adamant about it. The most successful purveyors of independence accomplish it with a certain amount of stoicism. Demanding that one's independence be *seen*, be appreciated, really exposes it for its near-opposite: a cry for approval. I prefer her in this black-and-white image, before she became quite so aware of her own hype.

This was the tail end of the New York of the late 1970s and early 1980s, an epoch in the life of the city that continues to fascinate, caveats of crime and poverty be damned. This was a city ravaged by suburban flight, financial implosion, and general neglect. It was also a city whose nearly complete submission to unearned opulence still lay ahead of it, and where gritty artists, writers, and musicians could still inhabit the place with a straight face. Madonna was a central character in this New York and specifically in the epicenter of the underground creative scene at the time, the East Village.

Starting with the Beats in the 1960s, the East Village emerged, literally, as a distinct neighborhood from the Lower East Side. In the 1970s, the club CBGB opened on the Bowery, showcasing bands like the Talking Heads, the Ramones, Blondie, and Patti Smith. In the early 1980s, artists like Keith Haring, Jeff Koons, and Jean-Michel Basquiat (whom Madonna dated) focused the city's progressive arts scene on the East Village. The writer Gary Indiana made his name largely through chronicling that neighborhood's arts landscape for the *Village Voice*. It wasn't a place for those looking to do things the conventional way, via the traditional channels—it was a tribe of its own, a tribe apart. Art galleries popped up in abandoned storefronts, drag queens held court, musicians pushed through new frontiers. Nothing was too outrageous, and nothing cost a lot of money. The make-shiftier the better. And in this mold, image was everything. Madonna was right in there, honing her look and performing with her band and networking in the local clubs.

Of course, the East Village myth, and especially Madonna's place in it, somewhat polishes over the truth. The East Village scene purported itself to be composed of a band of outsiders, rebelling against the moneyed establishment, living on the fringes of respectability. In reality, it was already on its way toward becoming fashionable: A *New York* magazine review of *Desperately Seeking Susan* in 1985 already contained a wistful reference to "pre-gentrification Avenue B." Downtown Manhattan had already taken hold in the popular imagination in a way that assured eventual migration there by a less avant-garde group of people—those for whom adulthood is primarily a series of steps from college graduation to marriage to children; the types of people who wear jeans only on the weekends. For the moment, though, it embodied that special moment when it begins to dawn on an entire social group that big things are possible. Madonna looked the part, in her hand-me-down, thrift-shop wardrobe, and her wide-eyed fixation on success. Her do-it-yourself look was seen by America at large to reflect the ethos of downtown New York. But there is little doubt that she was merely using that downtown image as a springboard to the very things it supposedly repudiated: wealth and fame.

Also, she was not, in the literal sense, of the East Village. Madonna—a former high school cheerleader, incidentally—lived in Queens for a year during her formative New York time, and after that on 37th Street, then the Upper West Side; all leading up to her first record release. She never actually lived in the East Village, it turns out; she moved to an apartment in Soho at the time of her first record deal. That's where she lived when this photo was taken. And those clubs where she famously cut her teeth? Danceteria was in Chelsea, Mudd Club in Tribeca, Max's Kansas City on lower Park Avenue. Our visions of her stomping around the lettered avenues may have more to do with *Desperately Seeking Susan* than anything rooted in accurate history. At least she did appear on the stage of CBGB once.

Still, despite the reality of it, when she burst into the national consciousness, it was largely due to the downtown aesthetic that she so consummately embodied.

And then, as Madonna's fame evolved, so did her relationship with the city. During the several years immediately following her breakout, she spent far more time in Los Angeles; her romantic involvements took on a decidedly West Coast hue, in tandem with her aggressive pursuit of a film career. Sean Penn, who would become her first husband, was rumored to abhor the eclectic, sexually convoluted company Madonna kept in New York. And as an international star, she became an international resident, touring, recording, and filming wherever around the globe those things took her. Eventually, she kept a triumvirate of homes in London, New York, and L.A., making England her permanent home. New York had long drifted from the bull's-eye position.

By the time she came back, it was a far different place that greeted her. In 2009, after her divorce from British film director Guy Ritchie, she returned to New York, purchasing a townhouse mansion on, of all places, the Upper East Side, that bastion of rote privilege. Madonna's trailblazing days were apparently over. She *became* the establishment, even as she complained that it had whitewashed the city. In 2008, she told *Vanity Fair*, "It's not the exciting place it used to be . . . It doesn't feel alive, cracking with that synergy between the art world and music world and fashion world that was happening in the '80s." Conceited as that may sound, it is hard to disagree with her. Illegal lofts were converted into designer lofts decades ago. Nightclubs are tailored to the guys in suits now, instead of providing an alternative to them. Music is made mostly in Brooklyn, as is anything that would remotely be deemed "underground." Manhattan today is strictly aboveground.

But then, as New York became more ostentatiously ordinary, so did Madonna. Gone is her capricious string of changing styles. Now, her personal style is interchangeable with any number of women for whom Jackie O would be considered an aspiration. Her blond hair falls perpetually shoulder-length, blow-dried and softly curled. She is most often spotted in either workout gear or a discriminating designer dress. The Madonna of today is in good taste.

It presents an amazingly stark contrast to the Madonna we first knew—the one who introduced lingerie-as-apparel to the world, and who wore a threadbare men's coat around the East Village, making it look like something enviable. And even if that early version is in some sense contrived, it's still the one I prefer. It's the only one that represents, to my mind, something that would have been nice to be a part of. It's the only one that inspires a yearning in me to have been there for—the innovation, the creativity, the general atmosphere of something new and different and possibly even great happening. To be part of a scene *just before* it gets exploited for the mainstream. Madonna here represents a version of the American Dream that competes with the more common, suburban, familial one.

This American Dream involves escape (*from* that more conventional one), independence, worldliness, the eternal chase for something bigger and better and brighter. Above all, it represents the pursuit not so much of happiness as of fame. This photo of Madonna memorializes that pursuit, endowed by New York City, on the verge of its fruition, just before she lost her last name.

Madonna is Boring and Lazy

Colleen Kane

IT WAS A cinch to admire Madonna in 1984. At age ten, I awoke each morning under her half-lidded, come-hither eyes. My Madonna poster, across from my bed, showed a close-up of her face with the hand posed at one side, the rag tied around her dirty-blonde hair, the dozens of black rubber bracelets, and the yellow nail polish. For me, Madonna introduced a previously unknown age range between teen-ager and mom, where you could do and wear whatever you wanted—and it looked really fun.

Madonna was Catholic, and so was I. But Madonna was a slut! The fact that she was the only Catholic slut I knew of shows how young I was. I didn't understand or approve of her, but I wanted to be like her. I didn't get what it meant to be "like" a virgin, but I did know I was supposed to be one until I was married, and that I should not be writhing around and moaning like a strumpet in front of God and everyone else. Still, Madonna was so cool; how could she be wrong? Furthermore, she was a fox. (Could the word "foxy" ever apply to *me* when I was older? The mind boggled.) To ten-year-old me, Madonna represented the exciting grown-up business I secretly obsessed about but wouldn't experience for years to come. Looking at her then was like looking ahead to a future me. But now I see her differently.

Cut to two decades hence. I'd had my own young and wild (in different ways) period in New York City. In July 2007, I was covering celebrities for an environmental magazine. Madonna headlined London's Live Earth concert to fight climate change. There she thanked Al Gore for his environmental wake-up call and said, "Tonight's concert is not just about entertainment, it's about a revolution. Amen."

But it was impossible not to notice the carbon footprint of her yearlong Sticky and Sweet Tour, which included 250 staff members, thirty wardrobe trunks, and four jumbo freezers to house ice packs for Her Madgesty's feet. The tour also included twelve seamstresses, sixteen caterers, about one hundred technicians and dancers, and a stage set, all flown around the world, with Madonna flying alongside in her personal jet. Jeez, Madonna Louise.

What kind of revolution was this? Wouldn't it have been cheaper to source those needs at each local tour stop? Even if Madonna spent a gazillion dollars for a greener tour, she could still afford to buy and sell most of planet Earth. (I did the math.) But embarking on a tour this extravagant after headlining the Live Earth event was a hypocritical move, not to mention plain lazy.

I know—it's incongruous to hear "Madonna" and "lazy" in the same sentence. Madge, who reportedly spends two hours a day working out. The woman who can sing and dance in concert for longer stretches than I can do, well, anything except sleep. Now, reconsidering her for the first time in years, she's no longer a cool role model; in fact, she's gotten kind of boring.

When called upon to appear at an awards show, the fifty-one-year-old Madonna seems to think to herself, *Which hot young pop stars do the kids like today—who should I pair with? Check, Justin, and check, Britney!* Oh, and *What's shocking and sexy—faux-lesbian kisses? Check!*

Straight women kissing each other to titillate viewers—you know who already thought of that? *Girls Gone Wild.* B-movies like *Wild Things.* The entire straight pornography industry. None of those are outlets known for pushing the creative envelope.

For tours, Maddy needs some provocative costumes. She could choose to rock some sleek, stunning new gowns or bodysuits designed especially for her, which other women could only dream of wearing. But no; it's time to trot out the knee-high, spike-heeled boots; the fishnets, the hot pants, the corset, the bra, the top hat, and the riding crop, and wear them all together at once. What tour is this, anyway? Blonde Ambition, Truth or Dare, or Sticky and Sweet? It's all of the above, apparently. Boring. Lazy.

Her visual message has become muddled, too, from trying on so many personas. But original-recipe Madonna, in her downtown DIY dance-punk get-ups, seemed to come from somewhere genuine, even if she didn't necessarily invent the look. A rosary worn as a necklace, and a hundred-plus O-ring bracelets piled on the arm at once? I never would have thought of such creative accessorizing without her helpful example.

But today, Madonna no longer represents anything I want. She's an unmatched master of image manipulation, but many of Madonna's latter-day looks (she's tried on every hat short of an astronaut's helmet) come off as contrived—like she's putting on a new look because she's expected to, not because she's feeling it.

The 2009 video for "Celebration" shows images of Madonna humping the air, intercut with shots of her clutching her crotch like a little girl who has to go pee-pee, like, *rightthisminute.* I can't claim to speak for fifty-somethings, but this isn't generally what they do, is it? Unless there's another unpleasant lady-problem I haven't yet learned about menopause?

The jumping and grinding behavior was believable when she was younger. But even back then, did Madonna *ever* party? Have fun with friends? Get drunk and eat a big plate of cheese fries? Is

Madonna *human*? Or is she just a singing, dancing, moneymaking sex machine?

Speaking of sex, there's her recent boy toy, Jesus Luz, who was twenty-eight years her junior. Does a simple young buck who barely speaks the English satisfy a mature woman's companionship needs? Go, Madonna . . . I guess. I didn't quite buy that someone so savvy is so horny at fifty-one that sex with a hot stud is all she desires from a partner. Was Madonna just doing what the public expected her to do, post-divorce? Was it a bonus that his name was "Jesus," which goes so marvelously with "Madonna"? Boring and lazy.

And let's talk about the ungraceful facial aging. Madonna's injection-riddled visage of the past few years brings her ever-closer to resembling a living Madame, the puppet that once hosted *Solid Gold*. Her distorted face and her recent photoshopped-beyond-recognition Louis Vuitton ads are huge disappointments coming from such an iconic "strong woman." She's not fighting the good fight; she's fighting a battle that can only be lost. (This is neither boring nor lazy, but delusional.)

Witnessing all of the above has been a gradual letdown. Madonna has aggressively transformed herself over the years, but all the while, I've morphed, too. In my mid-thirties, I want to savor life: discover new passion-inspiring places and friends and foods, repair some of the damage we humans have done to the environment, connect and share my experiences through writing and photography. I feel best when surrounded by my smart, funny friends, and I want to keep learning and improving and exploring and trying until I die at a ripe old age. Madonna was empowering to me as an uncertain, sin-burdened Catholic youth. She was about confidence and having fun being a girl. Now, as I start to see evidence that my own looks are not immune to the march of time, observing Madonna's battle against nature is the opposite of empowering. I don't have her millions to fight the pull of gravity on skin that can only remain elastic for so many decades. But I wouldn't want to imitate the grotesquery she's becoming in her fifties.

Madonna can't do much for me now except stand as an example for how *not* to age. Of course, she's still magnetizing to watch, albeit in a different way. Now I marvel that the surgeons have somehow made her eyes larger, and muse that there is such a thing as being too fit.

This is a harsh critique coming from someone who doesn't spend multiple hours each day in the gym, who neglects to execute brilliant business strategies, who has never once riveted millions with my actions. So if we are both boring and lazy, Madonna is way more accomplished at being boring and lazy than I am.

Touched for the Very First Time

Rebecca Traister

THE QUESTION I was asked Wednesday by more than one person was this: Is it too late to see Madonna?

They were asking me this because, at the last minute, my friend Sara had found tickets to Madge's final stop at Madison Square Garden on her Confessions Tour. I couldn't afford a Madonna ticket and I told Sara this and she said she would buy it and I would pay it off via a kind of social layaway plan. She also said, in a bracing way: "Look, I have never seen her. You have never seen her. And I don't want us to see her when she's sixty-five and it's too late, you know?" Yes, I said solemnly. I know.

I understand that there are a lot of people out there who have never seen Madonna and who don't consider it a missed opportunity. But I am a thirty-one-year-old American woman. I was nine when I watched a ratty-looking woman pleasure herself on a Venetian gondola while a panting lion looked on in the "Like a Virgin" video and my father, glancing at the television, asked, "Who *is* that?" I am sure that my father, who has barely glanced at a television since, has no memory of this. But I remember. Because while I didn't understand the first thing about who she was or what she was doing to that poor lion, I knew she was fascinating. And because my mother—who also never glances at the television and has never been able to remember anyone's name, including mine—stunned us all by informing him, "That's Madonna."

The conclusion to which I stumbled by following the logic of that exchange turned out to be coincidentally accurate: If my mother knew who Madonna was, then she was the most famous woman in the world. Many years later, she is the most famous woman in the world—at least the world I grew up in. Even without having been a truly devout Madonna fan (too young to be a wannabe, I was a wannabe wannabe), I managed to own every one of her albums back when people owned albums. Even songs I think I don't know the lyrics to—like "Music," or "Ray of Light," or "Take a Bow"—I know the lyrics to. Madonna has been the soundtrack to my life.

So I agreed with Sara that this was a pretty momentous event and besides, we had a hot ticket. They all sold out in four minutes or something, and this was the kind of concert the cool kids went to, and weren't we hip to be going at all. In short, I felt the way I probably should have felt at fifteen if I'd scored tickets to the Blond Ambition tour.

Which became abundantly clear when I happened to mention to my mother that I was going to see Madonna. "My goodness," she chuckled. "That's really some old-fashioned entertainment." That's right. My mother—the sixty-two-year-old woman who still occasionally asks me what ever happened to "that young rock 'n' roll guy, Billy Joel," which she still pronounces Billy Joe-Elle despite having been corrected a thousand times, *that* mother—was teasing me about being an old foggy because I was going to see Madonna.

Then my brother called. He's been calling a lot recently because he has a six-week-old son and chatting with a six-week-old gets boring fast, which makes chatting with your sister a lot more appealing. I told him I was going to Madonna. "Well, you're showing up a little late to that party, aren't you?" he said. I should mention that my brother is twenty-eight and cannot drive a car so I don't know where he gets off making fun of me. "No, I'm sure it'll be great," he said. "Like if Yente from *Fiddler on the Roof* got her own show for two hours." Then my brother underscored just how doddering we both are (as if the *Fiddler* reference weren't enough) by consulting with his six-week-old son as we spoke. "Do you think Madonna is still relevant to your generation, Noah?" he asked. "Do you think that the Material Girl still has the power to put asses in the seats?" I heard Noah burp loudly before hanging up.

Here is the thing: Because I have never actually been to a Madonna concert, and because going is something I considered doing at nine and thirteen and twenty-five, it is not something that makes me feel old at all. In fact, it makes me feel rather spry! Then again, here's another thing: I go to Bruce Springsteen concerts. All the time. As a matter of fact, I have seen Bruce Springsteen four times in the past three months. And what's more, some friends just yesterday proposed that we fly to Dublin to see him play in November, and to my immense surprise I said that seemed like a good idea, even though I have never been the kind of person who thinks that flying anywhere to see someone perform is a good idea, let alone if you have seen that person perform four times in the past year, let alone if that person is in his late fifties and you are completely aware that your devotion to him sort of dates you.

Also, in the past year, I have paid money to see Willie Nelson, Dolly Parton, and Prince. For the record, I have also seen Feist and Neko Case, though we left Neko Case early because it was standing only and sort of hot. And I thought about seeing Cat Power, but didn't.

But in any case, what I am saying is that I am not one of those people who go to shows by Modest Mouse or the Libertines. I feel comfortable admitting that my musical tastes are creaky.

But I somehow felt bad about the perception that Madonna is a creaky act. Maybe because it makes me feel old. Maybe because my radar was so off that I thought it was cool I was going to a Madonna concert when really it was fogeyish. Maybe, because seeing Madonna was something I'd wanted to do since I was nine, I got momentarily tricked into thinking I was nine again.

Anyway, I went. And I think it's a good thing I didn't see Madonna when I was younger, because I might not have been old enough to handle it. There have been a lot of reviews of the concert—which I assume never varies, since who could do anything spontaneous when you have fourteen tightly choreographed backup dancers in chaps?—but here is a rundown of what happened:

Madonna hatched out of a disco-ball egg that opened like a multi-faceted DeLorean; there were pulsing lights and reflecting surfaces; it looked like twelve disco emporia had vomited simultaneously all over the Garden stage. A team of shirtless, muscle-bound dancers clippety-clopped around in plumed riding hats; gymnasts did some impressive tumbling and jumping on uneven bars, and a woman in electric blue Middle Easternish gear convulsed in a cage. There was crumping. (OK, the truth is, I thought it was break dancing, but when I read Kelefa Sanneh's review of the concert in the *Times*, he said it was crumping.) At one point, Madonna donned a white Travolta suit and danced like Tony Manero on a lighted-up tiled floor; at another, she invited the audience to "suck George Bush's dick." Images flashed: of dead dolphins and tigers and falling horses. Of Bush, Dick Cheney, Nazis, Scud missiles, Klansmen, red blood cells. There was a roller-skating segment straight out of *Starlight Express*. It was the Folies Bergères, it was Bianca Jagger at Studio 54; it was the Moulin Rouge—if all those things were viewed at a distance, as if they were being broadcast when they were actually live.

After Madonna sang "I have a tale to tell," the first line of "Live to Tell," there were performance-arty monologues about falling, or being a gang-banger, acted out on jutting portions of stage by people who were not Madonna. In fact, there was a lot in the show by people who were not Madonna. Several minutes would go by in which Madonna was nowhere onstage but six people in loincloths were climbing jungle gyms or a guy in a turban was blowing a ram's horn and then all of a sudden Madonna—well-rested and in a new costume—would get lowered from a helicopter or shot from a cannon, or do what she actually did on Wednesday night, which was appear to sing "Live to Tell" hanging from a disco-ball cross dressed in a peasant blouse, a sequined belt and a crown of thorns.

You probably saw the pictures of Madonna on this cross when the tour started. I remember shaking my head in admiration; this woman's commitment to creating new ways to dismay the public is simply unrivaled. The trouble is she's made her own job so much harder. Whether she herself trained us not to flinch in the face of manipulated sexual and religious iconography or whether she has simply ridden the larger cultural shock wave past its crest, I'm not sure what her future as a provocateur could possibly hold. The self-crucifixion thing was a good try, but . . . eh. She may have to hang on until the day when, in a retirement gesture that will make Streisand cry in her *tsimmes,* she can disembowel herself onstage.

Anyway, back to the concert: After Madge came off the cross, she launched into "Sorry." The man in front of me—and believe me, he was practically the only man in front of me; everyone at this concert was female—started convulsing, face in his hands, Beatlemania-style. Then she stripped into a tank top and began singing, for real (which you could tell because her voice was out of breath, as it should be), and ground her hips into a chair. Madonna humped everything that stood still long enough for her to wrap her legs around it. At one point—and I do not think this particular disco egg is worth cracking open here and now—she rode a black man like a horse.

The concert was not at all like watching two hours of Yente from *Fiddler on the Roof,* unless updated productions of *Fiddler* have included scenes in which Yente whips a bare-chested Tevye with a riding crop and yells at the audience, "That's right, you motherfuckers, I love New York!" Which, I suppose, is possible. I never saw the version with Madonna's friend Rosie O'Donnell.

In 2004, Sanneh wrote about Madonna's Re-Invention tour that, "When you imagine Madonna, you don't see a single image but a time-lapse photograph, with one persona melting and warping into the next." It's a great line, and a great description of what I felt last night, watching Madonna live, for the first time in my life. When I look at her, it's hard not to imagine decades—of her life, and of my life—written on her body. That body. Her legs aren't even traditionally shapely anymore: Their muscles are serpentine and distinct; she's an anatomical enterprise as much as an aesthetic or athletic or musical one. I wonder if Madonna made that body so strong because she has to lug so much of her own baggage around on it every day.

Watching that body—not a ligament, let alone a strand of hair, out of place—it's hard not to think of the soft, ragged young woman who was content to hump a stage in a wedding dress back in 1984. I looked for that younger woman at Madison Square Garden. It was she, after all, who made this older woman—this freak of pop culture—possible. But if it was easy to recall younger iterations of the performer, it was tough to actually spot them onstage on Wednesday night. And I think that's how she wants it right now.

Madonna played almost all of her new album and only a handful of her classic songs; she seemed to be stamping her feet to convey that she is no nostalgia act. But in drawing such a severe line between her older and her younger selves, in successfully insisting that she's no foggy, she actually made me feel like more of one.

It was in her grand finale, "Hung Up," the best part of the night—that it felt like a concert at all. She let her hair down, literally and figuratively, and when she threw her leotarded bod around the stage, rubbing herself against a giant boom box, there was the first, and only, glimmer of authentic eroticism. It was then, for the first time, that she appeared to let herself get taken in by her own music, to lose just a shred of control. And for a second, she looked so young—like that girl in the New York clubs with her stupid leggings and torn gloves—and she seemed to notice at last that she had a flesh-and-blood audience and berated us, in her old S/M way, to sing along.

"Time goes by—so slowly/ Time goes by—so slowly/ Time goes by—so slowly." The crowd rose twenty feet in the air on adrenaline alone. And still she kept holding the microphone out: "Time goes by—so slowly."

And that was when I, or my nine-year-old self, got way overstimulated. Hearing words about time going by so slowly while staring at Madonna's preserved, warped body; considering all the long-forgotten cultural references on display—whatever happened to Tony Manero anyway? I was confused about why I was enjoying "Hung Up" more than "Like a Virgin," about why so much of the concert, especially the familiar songs, had seemed so distant but that this new song had brought her alive. And my brain began to expand and contract in sync with the pulsing lights and the rhythmic chanting—"Time goes by—so slowly"—and all I could think was that time goes by so quickly. And that sometimes, like tonight, it can fold in on itself, and remind us of how far away we are from our old selves, our old bodies, our old memories even as we experience things that bring the past to mind. And how this woman, who has been in my consciousness my whole life, seems to be trying to stop time—by singing about it and making her body impervious to it and making her career about the present, not the past. And then I came close to doing the most old-foggy thing I can imagine: crying at a concert. And just then she finally broke the trance with a final euphoric verse: "Every little thing that you say or do/ I'm hung up/ I'm so hung up on you."

"That was a great fucking song," Sara said to me, breathlessly. We walked downstairs, out onto the street, talking about the show. And then, as we exited Madison Square Garden, she turned to me. "You know what?" she said. "Maybe we saw her too late."

Immaterial Girl

Marisela Huerta

I GREW UP on country music. At six years old I would prance around the house dressed in my short frilly skirt, cowboy boots, and puffy nylon sports jacket with "Dallas Cowboys Cheerleader" on the back. I wore my long black hair hoisted high in two pigtails of giant ringlets. I don't know if it was adorable or weird for a little Mexican girl to be faking a Southern twang and swaying from side to side while belting out "Islands in the Stream":

"Sail away with me to another world
And we rely on each other—uh huh
From one na na na na na na—uh huh"

Kenny and Dolly were my favorites, but I sang along to everything from Reba to Hank Williams Jr. I had nothing against the pop and rock my friends listened to, I just liked country better. So did my entire family. As I climbed the ranks of elementary school, my friends began sharing stories of Bon Jovi concerts, raving about Madonna, squealing about which New Kid on the Block they wanted their boyfriends to be. I'd never heard of Bon Jovi, and I had no idea what the New Kids on the Block looked like. When my girlfriends squealed, I felt like a dork—a dork that listened to country music. With her parents.

But I wanted to fit in, so I stopped wearing my hair in curls and began vigorously watching MTV and VH1, cramming to catch up on all the years of pop music I'd missed.

It was 1991. Madonna's "Vogue" video dominated both music networks, and soon it was dominating my existence. I learned the dance. I memorized all her songs. Madonna now had me in her thrall.

Now don't get me wrong. I didn't dress like Madonna. I didn't wear Madonna buttons or scrawl her name on my binders or sport a fake mole. I was a fan, but I was a mature fan. I loved her for what she represented. I admired her—not for her foul mouth and sexual escapades but for her confidence and independence. Hearing her songs for the first time as a teenager, I knew they meant more to me than they'd meant to my friends who had listened to her earlier. I was seven when "Like a Virgin" was released; what could my seven-year-old classmates have possibly known about being touched for the very first time? But me? By the time I was into the song, Lord knows I understood exactly what she was singing about. Standing in front of my mirror, envisioning my overprotective Catholic parents, I tossed my hair from side to side and belted out "Papa Don't Preach": "You should know by now, I'm not a baby . . ."

I admire the hell out of my mom, but Madonna was a different kind of strong. Mom was a brilliant wife, mother, and homemaker—my lifelong hero. But I wanted to be independent, have a career, go away to college. I wanted to be strong and bold and sexy. I wanted to shed my insecure shell and climb into the skin of a grown, confident woman. Even mentioning sex in our house was taboo, but Madonna showed me it was okay for a woman to express her sexuality, okay for a woman to be successful, independent of a man.

By senior year, I had worn out both my cassette and CD of *The Im-maculate Collection*. By seventeen, I'd ripped out my proverbial pig-tails and busted out of my chastity belt. I also announced I was officially leaving El Paso to attend college. In Los Angeles.

Fast forward ten years. I was still in Los Angeles, now working for the Grammy Awards. I learned that Madonna would be performing at the upcoming awards show—a duet with Gorillaz. From the moment I heard the news, I was bouncing off the walls like a crazy kid on a sugar high. I couldn't talk about my excitement with anyone; no one would understand. But I was finally going to see her in person and I couldn't even articulate what that meant to me. Being a Grammy employee with an all-access pass, I could attend all re-hearsals, hang out backstage, stalk dressing rooms if I wanted to. I could watch Madonna rehearse. Private rehearsals—holy shit. I might even meet her. But what the hell would I say? Would I even be able to speak? There's a fine line between being a fervent fan and being a creep.

On the Friday evening Madonna was to rehearse, I trekked twelve miles in two hours through brutal rush-hour traffic from our office in Santa Monica to the STAPLES Center downtown. When I stepped inside the arena, all thirteen thousand seats were empty. The arena was entirely dark except for the fully lit stage. I gasped and slowly descended the bleachers, marveling at the twinkling lights. At the bottom, on the arena floor, the grandeur froze me, and I stood gaping at the massive space surrounding me. I'd walked into the arena a strong, confident woman but suddenly I felt small, like the girl in cowboy boots and pigtails, like a tiny organism inside a giant petri dish.

The arena was completely quiet. I settled on a row 150 feet away from center stage and stood beside the aisle seat. My stomach was doing cartwheels, and my lunch begged me to let it out. I looked around, desperately searching for co-workers, a familiar face, or anyone who looked as excited as I was, but the only other people around were some production guys in tool belts and clunky work boots, setting things up, taping down cables, and carrying heavy equipment.

They began to sound check, and the arena filled with the opening notes of Madonna's "Hung Up," which replayed over and over until they had the levels right. Chills ran down my spine; this was real. Each time the music started my heart rose, and when it stopped, my heart collapsed. I was so anxious, my nerves had nerves, and I tightly gripped the chair, hoping it might, by osmosis, absorb some of my anxiety. My eyes glazed over as the stage crew adjusted the lights. I felt lucky and innocent and young. What circumstances in my life had offered me this moment, this perfect moment?

My legs shook; my palms grew sweaty, and then I heard an unenthusiastic voice announce "Clear for full run."

It was time. Would it be everything I'd hoped for? Had I built up this moment so that it could never be enough? My heartbeat escalated so fast, I was sure it would combust, and then . . .

The computer-generated stage was set for the Gorillaz, who would open the number and appear onstage in their cartoon personas. Really? This? Now? I had to watch cartoons?

I inhaled. Fine. You can't just jump right into something this big. This was the calm-down period. This was my prom date putting me at ease, rubbing my knee, feeding me sweet talk and gentle kisses to alleviate the nerves. The Gorillaz song ended and a brief period of nothing but drum beats followed, then the familiar high notes of the synthesized opening to "Hung Up." And then it happened, slowly, a delicate figure in a sparkly lavender leotard ascended from beneath the stage floor. I saw a head of perfectly feathered hair. I erupted.

"Oh my God! Oh my God! Oh my God!" And in a deafening scream I declared to the empty arena, "It's Madonna—oh my GOD!" I went apeshit. I spastically shuffled around my chair, looking all around me, trying to connect with someone who would share my exhilaration, but there was no one but those old production men who couldn't care less. I shifted my attention back to the stage.

Madonna was dancing, and I watched, my mouth wide open, my heart stopped. Then she strolled sexily toward the animated characters still displayed onstage and began to interact with them. What? How was this possible? How could she walk *onto* their "virtual" set?

Then Madonna walked around Gorillaz and disappeared into thin air.

A couple of the production guys had stopped their work to laugh at me. A few more walked by and blew air through their teeth, embarrassed for me. As stupid as I felt, I turned to one of them and asked, breathlessly, "What just happened?"

Wearing a look of pity he answered "I hate to burst your bubble, but . . ."

The figure who had just mesmerized me wasn't Madonna; it was an animated, computerized 3D holographic image of Madonna—a projection. Madonna wasn't even there. For the real show, the animated Madonna would vanish, and the flesh and blood Madonna would appear with her dance crew, but that night they were rehearsing only the technical portion of the show. Everyone, it seemed, knew that but me.

"Sorry," one of the guys said, condescendingly patting my back, pulling the pin out and deflating me like a gigantic Macy's Thanksgiving Day balloon.

The rehearsal continued, playing and replaying the animated segments, over and over again, my disappointment growing with each take. I flipped over my all-access badge so no one would catch my name. This could not make it back to the office. I walked briskly up the empty bleachers, trying to ignore the snickering, giggling production guys.

Leave it to Madonna to remain, always, ahead of the times.

I ran outside, eager to get home to Google "3D holographic image." I still had a lot to catch up on.

"Vogue": Madonna's Creative Zenith

Amanda Marcotte

"VOGUE" HAS THE dual distinction of being both the best song and the last great song Madonna ever released. (Okay, I like the song "Music," but that was from an era when Madonna just bought other people's production skills with her ample wealth, and I don't think it counts as a Madonna Song in the way her '80s catalog does.) She tried her hand repeatedly at sugary ballads, but high-energy dance songs are her best: "Like a Prayer," "Material Girl," "Holiday," and "Like a Virgin." Her light but strangely commanding voice is perfect for dance music; I'd go so far as to argue strenuously that she has one of the best dance-floor voices since the era when Donna Summer and Diana Ross made a killing in disco.

With this specific talent, it's almost amazing that Madonna didn't leap on the house-music trend before 1990, but Madonna was never one to get ahead of a trend (that's a habit of innovators that tends to suppress record sales). House music's time in the pop-music spotlight was brief, but it left a glorious track record at the top of the charts:

"Groove Is in the Heart" by Dee-Lite, "Pump up the Volume" by Marrs, and even "Freedom" by George Michael were early house hits. And lest the "house" term confuse you, the modern image of house music may be that crap played in cheeseball clubs on "Jersey Shore," but when it was nascent, it was really different and more fun. The aforementioned group Dee-Lite identified as a house band— most of "Groove Is in the Heart" was composed by the DJ. Only the baseline and some of the vocals were contributed by live musicians; the rest was constructed of samples. One reason house is less fun than it used to be is that it's pretty much illegal to construct a song out of fifty different samples, but you could get away with it in the late '80s and early '90s.

In "Vogue," Madonna demonstrated her ability to take the current trends and remake them in her image. "Vogue" pulls in every trick that made late '80s–early '90s house so fun: the funky bass line, the drum machines and synthesizer creating complex layers, the steady hi-hat and regular hand claps, the prominent piano (with a brief solo, no less), and even a pseudo-rap that flirts with hip-hop without actually incorporating it. And, like a lot of less prominent house acts, the lyrics are pure fluff, about nothing more than the song itself, in this case calling you to do a kind of dance called "vogueing" that predated house and continues to be an underground phenomenon to this day.

"Vogue" brings everything both wonderful and regrettable about Madonna into a single, perfect package. As for her, Madonna is simultaneously the most overrated and underrated musical artist of the '80s. Overrated, of course, by academics and overanalyzers who wish to rationalize their love of bubblegum pop as a secret subversion. Most Madonna defenders—many of whom reside in these pages—genuinely work hard on their analysis and coax interesting insights out of the material. Madonna is construed as a subversive figure, bringing queer and sex-positive feminist imagery into the mainstream, selling it to little girls in suburban malls, recruiting one future radical at a time.

She's underrated, naturally, by the music-snob world, which has some overlap with the overanalyzer world, but tends to lean way more heavily male (sadly for me, since I consider myself in their numbers). Clinging to their Velvet Underground records, these snobs denounce Madonna as a hack, pointing out correctly that she stole all her aesthetics from actual subversives, mainly from the various New York subcultures of the late '70s and '80s.

Madonna's defenders have their retort: Those people were in the underground! Madonna mainstreamed their subversions, making them available to teeny-boppers around the world, giving them permission to play with fashion, gender, and sexuality. She may not have been the great innovator, but she knew how to get on MTV.

This rejoinder has always felt hollow to me, because an honest assessment of the '70s and '80s reveals that it was actually quite an incendiary time in pop music. It was, after all, a time when a kooky art-rock band like Devo could have a number-one hit. Madonna can't be given credit for mainstreaming the New York underground's blending of disco and rock, since bands like Blondie beat her to it. The people who did it first and did it better than Madonna didn't languish, beloved only by college radio DJs and the curators at Rhino Records—they made a lot of money at it.

And Madonna the fashion icon? Not so much. Cyndi Lauper's take on funky, vintage fashion was more inspired and had a longer impact on hipster street fashion. David Bowie had a full decade on Madonna in the game of the constantly changing image. Madonna the gender-bender? Annie Lennox was doing the woman-in-a-man's-suit thing years before Madonna, and let's not forget that way before Madonna played with gender, it was the era of boys in eyeliner right there on TV. Surely, platinum-selling artists like The Cure, The Human League, and Culture Club were a more destabilizing force, gender-wise, with their eyeliner and lace, than Madonna could ever be just walking around looking kind of masculine sometimes. Madonna didn't even really kick down the door of the "ladies doing it for themselves" music club, since the Go-Go's were the go-to band for that at the time. Even when Madonna entered the realm of borrowing Christian imagery for sexy purposes in "Like a Prayer," she looked like she belonged in the video for any hair-metal band that had been doing the same thing for years.

I also never really bought the idea that Madonna's in-your-face sexuality was earth-shatteringly subversive. "Like a Virgin" came out nearly a full decade after Donna Summer had a No. 2 Billboard hit with "Love to Love You," a song in which she faked an orgasm, in lieu of singing, for the entire track.

Still, none of this should detract from Madonna's importance as a pop icon. Madonna's genius was—in the '80s, at least—being derivative without being cheesy, which is much harder than it sounds. Should I sound like I'm damning her with faint praise, let me also say that music by people with this talent is sorely desired by record executives, who make lots of money off it, and more importantly, by DJs who need those perfect pop records to keep the party going. Picking music to play at a dance club is much harder than it sounds. The number of innovative artists you can play is restricted to those that are actually popular enough to get people dancing. Once you're down to that pool, you don't have enough music to fill up the time unless you play the same artists over and over again, and only hack DJs do that. What you need are knock-offs that are just different enough that it doesn't feel repetitive.

I recently had this experience when I had the fortune to DJ a fundraiser that was billed as an '80s dance party. My playlist was heavy with musicians I think of as the true innovators of the '80s: Prince, Run DMC, the Talking Heads. But there comes a point in every '80s dance party when you'd better go Madonna or go home. The song I chose was "Burning Up," which I've always admired for having a gritty, sexy authenticity that slowly turned more performance-oriented later in Madonna's career. The only reason I went there was that "Vogue" wasn't an option, having come out in 1990, past the deadline for a proper '80s party.

"Vogue" has captured some largely negative attention for being derivative, but not of house music—how can you really be derivative of a trend that's sweeping not just the country but the planet?—but of vogueing. Most of America probably thinks of the dance, in which striking poses like a model is turned into a fluid form of movement, as something Madonna invented for this song. In reality, it's rooted in dance styles developed in Harlem in the '60s, and it really took off (and lives on) in gay-dominated underground dance communities (one all-queer dance crew named Vogue Evolution specialized in vogueing and gained national prominence on MTV's "America's Best Dance Crew" in 2009). Because of this, and because of the amount of money Madonna made from positioning vogueing as a one-off dance craze like the Achy-Breaky Heart, "Vogue" is usually held up as a prime example of appropriation.

Madonna may have appropriated pieces of black, Latino, and LGBT culture for "Vogue," but that's not what makes the song the apex of her career. It's that, for the first time ever, she borrowed as much from herself (six years earlier) as from anyone else.

Sure, "Material Girl" doesn't sound much like "Vogue," the former being a New Wave–influenced pop song performed with traditional rock instruments, and the latter being pure house-for-the-masses. But with Madonna, image is half the game, and the video for "Material Girl" was about establishing Madonna as a Star by equating her with Marilyn Monroe, presumably because they're both bottle blondes with big boobs. The video is based on Monroe's famous performance of "Diamonds Are a Girl's Best Friend" in the movie *Gentlemen Prefer Blondes*, complete with the same dress, same set design, and similar choreography.

Unfortunately, the video for "Material Girl" isn't half as fun, because the materialism is undercut by a side plot created to reassure us that real-life Madonna isn't a gold digger, whereas Monroe's character never apologizes for using her looks to squeeze rich men for their money in *Gentlemen Prefer Blondes*. But most people don't remember the dopey side plot in "Material Girl," just the images of

Madonna-as-Monroe—Madonna laying claim to the glamour of old Hollywood, similar to how David Bowie borrowed the weirdness of B-film sci-fi to shore up his glam-rock image.

And in "Vogue," she does it again! Sure, the era of movies she harkens back to are the '30s and '40s (not the '50s, when Monroe worked), but the idea is basically the same: Madonna with perfectly coiffed hair and clothes, Madonna comparing her own glamour to that of the Golden Era of Hollywood. And even though she had used that trick before, it works beautifully this time around—even better than it did the first time.

The reason should be obvious: Madonna's genius is stealing ideas and remaking them in her own image. Madonna stealing from Madonna stealing from the Golden Era of Hollywood is like Superman taking steroids. She went, during the reign of that song, from being just Madonna to being Super-Madonna. And everyone hitting dance floors, from New York nightclubs to my junior high school dance benefitted. Just not those of us trying to put together '80s dance parties twenty years after the fact.

Unfortunately, the problem with hitting your peak is there's nowhere to go but down, and that has defined Madonna's career since "Vogue." The fun was gone after that song, which was a single for the *Dick Tracy* soundtrack and never had a proper home on a proper album. A few months later, Madonna released *The Immaculate Collection*, a greatest hits album, tantamount to an admission that a major phase of her career was over. *The Immaculate Collection* had two new songs on it, one of which was "Justify My Love," a tedious song that substitutes "whispery" for "sexy," and ushered in the Trying Too Hard phase of Madonna's career, a phase she's still in these days, more than twenty years later. Like I said, being derivative without being cheesy is really hard to do, and Madonna pulling it off for nearly a decade before fizzling out is to her credit. That the swan song of Madonna's career was "Vogue" is all the more reason for even the snobbiest of music snobs to offer her at least grudging respect.

Count Madonnicula

Lisa Crystal Carver

MADONNA DOESN'T HAVE a non-thieving bone in her body. She's a vampire. She steals from every subculture without giving credit. It started with Jellybean Benitez and the New York street scene. That was the only music, message, and fashion I liked of hers: "Borderline," "Lucky Star," "Burning Up." The rubber bracelets, star earrings, weird socks . . . I got fooled into thinking that was her. After she sucked that fun DJ/producer and his whole scene dry and moved on, the trick was up. Fad runs through Madonna's veins in place of blood.

She doesn't reinvent herself—there is no "self" to re-anything. She simply switches up who she steals from. Remember when she was appearing everywhere with Sandra Bernhard, and all that summer she was on talk shows, temporarily gay and funny? That woman is neither. She can't even hang onto one name. Her nicknames are Nonnie, Maddy, Mo, The Material Girl, Boy Toy, Madge (British shorthand for "Your Majesty"). She even legally changed her name to the Hebrew moniker Esther in 2004.

Because Madonna came before Britney, as far as whorey, evanescent pop singers who can't sing go, people assume that Britney nicked that nasal whine from the old lady. Nope. Britney has always sounded like a drunken, negligee-wearing, Long Island shut-in; she can't help it. Madonna, on the other hand, has never had a voice that sounds like hers. She tries low, high, middle, silly, and dead-serious tones; different producers keep punching different effects buttons. Sometimes, when she's live and desperate, she even tries them all in one song. The truth is Madonna ripped that nasal thing off Britney. Probably when she was making out with her. Madonna makes out with everyone, on camera and off—I guess that's how she sucks their essences.

Whether it's adopting gay men's vogueing, adopting an African child (I mean, geez—that baby had a dad!), or adopting an accent, she sneaks up on lesser-known people (which means everyone, for her), snatches the surface of their lives, and fashions a show or a children's book or a life decision from it. Remember when she moved to England and was suddenly doing photo shoots atop a horse (or off the horse, in the stuffy parlor) dressed to the teeth like an equestrian? No wonder she keeps falling off those horses and breaking things!

Remember the cone bra? Madonna didn't simply pull that straight off the Jean-Paul Gaultier rack. Another sexual, vocally challenged but very charismatic songstress did it way before Madonna, and way better. I'm talking, of course, about Lydia Lunch and her nail-adorned bra—stuck pointy-end out. Black leather. Scowl. So hot. If you're going to flaunt danger-breasts, it's so much better to do it all hagged-out, with threatening eyebrows . . . Not a blonde ponytail and a perky smile to take the edge off. Lydia's nail-bra sent a message: try to cop a feel and you will bleed from the palms like the Second Coming. What was Madonna gonna do with her goldie cones—haute-couture us to death?

But I'll tell you what makes me really mad, besides absolutely all of it: her chasing-Antonio-Banderas-around phase. She co-opted a whole culture pursuing one married man's drawers. When he resisted her advances, she hired a matador to masturbate to in "Take a Bow."

I admit, that bull was a handsome accessory, along with the matador's tight pants, epaulets, and cape. When I was young and first watched the video, that's all I saw—how elegant it all looked. But here's what I didn't know at the time, and Madonna must have, since she wasn't young and naïve like her viewers: Before bulls go into the ring, Vaseline is smeared on their eyes so they can't see; wet newspapers are stuffed in their ears; they're drugged and locked in a box for days to disorient them; then they're bled out by a series of men with knives before they even get to the matador, who stabs them some more before cutting off their tail and ears—sometimes while the bull is still conscious and the crowd throws empty beer cans at the poor, felled creature.

She treats living things as accessories, as if life itself isn't any more real than a screen or the pages of a magazine. I think she thought she was just playing another role—lady of the British manor—when she bought three thousand baby pheasants for her rich friends to shoot and kill for fun. But that wasn't a "role" for the birds. They died.

When your claim to fame is opening the world's eyes to variety in sex, I'd think it would be helpful to be able to play more than one part only through costume changes. Sexy boxer stroking herself. Sexy powdered-wig lady stroking herself. Sexy guitar-humper. Sexy pole-humper. "Quit masturbating, Madonna!" I want to yell. "Quit that sexy stuff! You're starting to irritate me!" I don't care for masturbation in my pop music. If it's not part of the storyline, it's just kind of embarrassing. Some things—well, that one thing—should stay shrouded in darkness and shame, just stay verboten, not trotted out as fashion. Let me feel guilty for at least two minutes a day. (I also hate anyone saying the word "dildo" out loud.)

Pretty much every woman who lost a parent early passes through the shallow attention-whore phase: bisexual, promiscuous, and able to give headline-creating blowjobs in bathrooms and backrooms all across this nation (and a couple others). In high school, I looked to Madonna to guide me through mine. With her fun sexual aggression and messing with gender identifiers, she was a female pop star switching from being object to objectifier. But then I grew up, experienced some life, and I understood that when you merely switch from being a prisoner to being a guard, no one is freed, not even yourself. Madonna never grew up. She did attention-whore better and funner than anyone, but she couldn't stop. That HEALTHY shirt she wore in 1985—when she raised her arm, not having shaved recently—how utterly happy she looked, dancing back then. It made you happy just looking at her; it made you healthy. That kind of raw, selfish, desire-full shallowness of youth she did so damn well got brittle and horrible when she clung onto it through the next three decades.

She got all that money and power and could have used it to change the world, but instead she kept doing the same thing-appearing as a hypersexual, in-control, heavily coiffed and corseted figure—so she could acquire more and more and more. Same with people. In her "Open Your Heart" video, Madonna initiated what looked like a ten-year-old boy into the porn industry. That boy is in his mid-thirties now, a decade and some-odd older than Madonna's recently dumped acquisition, a model named Jesus.

Maybe youth isn't wasted on the young; maybe it wastes the ones hanging onto it. You're not expected to be a whole person, a good person, at first. All you need to be is young. It's what comes after that's the hard part—learning kindness and thoughtfulness. You stop having good-looking sex; you learn how to connect with another human, learn how to be human.

You know who can really tell you about sex? Old people. Ones who have been through the Depression and war and losing legs and houses and family and who get put on antidepressants and morphine as they die of cancer, and then they really open up. People like that know what's precious. They're worth listening to on every topic, especially sex and love and even fashion.

Will you have this to remember? That moment in bed when you acquiesced to the loss of your youth, and found, by surprise, something so much more graceful in its place. You would have found yourself looking, as if for the first time, into someone's eyes, and there was no longer the invisible audience, there was no outfit, there was just . . . forever.

Dying people talk about the smallest things with such urgency and love—an airplane ride, the way a cloud looked as they lay in a field half a century ago, the smell of a certain meal a certain someone always cooked. Small kindnesses, petty slights. Life. The feel of an old saggy spouse crawling into your old saggy bed, one breast missing, desire whole. Every single thing that was left out of that *Sex* book. Every single thing that matters.

TRACK 6

Fighting Spirit

"I'm strong, ambitious, and I know exactly what I want.
Now, if that makes me a bitch, okay."

—MADONNA

Fuck You, Seattle

Bee Lavender

WHEN I WAS thirteen, my parents drove us forty-five minutes from our home on a rural wooded peninsula to a suburban-mall movie theater to see *Desperately Seeking Susan*.

I wasn't eating popcorn: One year after a surgery that removed a portion of my jaw, I could barely chew. This was just one of the small humiliations that had accumulated after I had been diagnosed with terminal thyroid cancer, undergone extensive surgery and testing, survived a recurrence of the cancer, and traded a death sentence for the murkier and far less glamorous reality of a rare genetic disorder. My neck was sliced halfway round, my jaw riddled with holes, and I had been diagnosed with a second, separate and distinct, type of cancer. The treatments had just started to remove the skin cancer ravaging my torso. Over the next three years I would have nearly four hundred biopsies.

I sat with cold hands tucked into each armpit, only half-awake until the movie started, and my perception of the world shifted in a sudden and irreversible way.

The film offered something that made every hair on my body stand on end: a glimpse of a world that might be out there somewhere—urban, messy, lawless; with cool, caustic boys on scooters, careless girls bedecked in ripped vintage clothes, and enormous empty warehouse apartments.

In the film, Susan was a trickster, a character with no motives, no back story, and no possessions except what she could carry with her or fit into a Port Authority locker. She was all gesture and blithe indifference. She took what she wanted, whether that was a bottle of room-service vodka, the contents of a wallet, a pair of studded boots, or sex on a pinball machine.

Roberta was different: constrained by tradition, rules, responsibilities, life. She had a place in the world, even if she did not like it. And then in an absurd flight of fiction, one knock to the head, a change of wardrobe: Roberta became Susan.

And that wardrobe change seemed to be all she needed. She found a place to stay, a love interest, a job based on her newfound clothes (and confusion). Even after she regained her memory and kept exclaiming, "I'm a housewife from New Jersey!" the truth was subsumed, not just to the cops or the people in her new life, but also to her husband and friends from home.

The movie proposed this radical vision: A costume can change not just perception, but reality.

Precisely when a thirteen-year-old most wants privacy and autonomy, I had lost all control of my body. Blood, vomit, pus, shit: Everything was discussed, examined, weighed, quantified. Doctors made the major decisions, my parents the minor. I had no choice in even the smallest details; not food, not even bathing. I was not allowed to immerse my skin in water, not allowed to shower. My mother washed my hair in the sink every third day, wrapping fresh scars in plastic to keep them dry and safe.

Other girls might have worried about their appearance, but I didn't need to bother. I knew that I was ugly—so mutilated, in fact, that I had a permanent gym class waiver to avoid having to disrobe and endure the mockery of my peers.

The surface is indeed superficial, but it matters—it is what you show the world, what you want the world to think and know. And the primary presentation of my essential self, then as now, were the scars. At the start of 1983 I looked garroted, as though I had been hung or strangled or cut in a knife fight. By the end of 1986, I would have hundreds of jagged red slashes and pearly white lumps trailing across my face, chest, shoulders, belly. Others were more obscure, hidden. But even if you couldn't see them, I could feel them. They throbbed.

Desperately Seeking Susan suggested: So what? Don't try to conform. Wear the costume, be a freak, because if someone is looking at your dress they are not looking at whatever you have hidden underneath.

★

Just after dawn on a wet gray Saturday morning a few weeks after seeing *Desperately Seeking Susan*, my parents dropped me off in a semi-deserted industrial town across the bay from our house. I was early, but not the first in line at the waterbed store, queuing up to buy Madonna concert tickets.

I recognized one of the boys in front of me, Marc. He had a locker near mine in the back hallway of a rural junior high school that resembled a penitentiary. I would never have dared talk to him at school—he was in the ninth grade, while I was a mere eighth grader—but that morning on the sidewalk, we struck up a conversation. He introduced me to his friend Scott, and we whiled away the hours chatting about music.

That is how it worked back then, back there. The music you listened to made a statement of intent: This is who I am. This is what I believe.

Arguably it was not a wise choice for a fourteen-year-old boy like Marc to declare a sincere love of Madonna. The taunt "fag" was a common and casual insult used to torment my new friends, but not necessarily because of the music they listened to. People our age didn't have the context. Even then it seemed extraordinary to me that "wannabe" and "poser" were two of the worst insults that could be leveled at a person. How do you define authenticity in your early teens, anywhere, let alone if you live in a failing shipyard town? Should we have worn steel-toed boots and welders' hardhats?

Madonna tickets secured, I went back to my routine of school, doctors—and drill team.

I had stopped riding the school bus because this kid named Troy tried to set my hair on fire. Lacking a ride for the eight miles home through dense second-growth forests, I was forced to find an approved afterschool club.

Technically, it was less a matter of joining the drill team (I was not issued a uniform, nor did I perform) as being drafted. The young, charismatic drama teacher in charge of the group caught me hiding behind the shrubbery once too often and put my idle hands to use running the tape player as the other girls snapped their necks and hips rhythmically to the latest pop tunes.

These girls were popular, the elite of the school, with a mongrel assortment of athletes as ballast for routines. The captain was Nikki, and her co-captain was Crystal. They, like all the girls on the team, had permed hair, blow-dried and feathered up into quiffs standing several inches above their heads.

My title was "manager," though I was neither in charge nor even a mascot. I was just there, tolerated, ignored, so long as the teacher was watching. This was the most desirable of all scenarios. If I had any goal at all it was to be unremarkable, invisible, vanished, gone.

Practice was held in the commons, a vast multipurpose room where we ate lunch and attended assemblies, with a three-story atrium and potted plants the size of small cars. I stood at a folding table next to the concrete planters, hitting the buttons on a boom box, flipping the cassette tapes, pausing and starting "Hey Mickey," "Eye of the Tiger," "Honky Tonk Woman."

Whenever the team took a break, I trailed behind them to the nearest restroom, where I watched as they painted their faces with cheap drugstore makeup and curled their hair with the butane curling irons they carried in white fake-leather purses.

I was not trying to fit in with the group (and the attempt would have been useless: Outside of drill team, these girls were among my most vicious tormentors). I was studying them in hopes of creating a reasonable camouflage. Belonging with the drill team without actually having to befriend them was conformity as strategy. If that required tedious long hours listening to adolescent girls' gossip, fine. If I could parse their mannerisms, clothes, concerns, I might be able to stay alive.

★

My new friends from the concert ticket line provided the first real social outlet I had in junior high, and I slowly edged toward the group of people who carried colored folders with pictures of their favorite bands cut out of magazines and taped to the front. These people shared my interest not just in Madonna but in the other things we had seen in stolen moments of the music video show *Bombshelter Video,* or heard on KJET radio: the Pet Shop Boys, Frankie Goes to Hollywood, Tears for Fears, The Clash, the Eurythmics.

They, like me, hid in the library or art room at breaks. We tried to go to dances and football games to fit in, but never quite looked right, even though we were buying our clothes at the same places as everyone else.

Madonna made popular music (though the popular kids in our school didn't like it) by trading on her sexual identity, and that fact upset our elders, but we were young: asexual, maybe yearning or experimenting, but unformed. She said, decide for yourself. Our parents did not necessarily agree.

We all existed in a liminal space of possibilities, with a profound lack of agency matched by a desire for control. We sorted ourselves according to bands, liking but not quite understanding what we were listening to. It would take a couple more decades before I figured out what the heck Morrissey was talking about in "Piccadilly Palare."

★

It was time for me to prepare for another round of cancer treatment. Most common foods were rigidly restricted, and I was taken off the medication that controlled my metabolism and kept me alive.

Starved of food and hormones, I could barely stay awake during the day. Classes, already fraught with social drama, turned into half-waking nightmares. I can't even offer anecdotes and stories, just vague semi-delusional moments of horror. You've seen the movies: Take it as a given that if my life were scripted by John Hughes, I would be worse off than the nameless neck-brace girl portrayed by Joan Cusack in the movie *Sixteen Candles*. I wouldn't want to read that story, and I certainly did not want to live it.

Outside of class, school was dangerous, even with security cameras in the halls. Violence was common, hazing and bullying were tolerated and often encouraged by staff. The worst of the scenarios, waking or dreaming, too often featured Troy, the kid who tried to set my hair on fire, or Nikki and Crystal, laughing—and the jokes often centered on me, because I could not defend myself. I was too weak to make a fist, and one tap would have shattered my jaw. I learned to be quiet, to watch and wait.

Some people believe there is nobility in suffering, and my family and doctors expected that my peers would respect my vulnerability. The reality is different; profound illness is deviance from the crowd, just like being too smart, too gay, too other. I was different, and different was bad. I was a target of harassment whether I tried to fit in or not. Too sick to succeed, and eventually too sick to care, I kept accounts, clocking each new humiliation.

My hair started to fall out, in strands and then clumps, and no amount of hairspray or sessions with a butane curling iron could hide the fact. One day, I locked myself in the bathroom at home with scissors and my father's rusty safety razor, hacking and slashing until half the remaining hair was gone.

I was too tired to even flip the tapes as the drill team prepared for the regional championships. Instead, I hid in a restroom the girls did not frequent, sleeping in a toilet stall with my forehead pressed against the cold metal wall.

★

The day of the concert finally arrived. It was the first concert I had ever attended, the first night of Madonna's Virgin Tour, and therefore the very first Madonna concert ever. I had a seat in the front row of the balcony, wedged in among my parents, an aunt, and the sole friend left from before the illness, a girl named Christine. The place was a cacophony of sound and activity, though I was drifting, not thinking about much except radioactive isotopes served in a Dixie cup and days spent in cold exam rooms holding perfectly still as enormous machines scanned my body one millimeter at a time.

I was so tired.

The theater filled with rippling waves of enthusiasm, girls in sequins and lace and sawed-off gloves, and I watched as they excitedly took their seats, clapping and hollering for their heroine.

Then something enormously startling happened: The opening act appeared, snarling white rappers from New York City. So foreign, so improbable, so wrong for this audience. They raced around the stage, waving their arms and shouting, and the crowd went calm in confusion, then started shouting back in anger.

This was the first time Seattle met the Beastie Boys, and the city was not amused.

I put my hands over my mouth, laughing so hard I could barely breathe.

The band held the stage a little longer until nearly all the little girls were booing, then they exited with the refrain "Fuck you, Seattle!"

In the interval between the opening act and the concert, the fatigue of the illness and the excitement of the night proved too much. I put my head down on the railing and fell asleep, missing the rest of the show.

It didn't matter—I was alive, I was there, and I still own the souvenir T-shirt.

★

One weekend afternoon a week or two later, we boarded a yellow school bus for the long drive to the other side of the county for the drill team regional championships. The team was psyched up and ready to prove it in their matching green-and-white polyester tunics and pleated skirts.

The venue was a windowless junior high gymnasium reeking of floor polish and sweat. We watched the clock, watched each other, the various teams whispering behind their hands about minor fashion differences in the sea of feathered bleached hair: a barrette here, a slightly less-than-white sock there.

Then it was time. My team marched out on to the gym floor in formation, hair and smiles perfectly organized, arms held stiffly at their sides, waiting for the music to start.

Standing behind the table next to other managers and the judges, I was supposed to cue their signature song, "Old Time Rock and Roll," by Bob Seger.

Instead, I hit the button and started the Willy Nelson and Julio Iglesias duet "To All the Girls I've Loved Before."

Nikki did not lose her smile as she turned her head and made eye contact with me, hatred burning behind mascara, lip gloss, braces. I stared back, then shrugged, not even pretending to search around for the correct tape.

She signaled and the group dutifully started their routine, not at all in sync with the music, half the girls unable to follow the intricate patterns without the cues of the beat.

After the judges issued a verdict (we lost), the girls huddled together, several crying. I stood against a wall, arms crossed, thinking of the scene in *Desperately Seeking Susan* when Madonna robs her sleeping date, tips her hat, and walks out of the hotel saying, "It's been fun."

Sabotage? Simple exhaustion? I don't know now, and I didn't care then. Whether choice or accident, it happened. Motives make no difference, and anyway, those girls were never going to play nice.

★

The fasting, medication, and tests that had made me too tired to watch the concert were leading up to an even more intense cancer treatment, scheduled for spring vacation to avoid interrupting my schooling. But then another unrelated anomaly was discovered, another surgery ordered. The doctors and my parents nodded and whispered and wondered: How to minimize the impact on my education? The experts wanted to perpetuate this idea of a normal education, normal adolescence, normal life. I was just about ready to accept the goal of remaining alive, maybe, because it seemed to mean so much to my parents. But normal, by then, was too much to ask.

Clutching the skimpy hospital gown tighter around my shivering body, the paper on the examination table crinkling and tearing as I shifted, I said, "I'm not going back. I will burn down the school if you make me."

Fuck you, Seattle.

The music was never as important as the delivery. The image. The style. Madonna offered a primitive and powerful idea of liberation, like many artists before and since. But her music was popular; it travelled vast distances, penetrated the forest where I lived. And, critically, her music was joyous. During the years when I had many legitimate reasons to feel sad, Madonna made music with an uplifting message: You can dance.

I made some friends, made some enemies, dropped out of school in the eighth grade. Later I went back, and that was probably the point: Wear the costume, and when it stops working, choose another.

There would be other songs, movies, concerts. Madonna embodied the dichotomy: virgin and whore, dutiful and independent, promiscuous and pristine. She did not require a lifetime of devotion—she did not even sustain her own relationships or defined interests all that long. Take what you need, and keep moving.

My life might have been the same without that concert, but it would certainly have had an inferior soundtrack.

The kids I met in line for concert tickets? We all moved away to find the urban, messy lives we were hoping for. Our friendships have unfurled across decades: adolescence, high school, college, emerging adulthood, coming out, marriage, divorce, raising our own children, travels across countries and continents. But though they are the friends who have known me longest, they (like anyone) only see the versions of myself I share and promote.

When I met one of those boys, decades later, in Europe, he asked, "Why didn't you tell me I was gay?"

I replied, "It was none of my business."

I asked if he knew I was in treatment for two different kinds of cancer in the '80s. He was shocked. "No!"

The disease wasn't what I wanted to show, and therefore, he didn't see it.

★

Last year, I visited my hometown. I was sitting in a coffee shop talking to my mother about plans for the future. The question was where to move next: I was having trouble deciding. This was a conversation I'd had with dozens of friends and colleagues all over the world.

London, Paris, Berlin—which should I choose? I said the words, then started to laugh wildly at the perversity of having the discussion in that place. I was still laughing when I realized that someone at the next table was listening.

I turned to look. It was Nikki, with shorter but still-dyed-blonde hair, jogging clothes instead of the team uniform, and she was staring at me with revulsion. Just like the day I caused the squad to lose at regionals.

I stared back for a sustained moment, and it was like we were once again wielding colored folders declaring our cultural affiliations.

Did Nikki recognize me, or was she just annoyed to have her morning interrupted by the loud chatter of an interloper, someone so obviously from out of town? I've lost my rural accent. My clothes, the things I carry with me, communicate that I do not live in the Northwest, or anywhere in the United States. I can't help it—that is just true.

I'm still the raggedy girl in spectacles, the drill team manager who hits the wrong buttons, dreaming of elsewhere. Nikki is forever the carefully groomed captain, the boss of her small syncopated corner of the world. Maybe there were no possibilities after all: Maybe we were simply what we were, and would always remain.

And maybe that is okay.

Madonna in My Corner

Ada Scott

THERE WAS MADONNA on the cover of another magazine: spread-eagled against a ring post, in leopard shorts that were more panties than boxing trunks, a black sports bra, and a cross dangling between her breasts. It was 2008 and Madonna's flair for self-promotion was as impressive as ever—she was looking mighty, and I hadn't been feeling mighty at all lately. I grabbed a copy of the magazine (celebrity news rag *LaLate*), brought it home, ripped off the cover, and taped Madonna to my wall.

As an eighteen-year-old in 1984, I could have been an extra in *Desperately Seeking Susan*. By day I was attending classes at Brooklyn College, and by night I roamed Manhattan's clubs, from Danceteria to Pyramid to the Peppermint Lounge. I didn't plan it this way, but in 1985, soon after Madonna married Sean Penn, I got married. When she divorced Penn in 1989, I divorced too. I guess we were both, well, too young to sustain young love.

Later, when Madonna adopted her daughter Mercy, I was a single mom taking care of my daughter by another man. I didn't travel across continents for my child, but just as Madonna went to Malawi to adopt, turning hopelessness into hope, I used my meager resources to create a good life for my daughter Chava.

Chava is no longer a child. She's old enough to take the bus home from school, old enough to hang out with her teen friends and, when it comes to music, she's old enough to choose what she listens to (and deliver opinions about what I listen to). With my daughter often out of the house desperately seeking her own Susans, I found myself with the kind of freedom I'd never had when I became a mother.

So I had time on my hands when I first saw that image of Madonna, looking fighting-fit and staring at me from the magazine rack. I'd wanted to get back in shape for a long time, so long that the desire was more about habit and less about truth. But when I saw Madonna, still looking young and strong in her fifties, still scowling for the camera, I thought, *why not?* Why not let this woman, whose music I danced to, whose gossip I ate up, whose films brought me to the theaters, why not let her push me in a new, selfish way to work my own body? Madonna's "Give it 2 Me" had just hit the air, and the song's lyrics spoke to me:

What are you waiting for?
Nobody's gonna show you how
Why wait for someone else to do what you can do right now?

I was old enough to know the importance of *carping* the *diem*, so I said again, this time out loud, "Why not?"

I knew a little about boxing. Some of my earliest memories were sitting in the living room with my mother and father on Friday nights watching the fights. While they drank cans of Schlitz and cheered their favorites, I played with my kid brother, holding open my palms so he could hit them with his small fists—my kid brother ended up winning the Golden Gloves. I was never an avid fan—I argued with my parents about the brutality of boxing—but when a match started and two men were fighting for their lives and for glory, I couldn't help but admire their spirit.

★

Two subway stops from my apartment, tucked under the shadows of the Brooklyn Bridge, is Gleason's Gym, one of the most famous boxing gyms in the world. Gleason's is home to many former and current champions, but the gym also offers white-collar boxing classes to nonfighters who want to get in shape and learn the rudiments of boxing. Though I grew up blue-collar (the fights on my streets were about violence, not fitness), I figured a white-collar class would be a safer introduction to the sweet science. Even from outside, standing on Front Street on a Saturday morning, I could hear the grunts of men and women working hard. When I walked up the stairs to the gym, which fills the second story of a former warehouse, I could smell the sweat.

Posted at the gym's entrance was a plaque with the poet Virgil's words (I must have had Madonna on my mind that morning because I read the sign as "Virgin," not "Virgil").

> Now whoever has courage
> and a strong and collected spirit in his breast
> let him come forth, lace up his gloves,
> and put up his hands.

Just as Madonna kept reinventing herself, I was ready to change: to update my body, to upgrade my mind, and to find something that heightened what I readily admitted was mundane—the life of another (somewhat disgruntled) single mom in the big city.

I moved my eyes away from Virgil's words and took in the boxing gym: three boxing rings; a dozen heavy bags hanging like thick pillars to develop power; a row of speed bags shaped like inflated teardrops to develop coordination; the whipping sound of leather ropes slapping the cement floor; the deeper sounds of men and women grunting; and the beauty of people in motion with physiques that were more dancer than Hollywood thug. I imagined Madonna walking into Gleason's. I saw her surveying the scene with her signature bravado, cocky confidence in her eyes, daring the world to question her blonde ambition just before striking a pose or jumping into a frenzied dance step. Madonna in my head, I steeled myself, collected my spirit, and walked in.

I changed in back and my shorts felt too long, my tank top too scant, and my sneakers too clean. When the trainer taught me the basic two-step of boxing, I felt awkward and foolish, especially when I saw the graceful movements of professionals dancing in the ring. And when I started to hit the bag, I felt weak. It was truly heavy, and my punches hardly moved the red pillar with the word Everlast printed down the side. There was nothing Hollywood about my first days in the gym, no soundtracks of power and victory. But I kept going back.

It's now been two years since I started working out at Gleason's Gym. I have worked with veteran trainers on my jabs and hooks and uppercuts. I have thrown thousands of punches at the heavy bags. I have learned to create my own music on the speed bag, the rat-tat-tat triple rhythm that fills every boxing gym. I have even sparred with some of my fellow white-collar fighters. My nose has been bloodied. My ribs have been bruised. And my muscles have lengthened and tightened. There are days when I leave the gym so exhausted I can hardly get down the subway steps to catch the A train back to my apartment, but by the time I do get home and dry out my hand wraps and shower off the sweat from the day's work, I feel young again— almost like a virgin, when the possibilities of life seemed possible.

Which brings me nearly full circle to my purpose here, to Madonna.

Part of staying in shape, part of every boxer's regimen, is road work. I force myself to run at least twice a week so when I do spar, I don't collapse from exhaustion. Boxing is really about balance and legwork, which is why Madonna would make a better prize fighter in real life than, say, a muscle-bound Stallone. I get bored of running the streets in my neighborhood, and when I have some extra time, I take the A train past Brooklyn into Manhattan, to Columbus Circle, where I can run Central Park's loop. One relatively early morning, climbing Cat Hill on the park's east side, I saw two runners approaching: a tall man and a small woman. The man wore shorts and a tank top. The woman wore sweats and sunglasses. Just before we passed each other, I recognized her face: Madonna, out for an incognito run with her bodyguard. I didn't stop to gawk. I didn't call out her name. I didn't ask for an autograph. I'm a born-and-bred New Yorker, too cool to lose my cool over a star, usually uninterested in celebrities. What I did do was look in her eyes—what I could see of them behind her tinted lenses—and nod my head. She nodded back. Of course she didn't know she was one of the catalysts for my Central Park run, but that moment of connection felt perfect.

Madonna striking a pose on a poster. Me striking a stance in a boxing gym.

I still have Madonna's ring-post poster above my bed. My daughter, now eighteen, mocks my home-decorating technique of taping magazine pages to the walls (along with the picture of Madonna pretending to be a fighter, I've taped photographs of real female fighters sweating real sweat). Chava rolls her eyes in exaggerated embarrassment when I walk around in tight T-shirts that show off my bantamweight arms, or when she catches me shadowboxing in the living room, kicking the ass of whatever opponent is in my head that day. Sometimes I even throw punches to the tunes of early Madonna, when she was just a kid coming up.

Madonna Louise Ciccone. She was always more than a could-have-been contender. Like the best champions, she inspired millions. She helped shape me in my could-have-been years when I was young and felt I could take on the world. She helped motivate me in my non-contender years when life as a single mom seemed a little too tough. And she got me to Gleason's Gym. It seems Madonna has been in my corner all along—sometimes directly, usually tangentially, a song playing in the background, a line of lyrics in my head.

Borderline: Madonna's Rebel Stance

Maria Raha

I'VE ALWAYS LOVED badasses.

And before her strange adoption drama in Malawi; before her rather unwitting embrace of Kabbalah; and before those acts belied her supreme narcissism, Madonna was, in my eyes, a definitive badass.

Her first album, *Madonna*, invaded suburban radio stations in 1983, when I was eleven years old. I had grown up listening to Joan Jett, Pat Benatar, the Go-Go's, and Blondie; I had always liked, respected, and dreamt of becoming like these women, whom I admired for their rough edges. In short, I liked women I was slightly scared of. And because of that, there was no good reason why I should have been so astounded by Madonna.

But I was.

That fascination had to do with the fact that most of the women prevalent in '80s pop culture had bodies that didn't look like my softening pubescent frame. The most admired women then were perfectly sculpted and toned—they fit the standards of beauty that were slapped, crammed, and cramped into magazines, from *Cosmo* to *Playboy.* The women of *Charlie's Angels,* plus Loni Anderson, Suzanne Somers, and Bo Derek—hell, even *The Dukes of Hazzard's* Daisy Duke—were entirely too perfect for any preteen to model themselves after. Besides, they bored me. They preened. They posed. They wore completely uninteresting, mostly pastel clothing, and curled their gleaming, mermaid-like hair. Even '80s rock stars, including Joan Jett, had angular, athletic bodies. But I was pale and freckled and sported insolent cowlicks; I had thick, short legs, wide feet, and broad shoulders—and I was always picked last for teams in gym class.

But Madonna seemed more like me than she did a celebrity. She had risen to infamy with a belly she wasn't afraid of. Unlike the compulsive tummy tucking of Jane Fonda's workout—and later, Suzanne Somers' ThighMaster—Madonna was initially unapologetic about that extra layer of chub. Instead of pretending that she didn't have it, she *showed it off.* She framed and bedazzled it with rhinestone belts and cropped T-shirts. She burst out of bustiers while my friends and I were busy trying to flatten our stomachs and hide our "flaws" from the world.

The more I was inundated with her early image, the more I found myself wanting to be brasher and less apologetic—*Charlie's Angels* be damned. And to hell with pastels. I wanted the same bows, hats, combat boots, rubber bracelets, and ragged skirts that Madonna wore. I wanted to stick out more than fit in. Suddenly, I wanted to take up *room*—a surprising thing for a girl at the height of an (extremely) awkward stage.

As Madonna's image and career evolved, so did my sense of self. I felt increasingly uncomfortable as I endured twelve years of Catholic school and attended mass every Sunday. I started to feel suffocated by unnecessary guilt and the church's unwillingness to progress. At the same time, Madonna's *Like a Prayer* era relied heavily on appropriated Catholic imagery, appalling my teachers and church leaders.

And in the face of the AIDS crisis, the ongoing abortion debate, and the resurrection of censorship in the late 1980s, that album and her insolence reinforced my own developing view of the Catholic Church as oppressive, patriarchal, and censorship-happy.

These views stoked restlessness in me. Luckily, I lived about two blocks from the Long Island Railroad, which shuttled me to New York City in forty-five minutes for about seven dollars. When I was seventeen, I began spending as much time there as I could. And it was then, when I began meeting more political, artistic, marginal people, when I started to witness true rebellion and began growing more isolated from the suburbs in which I had grown up, that I realized exactly how Madonna had gotten so far.

I would have had to be comatose to have missed the gaping chasm that existed between New York City and the suburbs. Obviously, this was pre-Internet: There was no easy access to non-mainstream culture. For me, mix tapes, magazines, newspapers, word-of-mouth, and eventually, long days wandering around downtown New York, introduced me to abundant, thriving subcultures populated by punks, drug addicts, poets, painters, activists, drag queens, drunks, and hustlers. I tripped over a world of progressive and experimental style, music, art, and politics that operated on its own, with open contempt for the middle-class suburbs that shored up its borders. I fell head-over-heels in love with outsiders and was almost instantly seduced by a city full of them.

But the more at home I felt in New York City, the more I grew isolated on Long Island—and the more Madonna made me *livid*. I wore clothes my peers couldn't understand. I saw films they had never heard of. My friends tolerated me enough to ask for advice on new albums or stores that were located downtown. But almost no one wanted to hear about the drag queens and junkies that decorated the streets. In true suburban spirit, they just wanted to be one tiny hair past the Joneses. And outside of urban America, my friends were exactly the type to whom Madonna appealed.

Madonna's suburban fan base could be fascinated with something that was new to them, something slightly different, without having to risk social rejection or venture into urban environments themselves. They could ignore the gay-friendly artistic lifestyle she flaunted, but love her music, which never strayed far from their comfort zone. Not only did the music keep her fans within their comfort zone, it also kept Madonna in hers. Marketable music isn't a bad thing on its own. But compared to the passionate struggle and sacrifices of other, more marginal artists like Keith Haring, Jean-Michel Basquiat, and Kim Gordon, her "rebellion" suddenly seemed calculated and cold.

The aforementioned people from whom Madonna lifted her image struggled for a lot less reward. For example, Haring addressed the political and social issues that plagued New York at the time—crack and AIDS being the most urgent. He painted in public, and both the messages and beauty were free. Not only was he making public art, he ran the risk of being arrested (and he was) for doing so. Basquiat spent much of his early life making public art, too—and living on the streets. Though musicians such as Sonic Youth's Thurston Moore and Kim Gordon have become icons of a different kind since the 1980s, they did so by holding fast to their vision, playing mostly for small (and confused) audiences, and tolerating the years it took for culture to catch up with them.

Unlike Haring, Basquiat, Moore, and Gordon, Madonna didn't take artistic risks. She released love songs and dance anthems that might set the inhibited free, but she never really reflected the times in sound, like the hip-hop that flooded the streets managed to do. Unlike the other artists with whom she mingled downtown, she never addressed her generation in her music. Madonna only dipped her toe in substance when she sang about an unexpected teen pregnancy in "Papa Don't Preach"—and reinforced the status quo when she insisted on "keeping the baby." It wasn't a rebellion that challenged the conservative culture of the 1980s, but it was *just enough* rebellion to tiptoe between shock and marketability.

Additionally, Madonna's rebellion never veered far from the visual, and appearance is what American culture has always used to distinguish women from each other (and from the norm). She might have given an accusatory glare, but it could also be misread for seduction. Her reliance on assertive sexuality made conservatives uncomfortable while enabling her to remain sexually available, an ever-fuckable fantasy to a swooning—and paying—audience.

The downtown '80s scene wasn't the only wave she rode. The release of the single "Express Yourself" in 1989 kicked off a decade of extreme notoriety for Madonna. She looked part pinup, part body-builder, and ultimately this was less accessible to young girls than her earlier images. She was also plucking more pieces from other subcultures than she had done before. One case of this lifting was "Vogue." While black queens were vogueing during drag competitions in Harlem, Madonna was making millions imitating them without the sociopolitical baggage that the lifestyle inevitably carried with it. Even her version of the dance was dumbed down: Harlem's vogueing took definitive skill, flexibility, improvisation, and spontaneity. It used mimicry and humor; it had its own language and symbolism. Madonna's version was humorless, rigid, simplified, static, and robotic. In some ways, her hijack of vogueing was a contemporary version of the white washed way the music industry promoted rock 'n' roll as "white" music, even though its roots were in black culture and blues.

But stripped-down choreography was her lesser offense. The Harlem male-to-female transgendered and transsexual community lived meagerly, fighting to "pass" as women when they could, partially for survival. They starved for their art and culture, and they risked their lives when they ventured to parts of the city that didn't accept drag as readily as the subterranean scene they moved in. For example, many of the lead subjects in the 1990 documentary about Harlem's drag circuit, *Paris is Burning*, either were murdered or died of AIDS since the film was made. Madonna, on the other hand, moved safely about that world, sent listeners into a robotic vogueing frenzy, and barely gave a nod to the Harlem queens that not only inspired the song, but invented what she turned into a nightclub craze. Not to mention how she made more money from that one single than a drag queen from Harlem is likely to make in a lifetime.

For all the ways in which Madonna spoke to me when I had a more limited frame of reference for female rebellion, I could finally see past the veneer. She was a collage of b-boy, punk, bohemian, gay man, drag queen, old Hollywood screen star, and heretic, not the free-spirited, free-thinking badass I had wanted so badly to model myself after. Because Madonna only toyed with social exile without fully committing to it, she hadn't truly taken *any* risk.

In the early 1990s, while Madonna blithely urged women to "express themselves" (to men, of course), a third wave of feminism bloomed—and so did a backlash. Along with other artists and activists, musicians such as Kathleen Hanna, Tobi Vail, and Ani DiFranco, plus bands such as Bratmobile and L7, faced scorn for their stands on abortion, reproductive rights, a more inclusive feminism that accounted for race and class, sexual harassment, and violence against women. The right wing deemed feminists fascists, hence the term "feminazi." Evangelical preachers such as Pat Robertson accused feminists of being witches and baby-killers.

For feminists of the third wave, empowerment wasn't as simple as finding a partner who would let them express themselves, as Madonna seemed to advise. Some of these women drew strength from challenging men perceived as allies for marginalizing women's issues in punk and indie music. These women rebelled by using the stage to explore issues such as rage about rape and incest, and they withstood vitriol from both the mainstream media and the punk/indie scenes.

The most prominent face of this new DIY feminism, called riot grrrl, was Kathleen Hanna, lead singer of the 1990s punk band Bikini Kill. Hanna became a bull's-eye for punks and indie rockers who revolted against the idea of feminist dialogue in punk rock.

Hanna, her bandmate Tobi Vail, and other women in their scene loudly encouraged feminist dialogues, inspiring hundreds of other young women. The media, of course, had a field day, boiling down feminism to simplified black-and-white terror tactics and quotes taken out of context.

I heavily identified with these outspoken, courageous, intelligent women who took risks and remained relatively marginalized due to their lack of compromise. Once again, the sexuality Madonna leaned on allowed her to keep her femininity intact—and her fame afloat— even as vocal, politically active, angry women with lesser public images were tossed to the wolves.

In the wake of that new feminist backlash, Madonna seemed more shrewd than cool, more constructed than spontaneous. Instead of being silenced or misconstrued, Madonna could move in and out of the feminist label as it suited her, and use it only enough to garner more attention. In the end, it was third-wave feminism that thrilled me, not the vague skimmed-from-the-top self-expression that Madonna promoted. Rather than being a rebel, Madonna simply played her cards right.

I still listen to that first album, though. I still love the rumpled punk-orphan image from her early years. The Gaultier bustiers she wore were gorgeous, and I still think she looked fabulous as a platinum blonde. But now I can see clearly that she was just a gateway to the real risk-takers and visionary women who would inspire me—the ones who saw a better way for us in life, politics, and art. Madonna might have influenced me as a girl, but real rebellion, and real feminism, made me who I am as a woman.

My Movie and Madonna

Caroline Leavitt

PICTURE THIS. I'VE just sold my novel, *Into Thin Air*, to a publisher, and suddenly I have a bona fide producer named Dan interested in making it into a movie. I lie my way into writing the script (I say I have written many scripts before, and when Dan realizes I haven't, the only thing keeping me on the project is the fact that I blurt out that I will work for free). People are excited, and then a new producer—we'll call her Adelle—comes on board, and things really start to spark, because Adelle just happens to also be working with Madonna on an indie film.

"What's she like?" I ask, and Adelle tells me she is a consummate pro, that she comes to work on time, that she knows not only her lines but the lines of just about everyone else on the set. "I carry your novel to work with me every day," Adelle tells me. She also carries her little girl, and she tells me that Madonna is really, really interested in both. "She's thinking about making her directorial debut,"

Adelle tells me. She nods enthusiastically. "And when she asked to borrow your book, I gave it right to her."

Adelle's smile is the size of Jupiter, but I've had my heart broken by Hollywood before. I know what that word "interest" means, and that and a dollar won't get you very far in the New York City subway. "She's reading you," Adelle tells me. "And no matter what you think of her, if she takes it on, you and your book will be famous."

That night, when I go home, I mull all this over. What *do* I think of her? Not that much, I'm afraid. I don't really like her music, which seems too boppy and synthetic and just plain overproduced for my taste. I don't really like her style, which seems calculated to me. I know from a friend of a friend who wrote the movie *Desperately Seeking Susan* that the star of that film was supposed to be the divine Rosanna Arquette, and supposedly Arquette felt that Madonna took over. All the press wanted to talk to her, not Arquette, and the film even began being called "The Madonna movie." ("She takes over everything," Adelle tells me. "But then again, she's Madonna.") Do I want this to happen?

I know already how producers change stories, and I begin to imagine what Madonna might do to mine. *Into Thin Air* is about a young woman vanishing into a whole other life hours after giving birth to her child. Would the Madonna-ization of it change my book into something I not only don't recognize, but don't like? Already, under Dan and Adelle, my main character has gone from a waitress to a phone sex worker (not my choice!) to a photographer. Characters that die come back to life and then are knocked off again. I know movie-making is a collaborative effort, but I can't shake the feeling: You don't collaborate with Madonna. She's too strong-willed. She calls all the shots, and maybe my job would be just to agree with her or not say anything at all.

I'm more and more wary, but Dan and Adelle are so excited that they almost never stop talking about it. Dan sits me down and tells me not to say anything to anyone about what might be happening concerning Madonna and my movie, that it must stay hush-hush until there is a firm deal in place. "But a story this big could leak out," he tells me. "Imagine the phone calls! We're talking *People* magazine! We're talking *The New York Times*! You have to be prepared when that happens."

"But I don't know anything about what's going on," I tell him. "I don't know what Madonna is thinking about my book, or when she might decide, or what she wants to do with my story." I ask if I can talk to Madonna about my book. I figure I can be smart and charming, plus—I admit, I really want to meet her. He looks at me as if I have asked him to run through Times Square without clothes on. "You're the writer. You don't really talk to anyone," he says. "And when you do, when the calls come, you say what we tell you to say."

"You can't be serious," I say.

"'Please talk to my producers.' That's all you say," he tells me. And that is that. I wait and wait, but the calls never come, and I confess, I'm getting a little peeved. I know that being associated with Madonna will boost my career, that some of her sparkle might even rub off on me. But it frustrates me that I have no contact with her, that I can't meet her and make a case for myself and my novel.

"She's reading it," Adelle keeps telling me. I think of Madonna reading and I wonder if she's imagining certain actors and actresses as my characters, if she's plotting out the visuals or even thinking about distribution deals. But I don't actually imagine we will be friends, Madonna and I. Or even that I might like her. I'm shy and bookish and her flamboyance bothers me because it seems like an act, an irritant to get a reaction. What would we ever talk about? I just want her to make my movie. "Don't tell anyone about your Madonna connection," I am warned again by my producers, and so I don't, though truthfully, I don't think anyone will believe me, anyway.

Two weeks later, while deep in a reverie about how I am going to convince Madonna to shoot the last act, I hear it on the TV news: Madonna is leaving on a worldwide concert tour. Heartsick, my fantasies crashing, I call Dan. "Oh," he says. His voice is dull and faded. "We were going to tell you. She decided to go make music instead of movies."

"But what did she say about the book? About me?"

"She said she was going on tour. That's Madonna for you."

So there I am. Does it bring me any sort of fame by association to know that Madonna read my book? Or had she not even read it, only skimmed it? Maybe she didn't even like it.

Suddenly, everything else about my film begins falling apart, as if Madonna is the first domino to fall, and look out now, because here come all the others. Dan falls in love with another new producer and they are talking about moving to France. Adelle is busy with a new film. Suddenly, no one is answering my calls or making any calls to me.

I think of Madonna, the way she simply tears off to do her tour when she could be directing a movie of my novel. And then I remember this story a friend had told me about her—something she had read in a magazine. When Madonna was struggling, she had been rejected by some record company executive. But instead of caving or feeling humiliated, she walked back into the office, ignoring the receptionist who tried to stop her, and she said to the executive, "Someday, you're going to wish you had said yes to me." I hate the Madonna who isn't going to make my film, but I like the one who stood up for herself like that. I like the way she was confident, that nothing was a slight to her—only a mistake, or a misjudgment.

In the end, Hollywood could have broken my heart. And Madonna could have, too. Instead, I choose to look at both in a different way. No one can make you feel small or wrong unless you allow it, and I'm not going to let that happen to me. I might have lost those producers, I might always wonder what would have happened if Madonna had directed my novels, but I don't give up, no more than Madonna did when that executive told her to get lost. I get new producers, and make new deals. I write more books, too. And yes, occasionally I think, "Someday, you're going to wish you said yes to me." But then I let it go.

You could say this change in me—this decision to never play the victim—was the one gift I got from Madonna when she almost, almost made my movie.

In Costume

Dana Rossi

REMEMBER HOW THAT lovely but basically powerless Diana Prince would go into a clearing, spin around, then suddenly her dress would disappear and she'd be wearing starry hot pants and a red-and-gold bustier, able to deflect bullets with her wrist bands and whip some not so good ol' boys into shape with her Wonder Woman Lasso of Truth?

Well, that's pretty much what I thought would happen if I tried to dress like Madonna.

Ever since I was little, I have been certain of two things. One, I definitely *did* see a ghost in my basement when I was five; and two, Madonna was the strongest, most unique, most uncompromising trailblazer pop music had ever seen, and deep down I always wished I were her. Madonna was fearless and unapologetic and in charge of both her naughty bits *and* yours. She gave a concrete visual to all my concepts of "cool," and I always thought her traits—chief among them fearlessness—would magically become mine the second I slipped on fingerless gloves or a bedazzled cowboy hat.

In October of 2001, I was invited to a costume party where everyone was "encouraged" to come dressed as a pimp. This was the beginning of the new millennium, a time when pimps had become a pop culture fascination again, but only to the point that they were considered wise-cracking, colorful street characters and not dangerous Svengalis hell-bent on making a dirty buck. I had never seen a live pimp before, so dressing like one would be especially challenging. Girls who just got out of college with a degree in musical theater didn't really interact with a lot of pimps—at least not that early in their careers. But fortu-nately for me, Madonna's *Music* album had just come out. And for "Music," its first single, the video showed her as a pimp-like character, hitting the strip club with her entourage, decked out all in white, com-plete with a cowboy hat and gold tooth. *I won't be dressing like her to be her, it'll just be like she's my "style guide",* I thought. Slick. Powerful. A one-woman rodeo with a steely stare and a fire in my pants.

I checked my closet and assembled an outfit that came as close as it was going to, since my closet was the most boring thing this side of the Gap. Black shirt, grey pants with pink pinstripes, black boots (from Payless—I'm so sorry, Madonna), a blue crushed-velvet knee-length coat, and a grey felt cowboy hat with black dots on it, all of which I sincerely hoped would scream, "Don't fuck with me, world!"

Just like Madonna.

I grabbed for my purse as I was about to leave the house, but re-considered—I didn't think either a pimp *or* Madonna would carry a purse from Express. So I decided to just take what I needed, stashing it in my pockets: fifteen dollars cash, my keys, and a full pack of Par-liament Light 100s.

I don't remember much about the party itself. I spent part of it alone on the bathroom floor singing "Linger," and most of it hiding in rooms or behind groups of particularly tall people to avoid flirta-tious advances from this guy named Greg.

Greg didn't deserve to be avoided. He was a quiet and down-to-earth guy dressed like a business-class pimp: three-piece grey suit, pink shirt, matching muted tie—and he wasn't spending the majority of his time trying to make people notice him, like so many other guys there. The problem was me—at that time, I was so uncomfortable with myself, my sexuality, even basic flirting, that it's a wonder I wasn't a virgin. It had only been a year since I'd needed three sedatives to ask a guy in *bell choir* out for coffee (which, admittedly, is not very Madonna-like). But I couldn't handle being both fear-inducing *and* vampy at the same time.

So I avoided Greg like a virgin avoids Fleet Week.

But he wasn't deterred. When the party started winding down around 4:30 AM, Greg insisted he walk me home to my apartment in South Philadelphia, which I definitely did not want. But I begrudgingly gave in, telling myself I was the one doing him a favor.

For most of the walk home, I didn't shut up long enough to hear another person sneeze. Talking incessantly is a crutch I lean on anytime I'm in a situation tinged with some kind of intimate overtone that I'm trying to skirt, and given my level of comfort when it came to anything related to S-E-X, I was trying to skirt this big-time.

So as we walked, I talked—about any and everything that popped into my head, from my favorite diner to a stoop where I once saw a guy masturbating. Finally, a block from my house, I realized I could just tell him, "It's five in the morning and you're so far from your house; I got it from here." *Oooh, you're so cool and detached, girl. Keep rocking that.*

I turned to launch *el grande* brush-off, and I noticed that Greg's eyes were fixed on something coming toward us. But before I had a chance to turn and see what he was looking at, a pair of large, solid arms softly restrained me, and a very gentle, quiet voice said, "Hold up, hold up, hold up."

It took me only a split second to realize that there were now two men in front of us, and one of them had a gun pointed at me.

Earlier that year, I had been walking this same stretch of road when I came up behind a scraggly guy walking in the same direction

I was. As I pulled even with him, I got a look and thought *Wow, he's homely,* before continuing on my way. But when I reached the next block, I heard furious footsteps coming up behind me and I felt a vicious yank on my purse, which I was wearing cross-shoulder. The culprit was the guy I passed, who was now yanking on my purse, seemingly trying to pull me down with it. But all he succeeded in doing was pulling me into the "power position"—legs wide, flat back, slight squat—that actually put me in control. I yanked up with all my lady balls and jerked my purse right out of his hands. He stumbled back, dumbstruck, and fell flat on his ass. As the now dominant animal in this kingdom where only the sassiest survive, I bent over him, looked him straight in the eye, and said, "Get up and run, bitch."

And he . . . did! He ran from me like a roach from Raid, and I was awesome because of it! I was strong and I was badass and I was tall, suddenly, for no reason. Armed with that new invincibility, I walked around for months high on the idea that I could defeat anyone—anytime, anywhere, anyhow.

Until, I was about to learn, it involved a gun pointed at me. Whether I was dressed like Madonna or not.

It was five in the morning, I was twenty yards away from my house, and I was looking back and forth between Greg and these two guys—the one who was doing all the talking, and the one who had the gun, so he didn't have to do any of the talking. I must have been in shock, because I heard Greg sharply whisper, as though he was repeating it, "They want your purse."

Then I remembered—*I didn't have my purse.*

I'd left it at home because it didn't go with my designer imposter version of Madonna's lady-pimp costume. So I reached into my pocket and pulled out everything I had—my keys, fifteen dollars, and a half-full pack of Parliament Light 100s. The talker started to frisk Greg, going in and out of the pockets of his three-piece suit (I guess Greg modeled his pimp on "investment banker"), and eventually retrieved two dollars and a blister pack of Eclipse gum. Before I could even give him my fifteen dollars, he snatched it out of my hand, and I immediately assessed the situation with more than a slight feeling that I was going to wet my pants.

Between the two of us, he had taken seventeen dollars and gum. It had been my understanding that it sometimes irritates muggers when you don't carry enough cash and prizes. So I thrust the one thing of value I had left at him—my half-empty box of Parliament Light 100s.

"Here," I coaxed him, my voice raspy.

And he turned, looked at me and said, "Oh, no thank you."

The thug holding the gun wasn't nearly as refined, and for the first time since the episode began he piped up and said to his partner, "Did you do her yet?" asking, I'm assuming, if he'd frisked me. There I was, dry-mouthed and terrified, and for some reason in the next moment, I reacted to the frisker the only way I felt was right. I did the only thing that made sense to both my brain and my body.

I stood there in silence and looked him right in the eye.

A coworker once told me a story she had read in the paper about a woman who was walking alone at night when she saw this guy making a beeline for her. Her intuition kicked in and she sensed he was bad news, so when he got close enough that he'd be able to hear her, she looked him square in the pupils and said, "How's your mom doing?" The question was so bold and so unexpected that he hauled ass out of there and didn't look back. I don't remember thinking about that story in this moment, and I certainly didn't ask this guy how his mom was, but I remember that standing there, and holding that person's gaze for as long as I could, was the most natural thing for me to do. And he had no choice but to mirror me.

It was the first time all night that I felt as strong as the person I was trying to look and act like.

The gun thug must have been very uncomfortable with all the silent staring, and he clearly had places to go, things to *do*, because he repeated himself—"Did you frisk her, motherfucker?" His partner, never breaking his gaze with me, just slightly shook his head and barely whispered, "No." Well, now the gun thug *really* had had enough of this scene, which was straight out of a bad Lifetime movie, so he gave up and said to Greg and me, "Fine. You two, turn the fuck around and run."

We turned around and . . . walked briskly. Which was not the instruction we were given.

"I fucking said *run!*" he yelled, and as I turned to bumble, "Right, yes, we will," I saw that he was standing with his feet shoulder width apart, gun raised and pointed at us as he started to count—One! Two! Three!

Now we ran. We ran up the block and around the corner to hide behind a building, lean against the wall, and exhale for the first time in ten minutes. Greg tried to lighten the mood, and said, "Have I told you how much I love that hat?"

He had, only about a million times that night. But when he said it this time, it dawned on me that if I had not been wearing it, I wouldn't have been dressed up like Madonna as a pimp. Which in turn meant that I very likely would have had my purse on me, and these two guys would have made off with a lot more than they had—and then some. I also realized that if I hadn't let this boy walk me home because I wanted to avoid an awkward situation, I would have been alone for this. I grabbed Greg and hugged him and we eventually let go to peek around the side of the building to make sure the men were gone.

They were.

We were alone, the both of us in ridiculous, ill-fitting costumes that surely made us stick out like Mormons at a truck stop. Greg looked nothing like a pimp. I looked nothing like Madonna as a pimp. And this hat and crushed velvet coat did little to deflect fear, fight off the bad guys, or make it appear that I'd been in charge all along, as I'm sure Madonna would have been. *But it's okay, she was with me anyway*, I reassured myself as I let Greg walk me to my door.

Burning Up

Wendy Nelson Tokunaga

I FIRST HEAR her voice on the in-flight entertainment program during a United Airlines flight from Tokyo to San Francisco. I like the song; it's got a catchy pop-rock, New Wave feel. Nice guitar solo, too. This girl's singing about how she's bending over backward, down on her knees, begging for some guy's attention. She's not the same. She's got no shame. She's on fire.

Who *is* this? I check the listings in the in-flight magazine: "Burning Up." Artist: Madonna. Madonna? I've never heard of this group. Kind of a cool name, though.

Back home in San Francisco I forget all about Madonna until I read a blurb in *Rolling Stone*. Madonna is not a group, but a she. Who names their kid Madonna? Must be a stage name. A fake.

One Saturday morning I'm watching *American Bandstand*, and at last I see Madonna. She's singing a song called "Holiday," and it couldn't be more different from "Burning Up." This sounds like dance music. Can't she make up her mind what she is?

Madonna's kind of cute but she's no Deborah Harry, I'm thinking as I watch. She's not the best dancer either; she kind of just shuffles and bops around. And her voice—well, Pat Benatar has nothing to worry about. And neither does that new girl Cyndi Lauper, who I'm certain will outsell and outlast this little flash in the pan.

And she doesn't play an instrument like Joan Jett or Chrissie Hynde or me. I pride myself on my strong voice. I'm a belter. But I started playing bass guitar in my band because I refused to be just the "chick singer." And since I write the songs, I want to be considered a real musician. I want to be taken seriously. I don't want to be a bimbo like this chick Madonna.

"What are your future plans?" Dick Clark asks Madonna on the TV. "To rule the world," is her answer. I roll my eyes. Could she be any more full of herself?

The next thing I know she's at the movie theater. On the screen. Some little film called *Desperately Seeking Susan*. So now she's an *actress*, too? Well, I have to admit that she steals the picture from that Arquette girl. It's impossible to take your eyes off her.

I'm too poor to afford cable, but when I catch glimpses of MTV at a friend's house, I find that Madonna is all over the little screen, too. In things called music videos. MTV shows a clip of her at a music industry conference. She's on a panel with John Oates of Hall and Oates. He doesn't know who the hell she is. She states with confidence that image and a video presence are imperative for pop musicians to succeed today. There's no avoiding it. Video is indeed killing the radio star. John Oates scoffs at her, saying music videos are a passing fad. He vows to have nothing to do with them.

While my band plays in little shitholes in North Beach and the Tenderloin, Madonna's performing on something called "The MTV Music Video Awards." She's a slutty bride in a wedding gown, humping the floor and singing "Like a Virgin." Is she serious? Has she no shame?

I know the truth. Madonna has to be a producer's creation. She must have slept with the right guy and then *Voilà!* A record deal. She didn't slog through the endless band break ups, drunk guitarists, psycho drummers, cockroach-infested rehearsal spaces, and crappy gigs playing in front of three people like me in my modest and failed attempts to release just one single. She simply waltzed into instant success and fame without paying her dues.

Later I learn that Madonna grew up in a small Michigan town, then bought a one-way ticket to New York, a place where she didn't know a soul. She played guitar and drums in all kinds of bands before she made it. She worked hard. She was determined. She didn't give up. She was on fire.

But she's just a singer, I sniff. She doesn't write her own songs. But then I discover that she does. She's written lots of them. "Burning Up," "Lucky Star." She cowrote "Into the Groove," "Like a Prayer," "Live to Tell."

Madonna becomes a permanent fixture in our collective face, a major force with which to be reckoned. No one can escape her. She is everywoman: a virgin, a vamp, a proud unwed mother, Marilyn Monroe in *Gentlemen Prefer Blondes*, a boy toy for a black Jesus. By now I have no choice but to give her props. My admiration. My respect.

I have even begun to like her.

The years pass and I burn out and eventually give up on my musical dream. I trade in my band, my songs, and my bass guitar for a different creative pursuit. I turn to writing short stories and novels. I spend years honing my craft, querying literary agents, garnering nothing but rejection after rejection. But I don't give up. There's something in me now that won't allow for that. And Madonna's still here. On the radio, in the movies, on the television, in the concert halls. She's been here all along.

Some two decades after I first heard Madonna on that flight from Tokyo to San Francisco I find myself in a writing workshop, still a couple of years away from when I will finally get one of my novels published. I don't remember why, but somehow the topic of Madonna has come up. After all this time she's still on top of her game, still causing trouble and creating controversy by just being herself. Some guy in the group says something disparaging about her. "You call that *talent?*" he asks.

My face flushes. My chest becomes hot, as if something fierce is emerging from deep inside me. I've got no shame. I'm on fire. "*You* try making number-one records for the last three continuous decades," I seethe. "*You* try maintaining that kind of staying power in something as fickle as the music business."

And later I wonder; where did *that* come from?

Thanks, Madonna. For everything.

Now I'm Following You

"To me, the whole process of being a brush stroke in someone else's painting is a little difficult."

—MADONNA

"I'd like to think I am taking people on a journey; I am not just entertaining people, but giving them something to think about when they leave."

—MADONNA

Madonna and Me

Susan Shapiro

MADONNA'S IN THE headlines again—with a new scandal, inappropriate lover, and baby. I knew she'd be back. That's because the Material Girl and I are sisters, kindred spirits, one and the same. We both lost our virginity at fifteen. She did it in the back seat of a Cadillac, and I did it in a dorm room at the University of Michigan—where she also went to school. And I didn't get straight A's either.

Madonna's from a Catholic home and I'm from a Jewish home, so we're into guilt. She had crucifixes, rosary beads, and saints. I had menorahs, mezuzahs, and Aunt Sadie. She had nightmares about Mother Superior. I couldn't get rid of Rabbi Schwartz. Maybe that's why we moved to Manhattan the same year to begin very similar careers—hers as a singer/dancer/slut and mine as a freelance writer. Although she's size-3 petite and I'm an 8 ½ on a good day, and she's now a multizillionaire megastar whose books sold 350,000 copies the first hour and I'm in the middle of a ten-year poetry book in progress, we're uncannily connected.

I first realized we were bonded when she starred in *Desperately Seeking Susan*. My name is Susan—but what's more, one of the girls in the movie orders a rum and Diet Coke—which has been my drink since the Korean grocery on the corner stopped carrying Tab. When I saw *Truth or Dare* I was amazed that she named her movie after the game I played at camp and she and I both practiced giving blow jobs by going down on a Coke bottle. That's because Madonna and I were never afraid to be strong and sexy at the same time. We're women who don't hesitate to use the "F" word when we feel like it. I too said it to David Letterman several times in a row (though from the other side of the screen).

Since being healthy can be a drag sometimes, Madonna and I have self-destructive doppelgangers. She went through her Marilyn phase. I have a thing for Sylvia. In fact, the night she was gyrating around in a white gown making a fool of herself at the Academy Awards, I put on all black, lit candles, stuck my head in the (unlit) oven and swooned around my one-room apartment moaning, "Oh Ted, how could you? Oh Ted."

I completely understand Madonna's relationships with Michael Jackson, David Geffen, Sandra Bernhard, Courtney Love, and Gwennie. I too have had troubled friends. Madonna and I took care of younger siblings so we both tend to surround ourselves with loony-tunes to nurture—she with her dance troupe and film directors, me with my Tuesday night writing workshop.

She cruises around the Lower East Side to pick up seventeen-year-old Latino boys and I too take daring risks others don't under-stand. Like the time I introduced myself to John Ashbery, told him I loved his work, and then quoted a poem by Mark Strand. Yet, despite our critics, Madonna and I have persisted in wearing our hearts on our sleeves over the years. I completed an epic, book-length sonnet called "I'm Still in Mourning," while she illustrated her sexual angst when she posed sucking on bananas with lesbian skinheads.

Not surprisingly, outgoing personalities like ours have inspired numerous authors to hold us under a microscope. An old mentor of mine published a poem called "PsychoTrauma III" in the *Sheepsmeadow Quarterly Review West* that alludes to our two-week affair. Similarly, Madonna has spawned nine trashfests I've read, which shed further light on our linkage: We both felt desperate and alone when we moved to the Big City. She posed nude for art students while I was emotionally naked in true-life confessionals for women's magazines. Though I never ate French fries out of the garbage at Burger King, I did eat their salad bar regularly, so I'm sure I tossed my remnants into the exact same can she was picking food out of.

I admit that our associations with the masculine gender have been a bit problematic over the years. Like Madonna, I used to be attracted to powerful men. Fred, an old lover of mine, once wrote a review for the *Beloit Poetry Journal* and Andrew was a teacher at NYU—with tenure. And we both dated older men named Warren. (Warren Schoenberg was a failed playwright from Queens, though he was just as vain.) Madonna and I were very upset when not one but three of our previous boyfriends ditched us and four days later showed up with quieter, more ladylike women. In her case, Sean, Warren, and Guy also had the nerve to marry and/or knock up their prim newbies. As a result, Madonna and I changed our hairstyles, went shopping, and took up aerobics. She goes to the health club six times a week and I'm there at least once a month, though there doesn't seem to be a correlation between tight abs and faithful guys.

Maybe that's because the losers won't go away. After we split up, Warren had the nerve to demand I return a green chair he gave me. When they called it a day, Guy wanted all her money. Madonna and I called our lawyers and shrinks, but later decided it wasn't worth the trouble. I gave him back the chair and she let him have the mansion. You'd think that would be the end. But no! Guy had the nerve to call her "It" in the press, the same week A-Rod took up with Cameron. Madonna's response was to take up with an even hotter blond and adopt another baby while I lost six pounds and left a curt message on Warren's machine, saying I might be free for coffee—next month. For control freaks who don't like surprises, I must say Madonna and I handled it all with poise.

Madonna, Myself

Mary K. Fons

IT MIGHT HAPPEN in London. She owns six homes there. It could happen in Paris, which would be nice. It wouldn't happen in Beverly Hills, because I would never willingly go to Beverly Hills, not even for her, but it might happen in Barcelona, because we are both women who enjoy Spaniards and modest servings of *patatas bravas* if we've exercised enough to deserve them.

If I am walking down a good street and see Madonna, it will most likely happen in New York City. My sister lives there, and even though Madonna has had trouble with its co-op boards and its baseball players, she can't stay away from New York for long. It's her oxygen tank. I'll see her in New York if I see her.

And though I send three of my best friends the new Madonna wall calendar every Christmas without fail; and though a sixth-grade Leia turned to me in her basement and told me she had a psychic vision that "Vogue" was debuting *that very minute* on MTV and we needed to go upstairs and watch it; and though Leia was right and our lives were changed forever; and though I see the entirety of my college experience when I hear "Music" (wildly inconvenient if I'm driving in traffic); and though I love her like I love the first boy who kissed me on the mouth, if I see Madonna walking along a New York City street, I will not say hello. I will not introduce myself. I will not approach her. My plan, for a long time, has been to keep walking.

Why, you ask? Not for the obvious things critics accuse her of. Madonna didn't disgrace feminism. I hope to God it would take more than a cone bra and some black backup dancers to do that. And she isn't a talentless hack; that the Madonna we know exists at all is proof that this can't be true. There may be pieces in this book that critique or tear Madonna down—for many folks she is the ultimate straw woman and everyone's entitled to their opinion, (even bell hooks).

When I say I don't want to meet my idol, my touchstone, the image that comforts me in dark times, I say it because I need an idol, a touchstone, an image that comforts me in dark times more than I need, say, an autograph. I want Madonna more than I want to meet Madonna. To continue to slog through this risky world—lo! how harsh and dangerous it can be—I need the Madonna that exists in my head, the amalgam of infinite, two-dimensional images, the endless montage. These images lifted me from my small Iowa town as a young girl, and they continue still to rocket me out of complacency and sog and into things like work, squats, riding crops. Those kinds of things.

★

We know what happens when Madonna meets a plebe. We've all seen *Truth or Dare* several times this year. We know that about an hour into the movie we'll be introduced to Maureen "Moira" McFarland. When this happens, any secret hopes we held of randomly meeting and becoming Madonna's BFF are over. Moira, world-weary but still scrunchied, goddammit, has called to (or has been called by)

Madonna for a brief reunion during a stop on the Blonde Ambition tour. Their meeting tells us all we need to know about what it's like to encounter Madonna if you're not already part of the inner cadre. Remember: This all happens in 1990. Madonna's been Madonna for several more decades since—it's doubtful the terms of a meet n' greet have improved.

The whole deal starts with tiny Madonna in costume backstage, getting her hair and makeup done. She's talking to Christopher, the brother who would eventually get all jowly and betray her in a crappy tell-all memoir.

Madonna is laughing. "Moira McFarland taught me how to shave my legs, let me borrow her stuffed bra, showed me how to use tampons—not very well, I might add—and taught me how to make out," she says. At some point, someone who I think is Alex Keshishian asks her how old she was when all this happened, but she doesn't respond. The film cuts to Moira's hotel room door. Her eyes widen, she conceals her lit cigarette. "Guys?" she calls to the kids squawking in the background. The cameras enter.

Two worlds, one collision.

They meet near the hotel elevators, or maybe it's a private suite, or a forest, or some ancient sea-faring vessel. It's hard to tell. Madonna comes in with the filmmakers, her handlers, and bodyguards. In the midst of all this, the two women embrace. Moira mumbles something about not being able to see because she doesn't have her glasses and Madonna tells Moira she's unfortunately unable to sit down even for a moment. At one point, Moira actually forgets how many children she has, then offers her old friend a "Madonna and Child" painting she's made and framed herself. Madonna blesses Maureen's pregnant belly, thanks her for the painting, and gets into the elevator, having never taken off her sunglasses.

This is what happens when you meet Madonna. You can't see, you forget you birthed five children, you offer a piece of your soul, then the big handlers take it—and Madonna—away forever. The bad news is that for you or me it would be way worse than that, because neither of us taught Madonna anything about tampons or sex in Bay City, Michigan, in the mid-1970s. If brassy, sassy "We-go-way-back" Maureen McFarland can't get more than a dismissive seventy-five seconds with Madonna, think what you or I would get. Half a blink maybe, and some of us might instantly birth five babies right there from sheer adrenaline, which I bet *still* wouldn't get her to sit down.

★

If you've ever tried to have a halfway pleasant holiday with the family or a killer birthday after age twelve, you know that despair and disappointment are the bastard offspring of fantasy and expectation. You want Norman Rockwell, you get Kmart. You want a confetti parade with candy tossed from a float, you get five bucks from grandma and an e-card from your dad. In your heart, you know everyone means well, but they're all super busy and after a while you are, too. So you learn to curb your holiday and birthday expectations because you're starting to piss people off. Who do you think you are, anyway? At a certain point you see some Buddhist quote in a coworker's email signature about how expectations create suffering and you start saying it to people when it seems appropriate. This is usually around Christmas or on their birthday.

But you fantasize anyway. In the weeks leading up to the holiday season, you daydream about some vague fireplace that may or may not actually exist, about throwing a Christmas cookie party, buying a knitting app. The night before your birthday, you catch yourself wondering for half a second if anyone might be planning something. There's nothing to be ashamed about. These fantasies save us from the truth, which is that it's plenty hard down here on planet Earth. If we can distract ourselves for a moment, we might find that we feel better on the other side, which means fantasy is a survival tool like water or oxygen or the Above & Beyond 12-inch remix of "Nobody Knows Me."

I needed Madonna when my parents were getting divorced and I could hole myself up in my room making up routines to "I'm Going Bananas" 'til I dropped from sheer exhaustion. I needed Madonna when my entire high school was line dancing to Garth Brooks. Oh, I was pissed about the gold tooth—it was hard enough to defend her as it was—but I stayed true and when the critics all admitted *Erotica* was some of her best work, I was justifiably smug. I needed Madonna when my heart was broken, again, and "Future Lovers" reminded me that there is probably a bigger love out/up there who will never just want to be friends.

But those Madonnas and the countless others she has been for me are all fantasies, all impressions. They're smoke signals or drawings in a book someone read to me a long time ago. Madonna the Actual Woman isn't my poster of Breathless Mahoney or my busted up *Ray of Light* CD. She's not the refraction of twenty-five years of my devotion and admiration. She's a five-foot-four-inch person. And, loath as we all are to admit it, she ain't that pleasant a person to be around, by all accounts. Apparently, you can't make an icon without breaking a few relationships—it's the price we pay for all those beautiful photographs, all those incredible nights on the dance floor pulsing to "Holiday," all the mid-1990s minds blown by the profanity, the Vanilla Ice moment, the schizoid pop that is *Music*.

Is it sad? Maybe a little. Like my fictional fireplace or my confetti birthday parade, I will likely never put my arms around Madonna or serve her spaghetti. But does she like hugging? Do I?

★

My friend Mark recently attended a 25th anniversary screening of *Desperately Seeking Susan* held by the Film Society of Lincoln Center. I got the full report via texts throughout the evening—it's the least he could do, seeing as how he gets a free calendar every year. He told me everyone was all a-quiver the entire night—there were rumors Susan herself would show up.

She never did. But she might have. And if I had been in New York that night, I would've been at the screening with Mark. It's quite possible that I might have walked out at the same time Madonna was walking in, or out, on water. And it would be the perfect opportunity to say, "Oh. Oh, geez. Hi. I admire you so much. Thank you." But I like my relationship with Madonna the way it is: entirely abstract. I don't want to break the spell. The way I see it, I've got two options: Either I do something so incredible with my life that Madonna wants to meet *me*, or I keep walking.

All right, maybe there's a third option. As soon as she turns away, I'll get out my phone and take a picture of her as she walks the other direction. It'll be a spot of blonde in a fuzzy mobile image, proof that she lives, and that I can live another day.

Where's That Girl?

Jamie Beckman

FOR THOSE WHO have never lived in New York City, all the rumors you've heard about insanely high rents and the exhausting hunt for an apartment that (fingers crossed) doesn't have a shower in the kitchen are true. Those of us without trust funds sandwich ourselves into the cheaper areas of town, bunking with three or four roommates on the Lower East Side, in Murray Hill, or deep in Washington Heights.

At age twenty-seven, when I'd had enough of my headmistress of a roommate in Midtown, I found my very own studio apartment in a neighborhood called Yorkville. On the far east side of the Upper East Side, my new apartment was three hundred square feet, max, recently renovated, with sparkling white-painted cabinets and new black-and-white tile, just like the ideal of a New York City apartment that often made an appearance in my teenage dreams.

Yorkville is a strange, quiet place, but I felt at home there. I was neither rich nor very glamorous, so I was among my people. Average-looking, somewhat melancholy couples with hand-me-down strollers meander down the sidewalks alongside recovering sorority girls still wearing their Greek letters. There are a few little old ladies waiting at bus stations and some low-rent nail salons, plus a riverside park that's a mecca for weekend joggers sweating it out over the sparkling water. The best restaurants have been around for ages—Elio's in particular, a white-tablecloth Italian place where I once saw Bob Costas.

Anyone who would describe herself as "cutting edge," a "club kid," or a "fashionista" would not be caught dead living here. It is, however, the perfect place to walk homeward after work from the 6 train, eat a piping-hot slice of pizza at Arturo's, grab a sixer of Bud Light at the incongruous 7-Eleven on the corner of 84th and York, curl up in your apartment, and plot your next career move. At least that's what I did. I loved perching there and listening to every second of my rich twentysomething life reverberate, keeping time with the bony tree branches right next to my orange fire escape.

And then something strange happened: Madonna decided to move to my neighborhood.

She didn't just plan to move in my general geographic direction. She literally purchased a home a few blocks from me, on 81st Street—a $32 million, four-story townhouse. What's even weirder is that Madonna chose the "cheap" side of Lexington Avenue—the decidedly unsexy side. Why? The tabloids lunged at the gossip:

> "'The townhouse is perfect for Madonna,' according to one source. 'She's trying to recreate London in New York City, and this is in the style of a London townhouse.'"
>
> —*The New York Post*, April 14, 2009

> "According to tattle tales who have been inside the house, the nearby Lexington Avenue subway line can be felt and heard as it rumbles through the tunnels, an unfortunate auditory issue we imagine will cost Miz Madonna a fortune to remedy."
>
> —RealEStalker.com, April 14, 2009

"The Upper East Side east of Lex [is] a jumble of soulless apartment towers, tenements and more dry cleaners, Duane Reade drugstores, and Citibank branches than the economy could possibly absorb, even in the best of times. Madonna's house falls on the dowdy side of the dividing line."

—*The Daily Beast*, April 22, 2009

I, however, was giddy. It was Madonna! *Madonna* was coming!

I had to go check out her new digs. I made plans to go see the place the very first Saturday after I heard the news. Pictures of the interior posted online showed opulent accoutrements: chandeliers, Oriental rugs, staircases with pristine carved banisters. Perfect for Her Madgesty. I couldn't wait to see what the outside looked like. I did some Internet research from my Madonna-adjacent headquarters at 84th and York. The address was plastered all over the newspapers, so it wasn't hard to find. I jotted the coordinates down on a Post-It note and told my boyfriend about my mission. He gamely agreed to tag along (as if he had a choice).

I shrugged on my khaki trench coat, he his navy-blue windbreaker, and we set off, Post-It in hand, to check out Madonna's magic kingdom.

We wound through the streets, past plain-looking groups of people wearing North Face fleece and brunching al fresco at cheap bistros on First and Second Avenues. After we had walked a few blocks, we stopped on an unassuming street full of unassuming townhouses.

"That's it . . . I think," I said, looking from my Post-It to the address across the way.

We stood, squinting in the afternoon sun at a big brick building four stories high. The plot of residential real estate was palatial by New York standards, but without context, it was just a brown brick box with painted brown wood accents. After all of the newspaper ballyhoo, it was a little underwhelming.

I was fascinated, however, by the two-car garage. I imagined shiny Benzes zipping in and out of there, her then-boyfriend Jesus Luz and her children inside the house, playing board games on one of those Oriental rugs, a piano tinkling in the background. The idea of Madonna setting up shop here—even if she were to turn the living room into a giant black-onyx disco, à la *Confessions on a Dance Floor*—felt cozy and familial.

My boyfriend and I stared at the place in silence for a few minutes.

"Well," he said. "Wanna go get brunch?"

When I signed the lease on my Upper East Side apartment, I was in search of a home. Somewhere to hunker down—a private enclave to shut out traffic noise, my roommate's chore list, and other people's opinions. If Madonna wants a retreat, a tragically un-hip cocoon where she can be herself without anyone watching, Yorkville has that on lock. Around Thanksgiving 2009, I moved to Williamsburg, Brooklyn: a place thick with self-described artists and supposed rebels—young, doll-faced hipsters wearing thick smears of red lipstick and torn-up black tights.

But forget any cultural superiority I'm supposed to feel living in Brooklyn; during the time that Madonna and I overlapped on the Upper East Side, my heart swelled with a bit more pride than usual about the neighborhood that I called home. In fact, I hijacked my fair share of conversations to tell people, if they weren't aware, that *Madonna* was my neighbor. I loved the area before, but now that she deemed it hers, too, it lent the entire area more legitimacy, as though the rest of the world had discovered how great it was to hang out that close to the East River. And it was great.

Sadly, I never saw Madonna casing out her new joint while I lived in the neighborhood, but I heard she recently put up an iron gate around the place to keep out peeping toms and the paparazzi. So much for mingling with the little people. Still, when I think back on my gem of a place on the Upper East Side, I'll always think of Madonna—and the fact that she followed in my footsteps. Literally.

Conversations I Will Never Have With Madonna

Kate Harding

"SO, I SAID I'd write an essay about Madonna," I tell my friend Anna, an editor who used to work at glossy magazines and celebrity weeklies, and thus knows from Her Madgesty.

"What's your angle?"

"I don't know yet. I was thinking of doing something about her ability to bounce back from failure-—"

"Reinvention, etcetera, etcetera," Anna interjects, sounding relieved that she's not the one who has to tell me, "Thanks, but we've already got something similar."

"No, I know everyone in the world has written about her reinventing herself. I'm talking about maintaining your ambition and self-confidence in the wake of abject fucking failure. Like, *Shanghai Surprise*–level failure."

Anna laughs. "I forgot about *Shanghai Surprise*."

"Everyone has! That's my point! But I don't know—I feel like I have about two paragraphs' worth of material on that subject, and then I'm back to not knowing what to say. Because my dirty little secret is, I just don't have strong feelings about Madonna, one way or another."

"There's your angle," says Anna. "That's one I've actually never seen before."

★

As a thirty-six-year-old feminist, I've come to feel the same way about Madonna as I do about porn. To wit, I get why some feminists will argue in favor of it, and I get why others insist it's degrading to women. I get that it's had a profound impact on our cultural expectations for women's behavior and appearance. I get that its enduring popularity across lines of class, race, and sexuality makes it a rich topic, worthy of serious discussion—and I get that it's really pretty weird for someone who writes about female oppression and empowerment to have no strong opinions on the subject.

And still, it's just sort of . . . not my issue.

I've found that most people will accept that dodge when it comes to discussing porn; when it comes to Madonna, though, folks want answers. How is it even possible to be neutral about one of the most influential and provocative women of the last three decades?

I don't know. *Shrug.*

★

In the interest of writing something more insightful, I visited Madonna's official website, looking for anything that might inspire passionate engagement, or even reignite the sincere appreciation I had for Ms. Ciccone circa 1986, when "Where's the Party?" was my favorite hairbrush-in-front-of-the-mirror jam. (Sure, I was eleven at the time, and my version of "losing control" was knocking back a Jolt cola and eating gummy bears until my stomach hurt, but when I sang "If you show me how/I'm ready now!" you'd better believe I meant it.)

Do you know what, out of all the elements of Madonna.com—photos and videos that once scandalized a nation, now-classic pop songs, a dissertation's worth of religious imagery, etcetera—actually caused me to gasp?

"Children's books! She writes best-fucking-selling children's books!" I holler angrily at my friend Gigi, who also happens to be my favorite local bartender and, in both capacities, often helps me work through writer's block.

"Everybody writes children's books now," says Gigi. "Jamie Lee Curtis, Katie Couric, Julianne Moore, Kelly Ripa, I think. They have a kid, and suddenly they're qualified to be authors."

And there it is, the root source of my uncharacteristically strong feelings about something Madonna's done: She's encroaching on my territory! I was fine when her umpteen self-reinventions only involved pursuits I have no real interest in, like acting and Jewish mysticism and going to the gym. But writing? I've spent the last twenty years learning how to be a writer, and all I've really got to show for it is one cowritten book and a handful of mostly defunct blogs. Madonna has written more than a dozen children's books in her spare time—like, as a hobby. I can't even finish crocheting a baby hat.

Gigi brings me another drink before I can ask for it.

★

"Did you see Lady Gaga at the Grammys?" asks my hairdresser, Corinne, as she, in her words, "restores my natural blonde."

"Naw," I say. "I usually just look at all the dresses online the next day." Also, I really hate making small talk into a mirror with a semi-stranger who's touching my head. But, like having a genuine interest in awards shows and claiming with an exaggerated wink that I don't color my hair, it's expected of a woman my age.

"You've got to watch it on YouTube," Corinne says, stabbing her paintbrush toward my reflection for emphasis. "She was exactly like Madonna from the high-ponytail-and-cone-bra era! It was unbelievable."

"Yeah, I keep hearing that the new song is a total Madonna rip-off."

It's true that I keep hearing it, but I don't actually believe it. I suppose I might have an easier time criticizing Lady Gaga for being derivative to the brink of copyright violation if everyone could agree on which song she supposedly plagiarized for "Born This Way." But in addition to "Express Yourself" (the most common answer), I've heard "Vogue," "Ray of Light," "Like a Prayer," and "Deeper and Deeper" mentioned—plus TLC's "Waterfalls," for that matter. Let me just throw a crazy idea out here: It's possible that Madonna songs are not quite as distinctive as her most devoted fans seem to believe they are, yeah? Who's with me?

As it is, I'm of the opinion that "Born This Way" does sound something like the Platonic ideal of a Madonna song, but not like an obvious retread of any particular one.

I mean, I don't know. *Shrug.*

"But you know what?" says Corinne. "They asked Madonna about it the next day, and she said it was all done with her blessing, and she thinks Lady Gaga is great."

"Well, that was gracious of her," I say.

What the fuck else was she going to say? I think.

This, how The Queen of Pop actually feels about an heiress apparent to her throne—one with a stronger voice and even more pronounced flair for the outrageous, no less—is something that interests me. So naturally, I'll never find out. Madonna is nothing if not a smart businesswoman, and the smart business move for a living legend is to humbly accept credit for a modest influence on your young successor and gratefully characterize any imitation as homage—even if "humble" and "grateful" belong in air quotes, and everyone knows it.

★

If I could talk to Madonna off the record—and if I were the kind of person to whom she'd tell the truth—I'd like to ask her about that. I would also ask:

- Does it kill you that Sean Penn is this big Oscar-winning star and director now, and everyone's pretty much forgotten about him hitting you with a baseball bat?
- Honey, what is going on with your face? Is it reversible?
- Would you have wanted kids if you couldn't afford round-the-clock nannies?
- Let's be real: A ghostwriter does the children's books, right?
- Will you buy me a house?

Madonna probably wouldn't like me very much.

But those are the kinds of conversations that might make me like her—or at least hate her enough to write a witty anti-Madonna screed in half the time it's taken me to get this far. I think I'd find her interesting as a person, but that's exactly how I'll never know her. And as a celebrity—i.e., a persona developed specifically to disguise everything human about her—she just doesn't turn my crank. I don't want to be her (I can't sing, I'm terrible with children, and sacrificing the quiet comforts of anonymity so completely would be my worst nightmare), or fuck her (I'm straight), but neither do I want to destroy her. And aren't those the basic options, when it comes to super-mega-giganto-stars?

What does it mean when we say we "love" or "hate" celebrities we've never met and never will? Either we identify so strongly with them that we imagine our own scarred and blemished skin glistening with reflected glory, or we decide that their very existence is such an assault on our values, the entire world would be improved by their absence. And the pedestal of superstardom is held precariously aloft by those two pillars; being neither "loved" nor "hated" is what drops one into the nobody-space between them. Madonna's career has survived nearly thirty years not just because she's a beautiful, ambitious woman with a knack for creating absurdly catchy pop songs, but because she infuriated Christians with her blasphemy and atheists with her woo; conservatives with her out-of-wedlock firstborn and progressives with her sketchy transnational adoptions; homophobes with her embrace of the gay community and the gay community with her embrace of reportedly homophobic Guy Ritchie. Etcetera, etcetera. The lady has a real talent for pissing people off.

And still, my envy of her publishing career notwithstanding, I don't hate her. Nor do I love her. The best explanation I can muster for my immunity to her provocations is that their cumulative effect reinforces how little I actually know about a woman who's been a regular presence at the periphery of my life since I was eight years old. One side effect of frequent reinvention, after all, is that the original model grows increasingly unrecognizable relative to the current one. Perhaps that was Madonna's goal all along, to erase any stray remnants of her genuine self that her public—loyal fans, passionate enemies, terrifying stalkers, and flattering admirers alike—might grab onto and greedily claim for their own.

I mean, I don't know. *Shrug.*

A Borderline History of My Relationship with Madonna

Erin Bradley

August 16, 1958

Madonna Louise Veronica Ciccone is born in Bay City, Michigan, home of Saint Stan's Polish festival, the founder of Avis Rent A Car, and geographically situated in what many refer to as "Michigan's Crotch."

May 5, 1976

I am born in St. Clair Shores, a Detroit suburb known for its beaches, marinas, and "Nautical Mile"—the perfect setting for a childhood spent avoiding the outdoors at all costs.

Late 1970s through early 1980s

Madonna moves to New York City and works odd jobs while trying to land a gig as a dancer. I'm already a dancer. My signature routine: 1. Put on Hall & Oates record. 2. Spin in circles. 3. Fall down while beaming head on coffee table.

My grandfather nicknames me "Keeker," which is Scottish for "black eye," or "grossly lacking in motor skill."

August 1, 1981

MTV makes its debut.

Summer 1983

I get my first taste of both MTV and Madonna when I see the videos for "Lucky Star" and "Borderline" at my friend Laurie's house (she has cable). I am in love. The music. The synchronized dancing. The outfits. I raid my mother's dresser for lace camisoles (she owns a total of two, both purchased at garage sales) and draw beauty marks above my lip with eyebrow pencil.

September 1984

Madonna performs "Like a Virgin" at the MTV Video Music Awards. My dad is watching from his La-Z-Boy. "This is ridiculous!" he says. "Pure sex." *Ummm, exactly.* An argument ensues. Eventually my mom lets me watch from her bedroom, where the screen's smaller but there's less commentary. She gives me Charleston Chews from her secret stash in the nightstand drawer.

November 1984

I round up all the rosaries in my grandmother's bedroom and attempt to wear them to Thanksgiving dinner as part of my kiddie "Boy Toy" ensemble. My mother puts a stop to it, explaining that the rosaries are, in fact, religious symbols, and not for accessorizing. I try bringing up the summer I went to Bible camp with a neighbor, but she effectively tells me to cut the shit and I take them off.

January 30, 1985

Madonna releases "Material Girl."

February 1985

My best friend and I choose "Material Girl" as the background music for our lip-sync and gymnastics routine in the school talent show. I prep for weeks in advance, making sexy faces in the mirror and turning my hair the color of a Number-2 pencil with Sun-In. Unlike Madonna, this does not earn me a slew of male admirers, though Andy Rubenstein does give me his fruit cocktail the next day at lunch.

April 1985

Shortly after our move to Pittsburgh, my parents take my sister and me to see *Desperately Seeking Susan*. I leave the theater with an unfortunate Junior Mints stain that looks suspiciously like poop on the back of my shorts, but I am otherwise buoyed by hope. My life is going to change from this point forward. I will dress how I want. Do what I want. Blast my armpits with hot air from a hand dryer in a public restroom and—this is critical—*I will own a poodle phone.*

April 1986

Nothing much has changed, mostly because I am a ten-year-old living in suburban Pittsburgh instead of a fictional twentysomething It Girl in mid-1980s New York. I have succeeded in getting my mom to let me wear more jelly bracelets, and my Cabbage Patch kid now has a jacket with a pyramid on the back, just like the one in the movie. I made it out of tempera paint and felt. The eye part of the pyramid keeps falling off and having to be re-glued, but otherwise it's pretty boss.

Spring 1987

Madonna's Spanish-inspired single "La Isla Bonita" and its accompanying video have renewed my interest in Latin men, which lay dormant since *CHiPs* was cancelled and I had to abruptly end it with Eric Estrada. Knowing zero about race and ethnicity, I do the samba in front of the mirror and serenade my (what I thought were) "Hispanic" lovers: Ralph Macchio (Italian), Henry Winkler (Jewish), and Scott Baio (Asshole).

December 1987

Madonna and husband Sean Penn file for divorce.

January 1988

Inspired by a Christmas vacation with my burnout cousins, I stage a dramatic breakup of my own. I decide that I must end it with pop music, putting away my childish posters of Michael Jackson and Cyndi Lauper and replacing them with more grown-up images of Aerosmith, Skid Row, and Guns N' Roses. Like an old teddy bear in corsets and lace gloves, Madonna is allowed to remain in the fold.

March 1989

Madonna catches flak for the controversial imagery in her "Like a Prayer" video. Many of my classmates aren't allowed to watch it. I am, and because of this I feel a sense of duty. I tape it on VHS and play it until the tracking wears out. I don't know if I learned anything about institutionalized racism by watching Ms. Ciccone dance in front of burning crosses. I did, however, learn that pushing your upper arms together and leaning slightly forward makes even paltry cleavage like mine look *enormous*.

March 20, 1990

Madonna releases "Vogue," spawning a dance craze consisting of a series of model-like expressions, movements, and poses.

May 18, 1990

I'm vogueing at the ninth-grade Spring Fling in a black-and-white silk polka-dot blouse with matching scrunchie and linen Bermuda shorts. Had Anna Wintour anything in her desiccated little stomach, I'm sure she would have vomited.

November 1990

I watch the extended, uncensored version of "Justify My Love" at a friend's house. It's boring, even for a horned-up fourteen-year-old whose access to titillating imagery starts and ends with her parents' copy of *The Joy of Sex* and a crumbling *Playgirl* of dubious origin. *Why is she doing this?* I wonder.

December 1990

Madonna is dating Vanilla Ice. I'm dating a redneck that speaks Ebonics and shaves lines into his eyebrows. Sign of the times, or are Madge and I on the same cosmic course?

Fall 1994

Madonna releases her sixth studio album, "Bedtime Stories." My parents release me to college. No one seems particularly thrilled about either one.

Spring 1995

Madonna is hosting pajama parties to promote her new album "Bedtime Stories" (clever, right? shut up) and studying up on Argentinean political leaders for her *Evita* role. I'm wearing pajamas and enrolled in Women's Studies courses.

Fall 1995

I walk into a campus head shop and buy my boyfriend a poster of Madonna topless. Yes, he's gawking at a nude woman that's not me and yes, it's an airbrushed and sexualized depiction of an unattainable ideal. My professor would be disappointed, but for some reason, I am okay with it. Maybe it's because Madonna looks happy—not like she's been drugged and beaten with an extension cord. Maybe it's because I've had this feeling, ever since I was a kid, that Madonna doesn't do anything Madonna doesn't want to do. It's what I've always admired about her. I'll learn later in class that this is called "sexual agency," but all I know now is that instead of the usual insecurity I feel around images of beautiful women, I just feel free. Sophisticated. Worldly.

October 1996

Madonna gives birth to her first child, Lourdes, and shacks up with fitness trainer/baby daddy Carlos Leon.

May 1997

I shack up with a mechanic and land my first white-collar job. An engagement soon follows. Maybe Madonna and I are growing up? That, or we have a thing for hot guys who fail at making money.

1997 – 1999

Madonna gets into Kabbalah. I pretend to get into (or at least not openly bitch about) my fiancé's family's Christian beliefs, which include "Adam and Eve, not Adam and Steve" and other sayings best confined to ignorant bumper stickers. Only time will tell who's the bigger sellout.

February 1998

Madonna releases "Frozen." In the video, she's dressed like an Indian princess who runs a sideline business in Renaissance garb. There's a flock of birds and lots of jam band-looking dance moves. I'm about to graduate from college and am finding it harder and harder to relate to this woman. The constant transformation is becoming a bit much. Was my dad right all this time? Is she really one big gimmick?

January 2001

Madonna shows up at the premiere of husband Guy Ritchie's new movie wearing a jacket with "Mrs. Ritchie" spelled out on the back in rhinestones. Is she having a laugh or trying to reassure the new hubby that her fame won't eclipse his manhood? I want to think it's the former but I have this uneasy feeling in my right ovary.

August 2002

Madonna may be settled in to domesticity, but I'm not. I leave my second big relationship in which I've managed to dodge marriage, and I move to New York. Among my first stops is the Port Authority Bus Terminal, where I try to recreate the armpit scene from *Desperately Seeking Susan*. Unfortunately, the nozzle on the hand dryer no longer spins around and I look like I'm trying to steal it for scrap metal. I leave the ladies' room heartbroken.

Fall 2003

Madonna French-kisses Britney Spears at the Video Music Awards, setting off a whole mess of controversy. Newly single in the city I feel has been waiting for me all my life, I French-kiss everyone, including but not limited to: my best girl friend, a bartender, a jogger in the middle of a run, a lawyer who works for Johnnie Cochran, and a union steward who talks like Elmer Fudd.

2004 – 2006

I'm working my butt off in advertising. Neon and all things New Wave are back in stores. It hits me that I'm no longer a kid scrounging through my parents' dresser for anything Madonna-esque. I have the freedom. I have the purchasing power. I can go as far with this as I want. So why am I buying cardigans? Damn you, being old.

March 10, 2008

Madonna is inducted into The Rock and Roll Hall of Fame. I am proud, though with the exception of *The Immaculate Collection* it's been about ten years since I've intentionally listened to any of her albums. Is it because her music's so clubby now? Or has she become one of those girls from high school who I don't hang out with anymore because she's way too into Pilates and her husband's a total pill?

2009 – 2010

Major shit is going down. Madonna's adoption of baby David is criticized in the press. She and Guy are getting divorced. Despite all this, Madonna continues to put out albums and go on tour. I'm starting to warm up to her again. It doesn't matter whether I approve of her *Confessions on a Dance Floor* leotard fixation or her prepubescent boyfriend. She just keeps going. I find this kind of consistency—even if it's from someone known for inconsistency—comforting.

July 30, 2011

Speaking of comforting, I am engaged now. And unlike my previous serious relationships, I'm going into this one full of joy and hope. I've become a saying on a hand-painted magnet you buy at the county fair. A Hallmark card. My guy is seven years younger and doesn't remember much about Madonna pre-"Vogue." I'm okay with that because Kurt Cobain is his Madonna, and that's not a bad substitute.

The Future

Although I can't imagine a world without her, I suppose one day I'll be watching the evening news or whatever passes for it and hear that she's passed on. I'll try and fail to explain the significance of this to my daughters, with that same searching look my mom gets when she talks to me about John F. Kennedy. Don't get me wrong; I like JFK, philandering richie or no. But with Madonna, I think you had to be there. And I'm glad I was.

Justify My Love

Emily Nussbaum

WHEN MADONNA CLIMBS out of the shining water in *Desperately Seeking Susan*, the audience gasps. At this recent late-night showing at 92YTribeca, the 1985 comedy holds up remarkably well—there's all that East Village New Wave energy, those dizzy scenes in Battery Park, the whole notion of New York as a machine that makes you more interesting the minute you enter Port Authority. But really, it's all about Madonna, squishing poor Rosanna Arquette right out of the picture. With her Italian nose and that jutting jaw and the baby-Elvis air of manipulation, Madonna is at once recognizable and something we haven't seen in years. She's a human wink.

Afterward, in the bathroom of 92YTribeca, I notice three girls from the front row. They'd been sitting dead center, but even from the back, they looked like the kind of people who knew they were attracting attention: a pale girl in black braids and a white eyelet dress, a tomboy in an oversize gold lamé baseball hat, the third in a bright orange romper. They are all in their twenties, they explain, coworkers at the same clothing store in Brooklyn. And in a chorus of enthusiasm, they gush over the Madonna of the movie, who is the reason they've come, their role model, their inspiration—even back in high school, which was not so long ago.

"She's so incredible!" they say. "So badass!"

One tells me dreamily that Madonna reminds them of the character Rayanne on *My So-Called Life*, another bad-girl catalyst—that special person who will bully us into becoming not better, exactly, but more exciting, with stories to tell. Yet when I ask what they think of Madonna today, they look uncomfortable and glance in unison away from me and into the mirrors.

"Now it's like, what do we have in common—?"

"I mean, she's twenty-six in this movie. She's a very hip fifty-year-old, but now it's just for show . . ."

Everything about the current Madonna makes them uncomfortable: the Kabbalah, the adoptions, the British accent. But they don't want to betray her. Maybe she couldn't always be "the girl you saw on Second Avenue." The plastic surgery troubles them the most, but then Orange Romper blurts out aggressively: "Hey, I'd do the same thing! I'd get surgery and Botox and . . ." She looks at her friends with a pugnacious air: "When you're that big a star, would you want everyone to see you that way, old and saggy, a has-been? What else could she do? Wouldn't you do it, too?"

Madonna has returned to New York.

This makes a strange kind of sense.

After all, Madonna Louise Ciccone's original arrival here, seven years before *Desperately Seeking Susan*, has long been one of Manhattan's primal myths. She was that brassy, motherless nineteen-year-old dance major from Michigan—the busty one with the unshaved armpits—who asked a cab driver to drop her where the action was. That was Times Square, late summer 1978. She jumped from the dance world to Danceteria, from the Russian Tea Room coat check to nude modeling, spending four years seducing and abandoning DJs, agents, and artists, impatiently waiting to become the famous person she clearly knew herself to be already. Terrible things happened to her (early on, a stranger forced her up to a tenement roof at knife-point and raped her), but that didn't sap her ambition, it fueled her: She kept snapping up influences like a magnet, pursuing a modern style of fame that was as much about her own charisma as about anything she created.

In those early years, with the rubber bangles and huge crucifixes hanging off her like bell tongues, Madonna was paired in the public imagination with Michael Jackson. For a while, they were twin MTV phenomena, each with an outsize, candy-cartoon quality, dancers as much as they were singers, crossing lines of race and sexuality (they even had that weird publicity date at the 1991 Academy Awards). But unlike Jackson, Madonna was no child star. She'd built herself; and while Michael Jackson's image was vulnerability, hers was proud control. She rejected the idea of being a victim, almost to a fault. Over the years, this vision of discipline as transcendence crackled, hardened, becoming at once awesome and alienating, creating a riddle for fans: How to reconcile that early Madonna with what she'd become?

Because now Madonna is back in Manhattan and, according to the gossip press, very busy: divorcing, adopting, hypnotizing baseball stars out of their marriages with Kabbalah, dangling Latino boy toys, occupying an uptown mansion and "shocking" people with bunny-eared fashion statements. I want to feel happy about this, since I am the kind of fool who gets excited by stars inhabiting my city. But instead, I feel unnerved, unsettled—thrown off by the Madonna who slouches toward the Upper East Side to be (for the thousandth time) reborn.

Now, bear in mind, for many years I adored Madonna, defended her to strangers—I was a fan, if not quite a wannabe. I graduated from high school the year Madonna exploded, and even in that initial incarnation it was clear that the woman was going to be a living collect-them-all doll collection. She seemed to shoot out new selves every six months—from Jellybean Benitez Madonna to Madonna of the Boy-Toy Belt, Unshaved Leaked Photos Madonna, Madonna masturbating on a wedding cake, bouncing beside the waves in "Cherish," dancing with the little boy in "Open Your Heart," *Who's That Girl* Eyebrows Madonna, Ideal Brunette Madonna (my favorite) saving Black Jesus in that incredible slip, Banned by the Pope! Madonna, "Vogue" Madonna, Fritz Lang Madonna, Wrapped-Plastic *Sex*-Book Madonna, Shame-Free BDSM Madonna, Sandra Bernhard–BFF Madonna, Bratty Letterman-Taunting Madonna, Self-Mocking *Wayne's World* Madonna, the Madonna Who Ate Your Exotic Culture ("Vogue," "Rain," "La Isla Bonita"), Abused Sean Penn Madonna of the Helicopters, Contrarian I'm Gonna Keep My Baby Teen-Slut Madonna, Secretly Pregnant While Filming *Evita* Madonna, Underappreciated *Dick Tracy*/Sondheim Madonna, Water-Bottle-Fellating *Truth or Dare* Madonna (with Warren Beatty accessory), Bad Actress Madonna (Wax-Coated/Mamet), Momma Madonna, Kabbalah Esther, British Madge, and on and on.

For years, Madonna felt like a slippery, elegant key to all feminine mythologies, a shape-shifter inspiring to any young girl (or anyone) who felt her shape shifting. In high school, I was friends with a Madonna wannabe, a girl who jumped right on the underwear-as-outerwear phenomenon. At a party, she confided in me about kissing strangers: She loved that BOY TOY belt Madonna wore—she got the humor of it, the wink. For so many women I knew, she was a living permission slip, suggesting not bravery, exactly, but something more accessible: bravado.

Besides, her music was fun to dance to and she fit nicely with a lot of things I liked, like third-wave feminism and reclaiming words like *slut* and *queer*. Half her songs were about orgasm ("Borderline," "Like a Virgin"), way before Christina Aguilera and Lady Gaga. And she had an intriguing ability to inspire startling hostility and contempt in men. One hippieish boyfriend hated her but couldn't say why, almost stuttering as he tried to explain: She seemed to be taunting him, he decided. A male friend who did like Madonna told me he felt required to have sex with her if asked: "It would be like being seduced by PepsiCo." (He meant this as a compliment.)

I enjoyed mouthing off in her defense right through the whole plastic-wrapped *Sex*-book period, until suddenly, somewhere in the late nineties, something bad started happening to my beloved multiple Madonnas, and my loyalty was severely tested.

The first shock was the morning I flipped through her children's book *The English Roses* in the now-closed Astor Place Barnes & Noble. *The English Roses* was the story of a sweet and perfect girl, Binah, picked on by a clique of jealous conformists. Then a fairy visits them and they discover that Binah is not merely prettier, but also kinder, simply better in every way, and they are ashamed when they peer through her window, only to discover that (a) she had no mother, and (b) she worked very, very hard.

It was her daughter, Lourdes's, envied-child-of-the-famous story braided into Madonna's tragic history of having lost her mother as a child—and the moral was that if you didn't like someone, you were just jealous. Except the book seemed oddly bullying in itself (the Roses were named after girls who went to school with Lourdes, after all). And the protagonist was the blandest, most passive good-girl on Earth, the opposite of Madonna: Patient Griselda Madonna, not Susan.

This was something new. Madonna had always been preachy (which kind of worked during the sadomasochism-is-freedom stage, when she chanted, "I ain't your bitch/don't hang your shit on me"), but now she'd turned downright sanctimonious—and worse, Millennium Madonna, unlike earlier Madonnas, was chiding her former selves instead of shedding them, turning those baby Madonnas (skanky, effervescently selfish visions!) into lessons. For a while, I wavered between Madonna Love and Madonna Hate. I did not much like British Madge, but I was okay with the pathos of the Guy Ritchie *Swept Away* era—there was something affecting about

Madonna's failure to be a movie star (her bossy self always poking through), and all those quotes about learning to compromise. That wasn't very Madonna, but it's not like I wanted Madonna to have a bad marriage. And who doesn't want to share, to grow? It's good to be unselfish! The selfless Madonna is less inspiring than the selfish one in so many ways.

But soon the bad Madonnas were pouring out in a rush: Lady of the Countryside Madonna, Tone-Deaf Antiwar Madonna, and particularly Hard Body and Plastic Surgery Madonna of the Purple Bodysuit. There were elements of this stream of Madonnas that I admired and feared, kind of the same thing when it comes to Madonna. There was Never Grow Old Madonna, turning fifty. There was Healthy Yoga Madonna, which I couldn't trust, because she was hard to distinguish from Baby-Cheeks Botox Madonna. There was Momma Madonna, to whom I was sympathetic, and I didn't have a problem with the Malawi thing per se, although it didn't look great from the outside.

But then, the world had changed.

For one thing, there was Angelina Jolie, who had emerged as an alternate Madonna, the Gallant to Madonna's Goofus, her cultish sanctimony somehow more earned. In every other previous iconic face-off—Madonna versus Cyndi Lauper, Madonna versus Britney and Christina—Madonna won, or, in the strange case of Britney Spears, seemingly sucked out her soul live onstage, a vampire-lesbian smooch that left poor Brit stumbling away into young motherhood and nervous breakdowns. (What kind of amazing celebrity act is it when you kiss Christina Aguilera and no one even notices?)

So yes, there was something amazing about her ability to suck the soul out of Britney Spears and also to survive the desire of all horses to kill her, à la *The Ring*.

And yet, I finally had to face the fact that the Madonna I had loved for years—who'd become to me, of course, not a real person but an abstraction, which I'd like to believe was her aim all along—was giving me chills of discomfort, just as she was returning to my city.

And of course, it was a new city as well, a Times Square filled with people rearranging the deck chairs.

So I wandered over to Love Saves the Day on Second Avenue, where Madonna's Susan traded her pyramid-embroidered coat for those tempting boots. (Why do all New York girl-fables center on footwear?) It was gone: closed shop in January. I checked out her recently purchased redbrick Upper East Side mansion in its peculiarly staid uptown location between Lexington and Third Avenue—and then went over to the Kabbalah Center, likewise quiet, with a maid mopping up as I flipped through the sequel to *The English Roses*. (Just as grating as the original.) And I called some people who I felt could argue me back into my more welcoming self.

"I totally love and worship Madonna," music critic Rob Sheffield tells me. "She brought New York to the rest of the country—the rest of the world, I guess." Long before he became a critic, Sheffield saw *Desperately Seeking Susan* at a mall in suburban Boston, and it defined Manhattan for him: "When you'd walk past one of those scenes, you'd feel 'Madonna has trod here.'"

Every time I start in on my troubles with her persona, Sheffield steers me back to her music. She propagated a unique fantasy, he says, "different from the punk idea, which was that you could become a decadent figure of cinematic tragedy, of sinister charisma." Madonna may have had punk trappings, might have dated Basquiat and mimicked Blondie, but her take on urban squalor was optimistic: not the "beautiful loser" but the disco winner. And while other disco stars longed to do gospel or soul instead, Madonna was a rare devotee: "She never stopped loving that particular sound."

Sheffield's never heard of *The English Roses*. As for Kabbalah, he points out, "You know, if she made bad records about being spiritually awakened, that's one thing—but she made a really good one, the *Ray of Light* album."

This is the way writer Wendy Shanker sees her, too: as a spiritual figure. Shanker's written an upcoming book about finding a guru, concluding that it is Madonna. ("I hope she thinks that's cool and not weird.") Like me, Wendy identified strongly with Madonna's vision of freedom, after a "conversion" experience at a Blonde Ambition concert; her most cherished memory comes from a brief job at MTV, when she found herself assisting the singer, yelling at the head of the network: "Madonna is going to do what Madonna wants!"

But unlike mine, Shanker's loyalty never faded. "Yeah, I think the Kabbalah stuff is crazy. But is that the craziest thing a celebrity has ever done? So Madonna wants to drink expensive water, so what? She wants to help a child, she pays for ten thousand orphans to get food! I don't know why people hate her so much."

It's the body, we conclude simultaneously. That aging/ageless body. "It's shocking to look at this picture on my wall, compared to the way she looks now," admits Shanker, describing a 1990 *Harper's Bazaar* portrait above her desk. "Somehow, she seems to stress people out. She still seems to have something to prove."

It's true. Maybe it's because I'm getting older along with her, but watching Madonna strut past fifty—hips grinding in high heels, posing legs spread—brings out anxious, contradictory emotions. It's become taboo to criticize stars for plastic surgery—both because it is their choice and because they have no choice—but each time I glimpse that grinning mask, I wonder why it's impossible for Madonna, with all her power, her will to shock, to ever stop "giving good face"? I try to persuade myself to admire her most New York qualities (ambition, workaholism); I tell myself she's a dancer, and this is what dancers do. But I feel exhausted just witnessing the effort it must take to maintain this vision of eternal youth.

Two days later, I find myself doing my daily Google search. Two workers died in an accident at her stage in France; she's broken up with Jesus Luz; also, the Poles are protesting because she's performing on a Catholic holiday. She's collaborating with the New York artist Marilyn Minter! A greatest-hits album drops this fall. And bloggers are examining her upper arms for indications of "bingo wings." Then I follow pointers on Twitter and find myself watching a YouTube clip of "Hung Up" from the 2006 Confessions Tour—one of many recent songs, I suddenly notice, studded with tick-tock sounds and countdowns—with Madonna doing seductive pelvic pops, then reaching out, drawing from her fans the eerie chant "Time goes by! So slowly . . ."

And hearing the roar of the faithful brings me back, all over again. Because, perverse as it sounds, the tougher Madonna gets, the more she invokes protectiveness and a kind of pride. In the eighties, during those endless debates about date rape and porn, she was our sacrificial anti-victim, jumping into the slut-pit before she could be thrown, magnetizing contempt: She'd play the tease, the porn star, the dominatrix, eager to control that imagery rather than let it swallow her. She predated and predicted *Girls Gone Wild* culture, blogs, reality TV, the whole exhibitionistic brand-me wave of modern female culture; she surfed over and then tried to surf past it. If she's hardened in the process, maybe that's because she was the first to step up and take it; she was a shield. Now she's catalyzing a new set of insults, that cougar-MILF catcall, with its attendant put-downs—she's "desperate," "pathetic," "trying too hard." And maybe she is.

Sometimes I think she is. But while other female icons fade, fold, or fossilize into camp, for better or worse, Madonna seems determined to do something unsettling and new: spin to the center of the dance floor, till the end.

About the Contributors

LAURA M. ANDRÉ received her PhD from the University of North Carolina at Chapel Hill, where she paid tribute to the Pepper's Madonna as often as she could. After a brief stint as a university professor, she now owns her own business and works for a bookseller specializing in rare and contemporary photography books. She has written for the anthologies *Ask Me About My Divorce: Women Open Up About Moving On* (Seal Press, 2009) and *Queer Girls in Class: Lesbian Teachers and Students Tell Their Classroom Stories* (Peter Lang, 2010). With Candace Walsh, she recently edited the anthology *Dear John, I Love Jane: Women Write about Leaving Men for Women* (Seal Press, 2010), and she is currently editing an anthology about women and mental health called *It's All in Her Head: Women Making Peace with Troubled Minds*. She lives in Santa Fe, New Mexico.

LESLEY ARFIN is the author of the drug-addled memoir *Dear Diary*. She has written for *Jane*, *Paper*, Jezebel.com, iD, *NYLON*, *Russh*, and is the former editor-in-chief of *Missbehave* magazine. She has also written many things on the Internet, which you can find by googling her name. Lesley is currently working on a television show and by the time this comes out, may or may not be based in Los Angeles.

CHRISTINE BACHMAN is a recent graduate of Middlebury College and currently works in the nonprofit sector in Boston. At Middlebury, she majored in Sociology and Women's and Gender Studies, and plans to attend graduate school to continue her studies in the Sociology and Queer Theory fields. She is deeply passionate about queer theory, queer culture, and feminism, and wishes to thank her parents for raising her in a world that constantly tests the boundaries between queer and normative.

JAMIE BECKMAN is a New York City–based freelance writer and the author of *The Frisky 30-Day Breakup Guide*. She has written about relationships, health, and lifestyle trends for magazines including *Glamour, Redbook, Men's Journal, Men's Health, First for Women*, and *Better Homes and Gardens*, and websites such as SheKnows and The Frisky.

ERIN BRADLEY is a writer and journalist living and working in New York City. She's written for and appeared in publications including *The Daily Beast, Nerve, Playboy, The Morning News*, and *College Humor*. Her book, *Every Rose Has Its Thorn: A Rock 'n' Roll Guide to Guys* is available on Amazon.com.

LISA CRYSTAL CARVER wrote a few books (*Rollerderby*, etc.) and a couple thousand articles, toured several countries (Suckdog), had a couple kids and husbands and houses, tried out a dozen different drugs and philosophies and pretty much each branch of the sex industry, bought and scratched or sold again many thousands of pieces of music . . . all this would have been so-o-o different had she accepted that full scholarship to be a history major twenty years ago.

GLORIA FELDT is a women's activist, speaker, and bestselling author of four books. Her latest, *No Excuses: 9 Ways Women Can Change How We Think About Power*, has been called "indispensable" by Gloria Steinem. The former president of Planned Parenthood Federation of America, she teaches "Women, Power, and Leadership" at Arizona State University. Find out more at www.GloriaFeldt.com and follow her @GloriaFeldt and on Facebook. She's married to Alex Barbanell; they share a combined family of six children and fourteen grandchildren.

MARY K. FONS is a full-time freelance writer, a nationally ranked slam poet, and has been a proud Neo-Futurist since 2005. She holds a B.A. in Theatre Arts from the University of Iowa. She is an original ensemble member of Chicago's Gift Theatre Company, Marc Smith's Speakeasy, and the Islesford Theater Project. A Green Mill slam champion, Mary teaches poetry workshops to high schoolers throughout Illinois and writes, directs, and performs approximately twenty-five weeks a year in Chicago's longest-running late-night performance art extravaganza, *Too Much Light Makes The Baby Go Blind*. A Driehaus grant recipient, and a LaMaMa E.T.C. Playwright Retreat participant (2010), Mary has performed her original work from D.C. to NYC, to Seattle and plenty of venues in between. She also cohosts the nationally-aired PBS program *Love of Quilting* and is creator, co-producer, and host of "Quilty," an online quilting show for rookie quilters at QNNtv.com. For the blog and more on Mary, visit www.maryfons.com. She wears her "Boy Toy" belt unironically.

STACEY MAY FOWLES is a writer and magazine professional living in Toronto. Her first novel, *Be Good*, was published by Tightrope Books in 2007. *This Magazine* called it "probably the most finely realized small press novel to come out of Canada in the last year." In fall 2008 she released an illustrated novel, *Fear of Fighting*, and staged a theatrical adaptation of it with Nightwood Theatre. The novel was later selected as a National Post Canada Also Reads pick for 2010. Her writing has appeared in various magazines and journals, and has been anthologized in *Nobody Passes: Rejecting The Rules of Gender* *and Conformity; First Person Queer; Yes Means Yes;* and PEN Canada's *Finding The Words.* Most recently, she coedited the anthology *She's Shameless: Women Write About Growing Up, Rocking Out and Fighting Back.* She is the former publisher of *Shameless* magazine, and currently works at *The Walrus.*

MARIA GAGLIANO is an editor, publisher, and writer based in Brooklyn, NY. By day, she's an editor at Perigee, an imprint of Penguin Group (USA), where she edits everything from pop culture books to craft beer guides. She is also cofounder and copublisher of *Slice,* a nonprofit literary magazine dedicated to helping new writers have their voices heard. Her food and culture blog, www.PomatoRevival.com, has been praised by Salon.com and Martha Stewart's blog network, Martha's Circle. Her writing has also appeared in *BUST* magazine, *Edible Brooklyn,* BrooklynBased.net, and *Slice,* among other publications. She can be reached at www.mariagagliano.com.

KATE HARDING is a Chicago-based feminist writer who coauthored *Lessons from the Fat-o-Sphere: Quit Dieting and Declare a Truce with Your Body,* contributed to *The Book of Jezebel,* and blogged for the late, lamented Shapely Prose (which she founded in 2007) and Broadsheet. You might also know her from Twitter (@kateharding).

JEN HAZEN is the music editor for *BUST* magazine in New York City. She's also the founder of ImitationObjects.com, a website which is basically her daily make-out session with music, bikes, art, design, and the city. Jen's work has appeared in *Time Out Chicago, JANE magazine, Chicago Sun-Times, Chicagoist,* and *Thought Catalog.* Other credits include a piece in the St. Martins book *Cassette From My Ex,* and quotes featured in the books *Girl Power: The '90s Revolution in Music,* and *How Sassy Changed My Life: A Love Letter to the Greatest Teen Magazine of All Time.*

SONIAH KAMAL was born in Pakistan and raised in England and Saudi Arabia. She came to the United States for her undergraduate degree and earned a B.A. in Philosophy with Honors from St. John's College in Annapolis, MD. Soniah's undergraduate thesis, an analysis of individual against society as seen in love and arranged marriages, was the recipient of the Susan B. Irene Award. Soniah wrote a weekly satire column (2002-2004) for the national newspaper *The Daily Times* in Pakistan. Soniah's short stories have been published in the United States, Canada, Pakistan, and India, as well as in collections published by Penguin India, Harper Collins India, and in the United States, by The Feminist Press. Soniah has lived in New Mexico, Maryland, Virginia, Colorado, Illinois, New Jersey, California, and presently resides in Georgia. For more of Soniah's work, visit www.soniahkamal.com.

COLLEEN KANE would rather hang out with Cyndi Lauper than Madonna, but has been known to bring the house down at karaoke with "Like a Prayer." She is a New Jersey-born writer who lives in Brooklyn, but is a citizen of the world. Read more at www.ColleenKane.com.

SHAWNA KENNEY is the author of *Imposters* (Mark Batty Publisher) and the award-winning internationally translated memoir *I Was a Teenage Dominatrix* (Last Gasp). Her work has appeared in *Ms.*, *BUST, Juxtapoz, AP*, the *Florida Review,* and various other outlets.

BEE LAVENDER was born and raised in the Pacific Northwest but emigrated to Europe in 2004, where she lives in London with her family. Her books include a memoir about danger titled *Lessons in Taxidermy* and the anthologies *Breeder* and *Mamaphonic*. Other work appears in numerous magazines, newspapers, anthologies, and radio programs in both the United States and the United Kingdom. Bee is the publisher of the online edition of *Hip Mama* and created and publishes Girl-Mom, an advocacy website for teen parents.

CAROLINE LEAVITT is the award-winning author of nine novels, most recently *Pictures of You.* A book critic for the *Boston Globe* and *People*, she lives in Hoboken, New Jersey, with her husband, the writer Jeff Tamarkin, and their young son, Max.

TAMARA LYNCH is a freelance writer and blogger focusing on interracial culture in New York City.

AMANDA MARCOTTE is a freelance writer and blogger who writes for Pandagon, Slate's Double X, and RH Reality Check. She's published two books, *It's A Jungle Out There: The Feminist Survival Guide to Politically Inhospitable Environments* and *Get Opinionated: A Progressive's Guide to Finding Your Voice (And Taking a Little Action).*

COURTNEY E. MARTIN is a feminist commentator and nationally renowned speaker. She is the author of *Do It Anyway: The New Generation of Activists* and *Perfect Girls, Starving Daughters: How the Quest for Perfection is Harming Young Women.* She is an editor at Feministing.com, and a senior correspondent at *The American Prospect.* She is also the coeditor of the anthology *Click: Moments When We Became Feminists.* Courtney lives in Brooklyn and owns a chin-length, platinum blonde wig in case the opportunity ever presents itself to dress like Madonna. You can read more about her work at www.courtney emartin.com.

KRISTIN MCGONIGLE lives in New York City. Her work has appeared in *Pindeldyboz, LIT* and various places online. She is currently at work on a novel.

EMILY NUSSBAUM is a contributing editor at *New York* magazine and writes primarily about pop culture, technology, and women's issues.

MARIA RAHA is the author of *Cinderella's Big Score: Women of the Punk and Indie Underground* and *Hellions: Pop Culture's Rebel Women,* both published by Seal Press. Her work has also appeared in the anthologies *Young Wives' Tales: New Adventures in Love and Partnership* and *The W Effect: Bush's War on Women*. She lives in Philadelphia.

DANA ROSSI's work has appeared in *Time Out New York, InDigest, The Retroist, Broken Pencil*, and *New York Press*, where a feature she wrote on actors understudying celebrities on Broadway won a 2008 New York Press Association Award. Dana is the host of The Soundtrack Series, a live storytelling event in New York where writers tell stories based on a song from their past. She was in the front row at Madison Square Garden for the *Confessions on a Dance Floor* tour. She swears Madonna looked right at her.

J. VICTORIA SANDERS is a journalist, lecturer, writer and librarian who lives in Austin, Texas. Her feminist criticism, personal essays, and book reviews have appeared in several anthologies, including *Click: When We Knew We Were Feminists* and *Homelands*. She has written for *Publisher's Weekly, Bitch* magazine, *VIBE*, half a dozen newspapers, and online for Feministing and The Root. She blogs at jvictoriawrites.tumblr.com.

ADA SCOTT received her MFA in writing from Brooklyn College. She has been published in numerous literary journals and is at work on a novel about boxing.

WENDY SHANKER's humorous, hopeful memoir about women and body image, *The Fat Girl's Guide to Life* (Bloomsbury USA) changed the way women around the world relate to their bodies. It has been published in ten languages including Italian, German, Spanish, Chinese, and Polish (but not French—because French women don't get fat). Wendy's byline has appeared in *Glamour, Self, Shape, Cosmopolitan, Us Weekly* (Fashion Police), alternative mags like *BUST* and *Bitch*, and on MTV. Her latest book, *Are You My Guru? How Medicine, Medi-*

tation & Madonna Saved My Life, was published by NAL Trade/Penguin. Find her online at www.wendyshanker.com.

SUSAN SHAPIRO is a popular Manhattan writing professor and the author of eight books, including *Overexposed, Lighting Up, Only As Good As Your Word, Secrets of a Fix-Up Fanatic* and the upcoming *Unhooked. Speed Shrinking* and *Five Men Who Broke My Heart* have both been optioned for films. Find her online at www.susanshapiro.net.

SARAH STODOLA is a writer and editor living in New York. She has written for *The New York Times, New York magazine, The Fiscal Times, Forbes Traveler, Slate, Stop Smiling* magazine and others.

SARAH SWEENEY is a North Carolina-bred poet and essayist. Her works have been featured in *Barrelhouse, PANK, Quarterly West, Best of the Web*, and more. Find her online at www.sarah-sweeney.com.

WENDY NELSON TOKUNAGA is the author of the novels *Love in Translation* and *Midori by Moonlight*, both published by St. Martin's Press. She is also the author of the nonfiction e-book *Marriage in Translation: Foreign Wife, Japanese Husband*. She holds an MFA in Writing from the University of San Francisco and teaches writing at Stanford University's Online Writer's Studio. Her favorite Madonna song is "Into the Groove."

ERIN TRAHAN was born in the same town as Madonna, grew up in the Cherry Capital of the World, and now lives next door to a descendant of a persecuted Salem witch. By day she is a writer and editor specializing in film and travel. She has contributed to *The Boston Globe*, New Hampshire Public Radio, *Girl Scout Leader Magazine*, NewEnglandFilm.com and has co-authored three Frommer's Guides to Montreal and Quebec City. As the editor of The Independent, an online magazine about film and its related books on filmmaking, she often serves on film festival panels and juries. By night she writes essays and poems and reads poetry submissions for AGNI. She earned an MFA in poetry from Bennington College in 2010.

REBECCA TRAISTER writes for Salon. She is the author of *Big Girls Don't Cry: The Election that Changed Everything for American Women* (Free Press).

KELLY KEENAN TRUMPBOUR is currently working on a memoir about her experience with infertility. She has published personal essays on Lifetime Television's mylifetime.com, the NPR-affiliated Stoop Storytelling Series, and D.C. Story League, audaciousideas. org, and *Urbanite* magazine. Her first book, *Working at Interest Groups and Nonprofits*, was praised by author and former White House Social Secretary Letitia Bladridge as "a walking primer of information . . . inspiring in its message."

JESSICA VALENTI, who was called the "poster girl for third-wave feminism" by Salon and one of the Top 100 Inspiring Women in the world by The Guardian, is the author of three books: *Full Frontal Feminism: A Young Woman's Guide to Why Feminism Matters, He's a Stud, She's a Slut . . . and 49 Other Double Standards Every Woman Should Know*, and *The Purity Myth: How America's Obsession with Virginity is Hurting Young Women*, which is being made into a documentary by the Media Education Foundation. She is the editor of the anthology *Yes Means Yes: Visions of Female Sexual Power and a World Without Rape*, which was named one of Publishers Weekly's Top 100 Books of 2009. Jessica is also the founder of Feministing.com, which *Columbia Journalism Review* calls "head and shoulders above almost any writing on women's issues in mainstream media." Jessica won the 2011 Hillman Journalism Prize for her work with Feministing.

CINTRA WILSON is a culture critic, author, and frequent contributor to *The New York Times*. Her books include *A Massive Swelling: Celebrity Re-Examined As a Grotesque, Crippling Disease*, the novels *Colors Insulting to Nature, Caligula for President: Better American Living through Tyranny* and the upcoming *Fear and Clothing: Unbuckling America's Fashion Destiny*, which will be released by WW Norton in 2012.

JAMIA WILSON is a feminist activist, organizer, expat-brat, networker, cartwheeler, truth seeker, and storyteller. She is currently Vice President of Programs at the Women's Media Center, where she amplifies women's voices and changes the conversation in the media. She trains women and girls so they are media-ready and media-savvy, exposes sexism in the media, and directs the WMC's social media strategy. Learn more at www.jamiawilson.com.

KIM WINDYKA also told her mom she was starring as Dorothy in a school production of *The Wizard of Oz* in order to get red shoes (she wasn't). She has written for *Metro Boston*, the *New Hampshire Visitors Guide*, the *Nashua Telegraph*, Orbitz and more, and still counts "Vogue" among her favorite songs of all time.

About the Editor

Courtesy of the author.

LAURA BARCELLA is a writer and editor who is perpetually trying to decide between San Francisco and New York. She has written about pop culture, feminism, and lifestyles for more than forty publications, including the *Village Voice, Salon, Time Out New York, ELLEGirl, BUST, NYLON, AlterNet,* and the *Chicago Sun-Times.* She's also the author of *The End: 50 Apocalytic Visions From Pop Culture That You Should Know About . . . Before It's Too Late,* a teen pop-culture book about the apocalypse (Zest Books, 2012), and has contributed to the anthologies *BITCHFest: Ten Years of Cultural Criticism From the Pages of Bitch Magazine, Somebody's Child: Stories About Adoption,* and the forthcoming *It's All In Her Head: Women Making Peace With Troubled Minds.*

In addition to being a longtime word nerd, Laura has been obsessed with Madonna since she was six. As a kid, Laura had Madge-themed birthday parties with decorate-your-own-T-shirt puffy-paint stations. She has also bought *almost* every album Madonna's ever made, despite her college-honed gravitation toward mopey indie rock.

You can learn more about Laura at LauraBarcella.com.

Acknowledgments

THE BIGGEST THANKS go to my parents, who always encouraged my writing efforts no matter how ridiculous those efforts seemed at times. I know my late dad would be insanely excited and proud of my work on this book.

Cheers also to all the friends, families, and therapists(!) who have listened to me discuss this project for years, from its inception as a rosy nascent idea, to my obsession discouragement when it looked like it might not happen. These folks encouraged me in so many small and large ways.

A massive thanks to my agent, Brandi Bowles, for her unwavering support of this project, even when it was deal-less. (And thanks to Erin for introducing me to Brandi in the first place.)

And kudos to my editor, Laura Mazer at Soft Skull, who helped me many times along the way, offering lots of strong feedback and advice throughout a winding process.

Thanks to Jessica Valenti for writing a kick-ass foreword despite being utterly swamped. And thanks to all the uber-talented contributors, who cheerfully endured countless revisions and tweaks to their essays. Thanks, too, to all the writers who submitted but didn't reach the finish line—there were so many great pieces! It was extremely hard to narrow it down to the thirty-nine essays that ended up in this book.

And finally, I must tip my hat to Madonna, the inspiration of this book, for being strong and controversial and always unfailingly herself. Obviously, this book wouldn't be here if she weren't.